Women's Empowerment and Microcredit Programmes in India

Women's Empowerment and Microcredit Programmes in India examines the value of microcredit-based self-help groups (SHGs) for women in India and provides an alternative model for women's empowerment programming.

The microcredit sector continues to boom globally – with private investors, governments and multilateral financial institutions all investing substantial amounts in self-help group programming. Nowhere is this more evident than in India, where the industry has further been deregulated in recent years. Much of the rationale for increased investment in microcredit is based on the idea that it improves 'women's empowerment'. But is this true? Researchers have fiercely debated the value of microcredit programmes for women, with some arguing that it is exploitative, and others contending that it is empowering. This book provides new insights into women's empowerment and microcredit programming, elaborating on the themes of power, dignity, mobility and solidarity. It takes a nuanced view of the complexities surrounding self-help group programming and women's empowerment and argues that the model of microcredit is key to whether it helps or harms women.

By focusing on the experiences and voices of microcredit self-help group members in West Bengal, India, this book elaborates on the idea of microcredit models existing on a continuum, from 'smart economics' to more holistic feminist versions of programming. It will be of interest to scholars in development studies, anthropology, sociology, gender studies, public policy and Asian Studies.

Annabel Dulhunty is a Lecturer at the Crawford School of Public Policy at the Australian National University.

Routledge / Asian Studies Association of Australia (ASAA) South Asian Series

Edited by Rahul K. Gairola, Murdoch University, Australia.

Published in association with the Asian Studies Association of Australia (ASAA), represented by Alexander E. Davis, Chair of the ASAA Publications Committee, University of Western Australia.

This series is published in cooperation with the ASAA to support and promote outstanding scholarship in the humanities, arts, and social sciences on South Asia, here widely understood as work emerging from or dealing with Bangladesh, Bhutan, India, Nepal, Pakistan, Sri Lanka, the Maldives, the Indian Ocean region, and comparative work on South Asia and its diasporas with and in other countries. The series publishes excellent, innovative research across a wide range of disciplines including history, politics and political economy, anthropology, geography, literature, sociology and social sciences, the fields of cultural studies, communication studies, security and surveillance studies, studies of religion and ethnicity, and women, gender, and sexuality studies. Interdisciplinary and comparative research is encouraged, and the Editor is also interested in work that stretches the interstices of area studies, identity studies, and technology studies in/ of South Asia into the 21st century.

Works in the series are published simultaneously in UK/ US and India editions, as well as in e-book format. Publications include single-authored monographs and edited volumes by authors based anywhere in the world.

Recent books in the series include

Women's Empowerment and Microcredit Programmes in India
The Possibilities and Limitations of Self-Help Groups
Annabel Dulhunty

Citizenship in Dalit and Indigenous Australian Literatures
Riya Mukherjee

For more information about this series, please visit: https://www.routledge.com/RoutledgeAsian-Studies-Association-of-Australia-ASAA-South-Asian-Series/book-series/ASAASAS.

Women's Empowerment and Microcredit Programmes in India

The Possibilities and Limitations of Self-Help Groups

Annabel Dulhunty

Routledge
Taylor & Francis Group
LONDON AND NEW YORK

First published 2023
by Routledge
4 Park Square, Milton Park, Abingdon, Oxon OX14 4RN

and by Routledge
605 Third Avenue, New York, NY 10158

Routledge is an imprint of the Taylor & Francis Group, an informa business

British Library Cataloguing in Publication Data
A catalogue record for this book is available from the British Library

ISBN: 978-1-032-41131-6 (hbk)
ISBN: 978-1-032-41130-9 (pbk)
ISBN: 978-1-003-35640-0 (ebk)

DOI: 10.4324/9781003356400

Typeset in Times New Roman
by Taylor & Francis Books

For Chris, Oscar and Ethan and for Milda and Emmeline.

Contents

Tables

Acknowledgements

I first and foremost wish to thank the women and men who shared their experiences with me from the communities in South 24 Parganas, Birbhum, Kolkata and North 24 Parganas. I am extremely grateful for their generosity, kindness and wisdom. I am also incredibly thankful to the NGO staff who shared with me their experiences and their time.

I also wish to acknowledge my PhD supervisors – Linda Bartolomei, Caroline Lenette and Eileen Pittaway – who guided me throughout my PhD with their excellent insights and mentoring.

I also am thankful to Sukanya Banerjee and Sunita Dey who accompanied me and aided me with translation. Their insights and support were incredibly valuable. I am also appreciative of Sayani Chakraborty for her further help with translation.

On a personal note, I want to remember Cooper Koffi who died from the immunodeficiency HLH at age two on 20 January 2018 and whose courage should always be acknowledged.

Finally, I wish to thank my beautiful family who I am so incredibly lucky to have and who mean the world to me. I thank my beautiful children, my bundles of joy, who light up our lives – Oscar and Ethan Peters. I am so grateful to my husband, Chris Peters, for his love, inspiration and constant support and belief in me. I am also so thankful to my Mum, Milda Dulhunty and my sister, Emmeline Dulhunty who have always provided unconditional love and care. I am so appreciative of my grandparents as well, Algis and Vida Kabaila, who I miss terribly.

1 Introduction

The SHG movement is all over India – it's a revolution!

Dipankar,[1] Project Coordinator of the NGO Shiksha, North 24 Parganas

We are meeting in a verdant hamlet, flanked by ripe banana plantations in North 24 Parganas, in West Bengal, India, yet only five kilometres from the border of Bangladesh. This area has fertile rich soil but is also on low-lying land, making floods a regular occurrence. Excited women have rushed to join the focus group discussion. They chat loudly amongst themselves, laughing and enthusiastic, laying out mats on the earth outside. The women joining come from a variety of backgrounds, but the majority are from 'scheduled castes'[2] – a phrase used to describe groups who have historically been discriminated against based on caste. Women are keen to explain the changes which have occurred in their lives since they joined a Self-Help Group (SHG), organised by a local non-governmental organisation (NGO).

In this focus group discussion, women detailed how prior to joining the SHG they '*weren't in a position to go out*'. They had been frequently confined to their homes, but joining the SHG had created a new social norm, increasing their mobility. They agreed with one young mother, *Taani*, who said:

> We all started going out of our homes, it was possible because of going to meet the (self-help) group – we would then go to the office, to the bank.

Another older lady, *Kaahini*, concurred and explained:

> Yes there used to be drama and they (the men) would say why are you going there, what are you doing?

After some time, however, the men began to accept that they were involved in the SHG and the women felt confident to challenge men in the community. Women recounted issues with a '*country liquor shop*', a small illegal stall set up by men in the community to sell alcohol. They described alcohol as

DOI: 10.4324/9781003356400-1

being a significant problem in their communities, with their husbands and sons drinking at the local liquor shop and using household money for alcohol. After being part of the SHG for some time, however, they felt emboldened and they '*smashed the shop*'. The women explained: 'Now if someone is drinking, we all go to protest'. Women also described that belonging to the SHG had helped them become involved with economic empowerment activities such as cloth making, harvesting banana plantations and purchasing cows. Belonging to the SHG also meant that they became more active in giving their recommendations to the *panchayat* (local council). Women explained that as a result of their efforts, the panchayat staff identified the flood prone areas, created an action plan to respond to flooding, developed a child care centre and undertook other vital actions in the community.

These positive examples were replicated in a number of other SHGs I visited and it was easy to understand why some people were very excited about the SHG model which revolves around microcredit but also frequently includes other activities. Yet I also visited SHGs where women felt that their situation had barely improved and their lives were hampered by class, caste and gender discrimination. Furthermore, I met with disbanded SHGs which had struggled under the weight of political differences between members. Other SHGs had fallen apart due to disputes about loans or the difficulties involved in administering the group.

These contrasting findings regarding the status of SHGs mirror the literature on microcredit and SHGs, where there are vastly different opinions as to the merit of these types of programmes. So what exactly is the worth of SHG microcredit programmes, particularly in their ability to 'empower' women? In this book I answer this critical question and the extent to which SHGs are able to spark transformative change. I examine this question by exploring the key themes of power, mobility, dignity and solidarity in addition to the types of *models* microcredit programmes operate under. While answers to this question are not clear cut, each empirical chapter elaborates on one dimension of microcredit programming which either enhances women's empowerment or limits it. This helps paint a nuanced picture of microcredit SHG programming and enables me to make detailed recommendations for women's empowerment programming throughout the book and in the final chapter.

Microcredit on the World Stage

In 2006, Mohammed Yunus won the Nobel Peace prize for establishing an innovative microcredit programme with the Grameen Bank in Bangladesh, catapulting microcredit on to the world stage. While microcredit had existed before the foundation of the Grameen Bank in 1983, it was Yunus who brought global attention and investment to this idea. Before long, most countries in the Global South had various kinds of microcredit schemes in operation – with programmes designed to make it easier for individuals experiencing poverty to access credit. These programmes were variously funded by national and state governments, NGOs, bilateral donors such as the United States Agency for International Development (USAID) and International Financial Institutions (IFIs) such as the World Bank.

Microcredit has been highly acclaimed as a solution by some, not only for assisting individuals out of poverty, but also as a means of empowering women (Asian Development Bank, 2020). In many countries, patriarchal constraints meant that it was previously only men who were eligible for loans, entrenching women's position within the unpaid domestic sphere. Women were thus bearing the brunt of poverty. Many stated aims of microcredit programmes include that they aim to lift women and their families out of poverty by encouraging enterprise and small business initiatives. In addition, in countries like India where the vast majority of the workforce work in the informal sector (National Sample Survey Organisation, 2011–12), both women and men can remain trapped within exploitative working conditions and easily can become unemployed as a result of injury or lack of work opportunities. Due to gender discrimination, poor women have even less bargaining power and options than poor men within the workplace and at home (UN Women, 2022). As such, microcredit was seen as a means to provide options and choice to the poorest communities, particularly women who experience multiple forms of discrimination.

Many microcredit programmes were designed as group loans (in part to try to ensure repayment and so that risk could be shared amongst the group). Numerous NGOs and government departments designed SHG programmes whereby an SHG of between roughly ten to 20 individuals would access a collective loan and each individual would contribute to repayments. Many of these SHG programmes were designed for women only. This was either with the intention of directly 'empowering' women or was based on the belief that women were more likely to spend and manage the funds from an SHG in an 'appropriate' altruistic way, with greater concern for community wellbeing (Calkin, 2015). SHG programmes have been established by a variety of actors (from government to NGOs) and in some cases, these programmes include a much larger assortment of activities than microcredit. Many NGOs in particular have linked broader health, gender equality or education programmes with microcredit activities. These programmes are termed 'credit plus' (Holvoet, 2005; Mayoux, 1999) in this book, in acknowledgement that they combine access to credit with a variety of initiatives.

The advent of global microcredit was initially met with much (albeit not universal) support. In the past decade, however, there have been a growing number of critiques as to the value of microcredit – both for the purposes of alleviating poverty and for empowering women. The 2010 crisis in Andhra Pradesh precipitated much criticism of the sector. A host of microcredit borrowers dying by suicide in the state led to the shutdown of the entire microcredit industry in Andhra Pradesh for a time, while the Government and the Reserve Bank of India (RBI) investigated microcredit practices. Essentially, the lending practices of SKS Microfinance, the largest lender in Andhra Pradesh, were predatory, with SKS shaming and hounding clients for repayments (Mader, 2013). At the same time as borrowers were despairing, SKS Microfinance reported a revenue of over 10 billion in FY11 (Mistry, 2022). This crisis led to a tightening of the rules by the RBI, however, it is important to note that just recently in April 2022, the RBI has loosened some of these restrictions.

The case of Andhra Pradesh was not the only example of predatory lenders globally – there have been multiple instances of widespread debt distress and despair in places such as Sri Lanka, Cambodia and Mexico (Heller, 2021). The idea that microcredit is an exploitative industry designed to financialise poverty, with investors seeing the 'untapped' billions as an investment opportunity (Federici, 2014), has hence gained traction. Criticism has highlighted the extent to which private capital has been driving the microcredit industry and predatory lenders have abounded (Bateman et al., 2019). Predatory lenders will charge exorbitant interest rates and will harass and shame clients into repaying. While a number of lenders may not be predatory, microcredit is such a large market that it attracts numerous private initiatives. Within this array of lenders, if regulation is weak (or loosened, as it recently was in India), there are likely to be predatory lenders in this group.

In addition to criticisms that microcredit is fundamentally exploitative, a growing collection of studies have argued that microcredit just doesn't work – or at least that it does not achieve the claims which microcredit advocates have made. A number of studies have indicated that there is no correlation between being part of a microcredit initiative and reduced poverty (Banerjee et al., 2015; Meager, 2019). The case linking women's empowerment with microcredit is also ambivalent, with numerous contrasting findings (Brody et al., 2017; Duvendack & Palmer-Jones, 2016). Many of these studies, however, have focused on singular approaches to microcredit, not credit-plus models. Is there a case then to be made that credit-plus models are empowering for women? Particularly as many credit-plus models are not driven by profit, but are instead operated by non-governmental organisations?

In this book, I show that there are mixed findings about the extent to which microcredit-plus programmes empower women. Ultimately, this research indicates that the benefit gained from belonging to a microcredit based SHG is primarily based on developing networks and solidarity with other women in the SHG, whereby women can use this as a platform for collective action in their communities. Other benefits accrued from the wider training programmes offered by the NGOs and their support of women to become active leaders in their communities. While women derived value from functioning SHGs, there were numerous instances of SHGs being abandoned and deemed too difficult to maintain. In this book I elaborate on the complexities of microcredit-plus programming and its relationship with women's empowerment.

To better determine whether credit plus models of microcredit can be empowering, the very notion of empowerment must also be better understood and analysed. In this book I outline different approaches to women's empowerment. The idea of 'women's empowerment' is indeed ubiquitous. Almost all microcredit programmes claim to 'empower' women, but what does this really mean? Despite the excessive use of the word 'empowerment', it differs in meaning substantially – from a mere gaining of skills and economic improvements (Buvinić & Furst-Nichols, 2016) to a holistic, radical changing of one's life (Sardenberg, 2008). Feminist and Gender and Development (GAD) scholars have generally challenged the idea of economic empowerment and instead argued that empowerment must be based on ideas of power and the challenging of power relations (Batliwala, 2007; Cornwall & Rivas, 2015). This book examines women's empowerment in microcredit initiatives through contrasting feminist, holistic empowerment models with recent trends in 'smart economics'. 'Smart economics' is essentially an instrumentalist argument for empowering women economically. The rationale behind 'smart economics' is that by improving women's economic empowerment, overall community wellbeing and economic growth will be achieved (World Bank, 2012). This book addresses these different approaches and I argue that effective programming aiming to achieve any form of 'empowerment' must take a holistic view considering different forms of power. In this book I also assess the nexus between mobility, empowerment and social norms and the crucial and frequently overlooked role of dignity in empowerment. Finally, this book examines the main benefit of SHG programmes, in creating a space for solidarity, companionship and collective action.

West Bengal and Self-Help Groups

While SHGs and microcredit are a global phenomenon, this book is situated in the eastern state of West Bengal in India. It is hence important that I provide some background information here to establish the contextual environment for SHGs in the state. West Bengal has had a diverse reputation throughout its history – known alternately for being an intellectual hub of culture and the arts; a troubled state embroiled in various refugee crises and Maoist insurgencies; a state battling poverty, particularly in its overcrowded capital, Kolkata; and a highly politicised state, where every individual eagerly supports a political party. As India's fourth most populous state, it makes for an important case study for microcredit SHG programming. As throughout most of India, SHGs have been prioritised as a 'development' strategy in the state. In addition, governments in West Bengal have a long history of claiming to uplift the poor and marginalised, with SHGs but one component of state reforms.

West Bengal has a large rural population and their political support and engagement has been necessary to sustain both the thirty-four year rule of the Communist Party of India Marxist (CPIM) from 1977 to 2011 and the All India Trinamool Congress (TMC) government since 2011 (Bhattacharyya, 2011; Roy, 2013). The need to harness support from rural disadvantaged populations also resulted in a devolution of power to panchayats (local councils). Indeed, West Bengal is highly politicised, with citizens being politically active in even the most isolated communities (Bardhan et al., 2010). These factors all contribute to the dynamics of SHG programming in West Bengal, which I shall detail throughout this book.

Over the past 30 years there also have been a series of economic reforms in West Bengal which have impacted poor communities. The CPIM undertook a number of land reforms and redistributed land titles. This benefited poorer communities in rural areas, many of whom were able to hold small plots of land. Despite these changes, however, the redistribution was only of fairly small parcels of land which were not economically viable for agricultural projects (Guha, 2021). Today, many poor communities, particularly scheduled caste or tribal communities, do not own land but work as daily wage labourers on the land of others.

In the past 20 years, the burgeoning middle class of West Bengal have increasingly been supported by the ongoing neoliberal policies in the state (Das, 2019). While West Bengal held back from India's liberalisation reforms for some time, by the mid-2000s, it's economy was opening up significantly. In the second half of the 1990s, the government formed 'Special Economic Zones' which enabled land to be cleared for industry and decreased regulations in these areas. In part, Mamata Banerjee's party, the All India Trinamool Congress (TMC) was able to build on the discontent of citizens in rural areas following these CPIM led reforms. While the CPIM were liberalising the economy, Mamata Banerjee of the TMC styled herself as a champion of the rural people, calling herself '*Didi*' (elder sister) (Bose, 2012). However, once elected, Banerjee began a campaign of 'modernising' the city and focusing on middle to upper class interests such as 'beautifying' the streets (Jack, 2015). While shopping malls and gated communities have spread with the rise of a larger middle class, those trapped in poverty cycles were less able to benefit from these transformations and in many places were disadvantaged by them – such as when informal housing settlements and roadside work stalls were proclaimed 'illegal' and demolished for the sake of urban 'renewal' (Routh, 2014). While the poor have been excluded from many of these development programmes, the state government instead vigorously promoted SHGs as a critical mechanism to promote pro-poor growth and redress disadvantage (Department of Panchayats and Rural Development 2021).

The state and national governments have treated the expansion of SHGs and microcredit programmes with great fervour (Chaudhuri, 2018). SHGs became popular in India in part because of the influence of the popular

Grameen Bank microcredit programme in neighbouring Bangladesh and in part due to the deemed success of earlier schemes in India. While small scale SHG programmes existed in India since the 1970s, SHG programming significantly expanded after the National Bank for Agriculture and Rural Development (NABARD) implemented a scheme between banks and 500 SHGs in 1992. A Department of SHGs was created in 2006 in West Bengal and by 2020–21, microcredit loans had been distributed to almost 900,000 SHGs (Department of Panchayats and Rural Development 2021). The focus on SHGs as a means to address the needs of poorer women comes in the context of wider trends in India and indeed in West Bengal where women's female labour force participation rate has been reducing over decades (Goswami, 2019), with women predominantly working in informal sectors in insecure and unstable work (Chakravarty, 2018).

The popularity with which SHGs were implemented shows no sign of abating. SHG programmes vary widely in their set up. On one side of the spectrum, SHGs act as mere conduits of microcredit, with no other purpose than channelling the disbursement of loans. At the other end, SHG members engage in a wide range of community development activities from income generating projects to educational training programmes. SHGs can be linked directly with banks and microfinance institutions (MFIs) or they can be managed by government departments or NGOs, which act as intermediaries between communities and financial institutions. There is slippage between models, but generally, in West Bengal, government-run SHGs work with groups on financial activities only. Government-run SHGs focus on linking the SHGs with microloans from banks – loans are frequently given for small scale agricultural or microbusiness activities (Ministry of Rural Development, 2021). Government-run programmes generally focus only on linking women with credit. By contrast, many (though not all) NGO programmes include a broader range of activities.

Some recent studies on SHGs and microcredit groups in West Bengal illustrate the different models of microcredit and the varying opinions as to its worth. Paromita Sanyal's studies (2009, 2014, 2015) have highlighted the benefits of SHGs in connecting women who were previously isolated. SHGs were able to provide a basis for members to engage in collective action against domestic violence or for the provision of public goods. Chakravarty and Chaudhuri (2012) similarly argue that SHGs formed a platform for women to protest against witch-hunts. Sen and Majumder (2015) took a pragmatic view and argued that women have been able to subvert the neoliberal aims of microcredit programming and use it for their own ends. Kar (2018) examined women's interaction with microfinance institutions more broadly and found that the strict rules for credit management hampered the extent to which these loans benefited women. Lahiri-Dutt and Samanta (2006) illustrated that caste tensions created issues in the maintenance of SHGs, as well as political and religious divides. These studies provide a brief snapshot of microcredit programming, a topic I explore in greater depth in

Chapter 4. In this book, I draw on these studies, amongst others, to illustrate the competing tensions within microcredit SHG programming and to explain how attempting to improve women's empowerment is a difficult enterprise.

Introduction to the Case Study

This book is based on in-depth research I undertook with women belonging to SHGs in West Bengal and with men in their communities. It is also drawn from interviews I conducted with NGO staff members and consultants working on SHG programmes. It is important to note that I come to this research as an outsider, as a foreigner. My views are necessarily shaped by my experiences as an outsider, as an Australian from a European background, with no Indian heritage. This book is drawn from my PhD which was based on empirical research in West Bengal. I chose to base my research in the state because I had had a long history of visiting the area since 2001 and had been fascinated by the various developments and changes which had occurred in the previous decade. It was also in West Bengal and Bangladesh where I first began working on gender issues in 2006 as a 'Gender Development Officer' in a volunteer position with an international NGO. In this role I would meet with women's self-help groups. After this position, I had also returned to the area for humanitarian and gender related trainings and conferences. In conducting research I was conscious how being an outsider shaped my experiences. On the one hand, I was outside of the local caste and class hierarchies, yet I was also clearly different and an outsider, coming from a position of privilege. I have grappled with what this status has meant for this research and it is clear that my analysis will always be shaped by my standpoint and status as an outsider (Manohar et al., 2019). It is important then that I make no claim to be sharing one objective overarching truth, but instead to acknowledge that my recommendations and viewpoint must necessarily sit alongside others, to contribute to a multitude of visions and ideas about women's empowerment and microcredit SHG programming.

I carried out this research with women and men from SHGs in three primary locations in West Bengal: Kolkata, South 24 Parganas and Birbhum. I also conducted further secondary research in North 24 Parganas. I went on two separate research visits in 2014 and facilitated focus group discussions and one to one interviews with primarily the same communities each time.

I mainly focused on SHGs which had been formed by the NGO, Swadhinata Program Team (SPT).[3] SPT was a recently nationalised NGO which had connections with member organisations in other countries and was affiliated with a global headquarters in Europe. SPT had commenced working in West Bengal in the 1970s, primarily focused on humanitarian assistance. Since that time, SPT's programming grew to include broader community development initiatives. SPT adopted an explicit 'rights-based approach' focused on promoting the rights of impoverished communities in India.

I also conducted secondary focus group discussions and interviews with participants and staff from three other organisations:[4] Shiksha, Sochetana and Sahosh. In total, I spoke with 109 women who were part of SHGs established by SPT during the first research visit and with 129 women and 57 men from the same communities during the second trip. I also talked with 59 women and 11 men from SHGs set up by other organisations and with 19 staff or consultants working with NGOs.

There were ten primary communities which I visited both times which had SHGs which had been established by SPT. These ten primary communities had completed the SPT Transformation programme. Two communities were in Kolkata, five in South 24 Parganas and three in Birbhum. Across all locations, the SPT Transformation programme included the establishment of SHGs as a key feature. The programme delivery was different across locations but the core components were the same and revolved around the development of SHGs. The programme had broad objectives, aiming to redress the problems of chronic poverty, poor health, social discrimination and household debt. These programmes focused on the holistic wellbeing of communities. SHGs operated by SPT were generally either all-female or all-male, with ten to 20 members. Most SHGs were all-female. SPT staff emphasised that female SHGs were more effective as government schemes that SHGs could access mainly focused on women. Furthermore, many men migrated either seasonally or travelled far each day for work and men appeared to be less interested in joining SHGs.

SPT provided support to both individuals and groups for microenterprises. SPT also funded group projects within communities. Examples of individual loans included funds for setting up a grocery store, a van, a paddy processing unit, materials for fish farming or poultry raising. Examples of group loans included finances for SHGs to rent out decorations or utensils for festivals, or for SHGs to stock grains for sale when prices were high. SPT would provide mentoring for setting up and running of the microbusiness during the life of the programme. In many cases, SPT also purchased agricultural equipment (e.g. diesel or treadle pumps) for communities, which was owned by the SHG. SPT also supported the broader community in conducting training programmes, such as on using sustainable agricultural practices to improve agricultural outputs.

For my research, I used a constructivist grounded theory methodology (Charmaz, 2014) which is based on being fairly open to exploring what themes arise out of interviews and discussions. Rather than setting strict research questions, I aimed to focus on the testimonies of women belonging to SHGs to see what was important to them. I focused my research on women from scheduled castes, though most SHGs had a mix of women from different caste backgrounds. My first visit was based on exploring broader themes of how women experienced belonging to the SHG and any changes which had occurred in their lives. I then analysed these findings and created more detailed questions for my second research visit to probe these initial ideas. During the second visit I also used Participatory Rural Appraisal (PRA) techniques (Chambers, 1994). I facilitated a time-use activity, the drawing of a safe movement map and analysis of a decision-making chart to further examine ideas which had emerged from the first visit. I purposefully used PRA tools during the second visit which created an entirely different dynamic from simply asking repeated questions. Participants were much more engaged and I could ask follow on questions more naturally. In addition, PRA tools enabled me to approach sensitive topics in a different way that was less confrontational than standard interviewing and it enabled for a greater diversity of people to speak, who may have been less comfortable talking in a focus group situation.

Outline of the Book

This introductory chapter has explained the key aims of the book and given contextual background information as to the status of microcredit and the situation of SHGs in West Bengal. The next chapter, Chapter 2, introduces the reader to the various debates around the topic of empowerment, and then outlines a brief history of women's empowerment initiatives, from Women in Development (WID) to Gender and Development (GAD). Chapter 3 then explores the many contributions of feminisms in India, particularly Dalit feminism. Chapter 4 takes a deeper dive into the microcredit debate – outlining the differences in scholarship and opinion. The next five chapters then focus on the case study of SHGs in West Bengal. These chapters are based around the five key themes of: microcredit modalities; community development modalities; dignity; mobility and solidarity. Chapter 5 illustrates how different modalities of microcredit programming operate either on the basis of a 'smart economics' ideology or on the basis of more holistic feminist credit-plus approaches. Chapter 6 then investigates how microcredit and SHG programming are framed by different models of community development. Chapter 7 demonstrates how questions of dignity must be central to the idea of empowerment and SHG programming. It also outlines the intersection between women's care work, paid work and SHG programs. Chapter 8 focuses on the way that SHG programming must contend with entrenched patriarchy. This chapter also details the extent to which SHG programmes can improve women's mobility and household decision making and the limitations to these programmes. Chapter 9 addresses the most positive feature of SHGs and women's empowerment programming: the potential of SHGs to create networks of solidarity and community, in addition to providing a platform for collective action. Lastly, Chapter 10 concludes the book by examining future possibilities for SHG and microcredit programming and by providing recommendations for practitioners and scholars.

Notes

1 Pseudonyms are used for all research participants and aliases for organisations.
2 The term 'Dalit' is also used in this book, though this term is used less in West Bengal than 'SC' which stands for scheduled castes.
3 I have used aliases in this book, including SPT.
4 Aliases are used for these organisations as well.

References

Asian Development Bank (2020). How Microfinance Is Helping Poor Households and Businesses Survive and Thrive: 6 Things to Know. https://www.adb.org/news/features/how-microfinance-helping-poor-households-and-businesses-survive-and-thrive-6-things.

Banerjee, A., Karlan, D., & Zinman, J. (2015). Six Randomized Evaluations of Microcredit: Introduction and Further Steps. *American Economic Journal: Applied Economics*, 7(1), 1–21. doi:10.1257/app.20140287.

Bardhan, P. K., Mookherjee, D., & Monica, P. T. (2010). Impact of Political Reservations in West Bengal Local Governments on Anti-Poverty Targeting. *Journal of Globalization and Development*, 1(1), 1–38.

Bateman, M., Blankenburg, S., & Kozul-Wright, R. (2019). Introduction. In M. Bateman, S. Blankenburg, & R. Kozul-Wright (Eds.), *The Rise and Fall of Global Microcredit: Development, Debt and Disillusion* (pp. 3–23). Routledge.

Batliwala, S. (2007). Taking the Power out of Empowerment – an Experiential Account. *Development in Practice*, 17(4–5),557–565. https://doi.org/10.1080/09614520701469559.

Bhattacharyya, D. (2011). Party Society, Its Consolidation and Crisis: Understanding Political Change in Rural West Bengal. In A. Ghosh, T. Guha-Thakurta, & J. Nair (Eds.), *Theorising the Present: Essays for Partha Chatterjee* (pp. 226–250). Oxford University Press.

Bose, S. (2012, 26 September). Class, Culture, and Politics: The Making of Mamata Banerjee. http://eprints.lse.ac.uk/75478/1/blogs.lse.ac.ukClass%20culture%20and%20politics%20The%20making%20of%20Mamata%20Banerjee.pdf.

Brody, C., de Hoop, T., Vojtkova, M., Warnock, R., Dunbar, M., Murthy, P., & Dworkin, S. L. (2017). Can Self-Help Group Programs Improve Women's Empowerment? A Systematic Review. *Journal of Development Effectiveness*, 9(1), 15–40. https://doi.org/10.1080/19439342.2016.1206607.

Buvinić, M., & Furst-Nichols, R. (2016). Promoting Women's Economic Empowerment: What Works? *The World Bank Research Observer*, 31(1), 59–101.

Calkin, S. (2015). "Tapping" Women for Post-Crisis Capitalism. *International Feminist Journal of Politics*, 17(4), 611–629. https://doi.org/10.1080/14616742.2015.1071994.

Chakravarty, A., & Chaudhuri, S. (2012). Strategic Framing Work(S): How Microcredit Loans Facilitate Anti-Witch-Hunt Movements. *Mobilization* 17(2), 175–194. https://doi.org/10.17813/maiq.17.2.f54x1h0622750028.

Chakravarty, D. (2018). Lack of Economic Opportunities and Persistence of Child Marriage in West Bengal. *Indian Journal of Gender Studies*, 25(2), 180–204. https://doi.org/10.1177/0971521518761430.

Chambers, R. (1994). The Origins and Practice of Participatory Rural Appraisal. *World Development*, 22(7), 953–969.

Charmaz, K. (2014). *Constructing Grounded Theory* (2nd edition). SAGE Publications Ltd.

Chaudhuri, S. R. (2018, March 11). West Bengal Govt Targets Rural Woman with Rs 700 Crore Shg Scheme. *Hindustan Times.*

Cornwall, A., & Rivas, A. M. (2015). From 'Gender Equality and 'Women's Empowerment' to Global Justice: Reclaiming a Transformative Agenda for Gender and Development. *Third World Quarterly*, 36(2), 396–415. https://doi.org/10.1080/01436597.2015.1013341.

Das, R. (2019). *Neoliberalism and the Transforming Left in India: A Contradictory Manifesto.* Routledge.

Department of Panchayats and Rural Development (2021). Department of Panchayats and Rural Development, Government of West Bengal. http://www.wbprd.gov.in/index.aspx.

Duvendack, M., & Palmer-Jones, R. (2016). Micro-Finance, Women's Empowerment and Fertility Decline in Bangladesh: How Important Was Women's Agency? *The Journal of Development Studies*, 53(5), 664–683. https://doi.org/10.1080/00220388.2016.1205731.

Federici, S. (2014). From Commoning to Debt: Financialization, Microcredit, and the Changing Architecture of Capital Accumulation. *South Atlantic Quarterly*, 113(2), 231–244. doi:10.1215/00382876-2643585.

Goswami, D. (2019). Low and Declining Female Work Participation: The Case of Rural West Bengal. *Journal of Labor and Society*, 22(2), 325–343. doi:10.1111/wusa.12411.

Guha, A. (2021). The Caste Question in West Bengal Politics: Continuing Inconsequentiality or Rising Relevance? *Contemporary South Asia*, 29(3), 376–400. doi:10.1080/09584935.2021.1886247.

Heller, P. W. (2021). The Lessons of Microcredit. In K. Wendt (Ed.), *Theories of Change: Change Leadership Tools, Models and Applications for Investing in Sustainable Development* (pp. 153–168). Springer.

Holvoet, N. (2005). The Impact of Microfinance on Decision-Making Agency: Evidence from South India. *Development and Change*, 36(1), 75–102. doi:10.1111/j.0012-155X.2005.00403.x.

Jack, I. (2015). What Will Turn Kolkata into a 'London of the East'? A Ferris Wheel, of Course – and a Lick of Paint. *The Guardian.* https://www.theguardian.com/commentisfree/2015/aug/01/what-will-turn-kolkata-into-london-of-east-ferris-wheel.

Kar, S. (2018). Securitizing Women: Gender, Precaution, and Risk in Indian Finance. *Signs*, 43(2), 301–325. https://doi.org/10.1086/693537.

Lahiri-Dutt, K., & Samanta, G. (2006). Constructing Social Capital: Self-Help Groups and Rural Women's Development in India. *Geographical Research*, 44(3), 285–295. https://doi.org/10.1111/j.1745-5871.2006.00390.x.

Mader, P. (2013). Rise and Fall of Microfinance in India: The Andhra Pradesh Crisis in Perspective. *Strategic Change*, 22(1–2),47–66. https://doi.org/10.1002/jsc.1921.

Manohar, N., Liamputtong, P., Bhole, S., & Arora, A. (2019). Researcher Positionality in Cross-Cultural and Sensitive Research. In P. Liamputtong (Ed.), *Handbook of Research Methods in Health Social Sciences* (pp. 1601–1616). Springer Singapore. doi:10.1007/978-981-10-5251-4_35.

Mayoux, L. (1999). Questioning Virtuous Spirals: Micro-Finance and Women's Empowerment in Africa. *Journal of International Development*, 11(7), 957. https://doi.org/10.1002/(SICI)1099–1328(199911/12)11:7<957:AID-JID623>3.0.CO;2-%23.

Meager, R. (2019). Understanding the Average Impact of Microcredit Expansions: A Bayesian Hierarchical Analysis of Seven Randomized Experiments. *American Economic Journal: Applied Economics*, 11(1), 57–91. doi:10.1257/app.20170299.

Ministry of Rural Development (2021). Deendayal Antyodaya Yojana. https://aajeevika.gov.in/en/content/faq.

Mistry, J. (2022, 4 April). Rbi's New Guidelines to Make Microfinance Stronger. *The Economic Times.* https://economictimes.indiatimes.com/markets/stocks/news/rbis-new-guidelines-to-make-microfinance-stronger/articleshow/90639257.cms?from=mdr.

National Sample Survey Organisation (2011–12). 2011–12 Employment and Unemployment Survey. https://catalog.ihsn.org/index.php/catalog/3283 (accessed 12 December 2022).

Routh, S. (2014). *Enhancing Capabilities through Labour Law: Informal Workers in India*. Routledge.

Roy, D. (2013). *Rural Politics in India: Political Stratification and Governance in West Bengal*. Cambridge University Press. doi:10.1017/CBO9781107326316.

Sanyal, P. (2009). From Credit to Collective Action: The Role of Microfinance in Promoting Women's Social Capital and Normative Influence. *American Sociological Review*, 74(4), 529–550. doi:10.1177/000312240907400402.

Sanyal, P. (2014). Credit to Capabilities. doi:10.1017/cbo9781139939461.

Sanyal, P. (2015). Group-Based Microcredit & Emergent Inequality in Social Capital: Why Socio-Religious Composition Matters. *Qualitative Sociology*, 38(2), 103–137. https://doi.org/10.1007/s11133-015-9301-8.

Sardenberg, C. (2008). Liberal Vs. Liberating Empowerment: A Latin American Feminist Perspective on Conceptualising Women's Empowerment. *IDS Bulletin* 39 (6), 18–27. https://doi.org/10.1111/j.1759-5436.2008.tb00507.x.

Sen, D., & Majumder, S. (2015). Narratives of Risk and Poor Rural Women's (Dis)-Engagements with Microcredit-Based Development in Eastern India. *Critique of Anthropology*, 35(2), 121–141. https://doi.org/10.1177/0308275x15569850.

UN Women (2022, 1 February). Poverty Deepens for Women and Girls, According to Latest Projections. https://data.unwomen.org/features/poverty-deepens-women-and-girls-according-latest-projections.

World Bank (2012). *World Development Report: Gender Equality and Development.*

2 Women's Empowerment and Feminist Movements

Women's empowerment is such a frequently repeated phrase in development circles that it is difficult to establish exactly what it means. A whole host of development actors claim that their various programmes 'empower' women (Cornwall, 2016). Certainly most descriptions of microcredit and self-help group (SHGs) programmes state that they aim to improve 'women's empowerment'. In addition, many see women's 'empowerment' as critical for development more broadly – claiming that it will improve women's labour force participation rate, broader economic growth, children's development and societal wellbeing (World Bank, 2012). Yet what exactly is 'women's empowerment'? In this chapter I explore this idea and the contested debates around this term. Empowerment is a difficult idea to define. On the one hand, it seems straight forward – to be empowered is to have power, yet, in reality, empowerment has come to mean many different things to various actors. In this chapter I provide an historical overview of these differences and the key debates surrounding women's empowerment from significant movements such as 'Women in Development' (WID), 'Women and Development' (WAD) and 'Gender and Development' (GAD). I also attempt to lay the foundations of a conceptual framework for a meaningful understanding of 'women's empowerment' and accompanying feminist movements.

Women's Empowerment

'Empowerment' has come to represent many contrasting ideas both in theory and in practice. While there are numerous interpretations of empowerment, two main ideas are frequently juxtaposed: that of economic empowerment and that of feminist empowerment based on redressing power inequalities. These dissimilar philosophies have permeated various approaches to addressing women's equality in development from WID, to WAD and GAD. By the 2000s, the term empowerment was ubiquitous. As Srilatha Batliwala (2007, p.557) argues: 'Of all the buzzwords that have entered the development lexicon in the past 30 years, empowerment is probably the most widely used and abused'. Hence, it is now difficult to find a development programme targeted

DOI: 10.4324/9781003356400-2

at women or even an overarching aid strategy which does not mention the phrase 'women's empowerment'. It is an idea which is thoroughly embedded in multiple layers of development architecture.

Initially, however, empowerment was seen as both a radical and a political idea. Batliwala (2007), for example, highlights diverse origins of the philosophy of empowerment, including the Veerashaiva movement in the 12th and 13th centuries which called for an end to hierarchies of power. Batliwala and others such as Celia Sardenberg (2008) also highlight the significance of Latin American social movements, such as Latin American feminism and liberation theology. In particular, Paulo Freire's work on critical education was foundational for this radical conception of empowerment. In his book *Pedagogy of the Oppressed*, Freire (1970) argued that elites used a 'banking' model of education, where they taught poor communities with the aim of subduing them, so that the poor didn't question their environment. Freire maintained that a radical approach to education was needed whereby students joined 'learning circles' and were encouraged to critically question their environment instead of engaging in rote learning, During this process of critical questioning, Freire (1970) argued that a process of *conscientização* (consciousness raising) occurred, where individuals come to be aware of the injustices in their surrounding environment and of their own place in the world. While Freire's theories have received criticism for their lack of gender or racial analysis (Stromquist, 2014), these methods certainly were highly influential for the 'consciousness raising' of feminist movements in the 1970s (Sardenberg, 2008).

Despite its radical origins, feminists have argued that the idea of empowerment was essentially 'hijacked' or 'co-opted' from the 1990s onwards (Cornwall, 2007b). The term became part of the mainstream aid and development lexicon, with all programmes aiming to 'empower' women. Crucially, empowerment was also viewed as a process which did not require state resources, in some cases it could even be interpreted as *anti*-state and essentially conservative (Batliwala, 2007). In this way, empowerment could be seen as a kind of individualistic process of improving oneself without requiring outside help. Development programmes could thus focus on giving women access to credit, for example, without identifying any structural barriers that needed changing. Hence, even corporations had begun to use the idea of empowerment, such as Nike's Girl Effect campaign (Wilson, 2015). The term 'women's empowerment' has thus been used by such a broad range of actors with markedly different political viewpoints (Rowlands, 1997) that it has almost become meaningless in its usage. It is no surprise then, that the term 'empowerment' has been criticised as a vacuous 'buzzword' (Cornwall, 2007a).

In addition, in the past decade, the term empowerment has been frequently reduced to mean *economic* empowerment. With the World Bank's 'World Development Report 2012: Gender Equality and Development', the idea of 'smart economics' has gained ground, whereby women's empowerment is argued to be of benefit not only to women, but to improving the economy at large (Chant & Sweetman, 2012). Women's empowerment has thus become *instrumentalised* – rather than focus on women's rights as important in and of themselves, improving women's access to the mainstream economy is thought to lead to larger prospects of societal wellbeing and economic growth (Eyben & Napier-Moore, 2009). This instrumentalist idea has gained traction in a number of areas, particularly amongst multilateral and bilateral development agencies. Hence, Women's Economic Empowerment (WEE) has become something of a 'phenomenon' in recent years, with the Secretary General of the United Nations developing the High-Level Panel on Women's Economic Empowerment in 2016. The High-Level Panel argue in their report that 'women's economic empowerment is the right thing to do and the smart thing to do' (Secretariat, UN Secretary-General 2016, p.1). This echoes the idea of 'smart economics', based on the notion that empowering women is 'smart' because it is seen to lead to prosperity and economic growth. The economic empowerment of women is framed as a catch all solution and as containing a 'multiplier effect that spurs economic growth and contributes to global peace and stability' (United States Department of State 2022, p.1).

Despite this co-option, feminists have argued that empowerment should be reclaimed to better reflect its radical origins. Celia Sardenberg (2008), for example, helpfully distinguishes between 'liberal' and 'liberating' empowerment. In this conception, liberal empowerment follows liberal feminism and is concerned with including women within pre-existing social and economic structures. Liberal empowerment focuses on equality of opportunity and on ensuring that women aren't overlooked or excluded. Liberating forms of empowerment, by contrast, aim to dismantle societal structures of oppression, not to merely integrate women within their framework. Liberating forms of empowerment are thus inherently more confrontational (Cornwall & Anyidoho, 2010).

As the notion of women's empowerment has become somewhat subsumed by ideas of economic empowerment and has moved away from radical ideas of shifting power imbalances, some have argued that we need to return to the idea of women's *rights.* Carella and Ackerly (2017) for example, argue that in the focus on 'investing in women' or women's empowerment, women's intrinsic rights have been ignored. They argue that we need to reframe our attention to building on the gains of a Rights Based Approach which was adopted in the 1995 Beijing Platform for Action (Carella & Ackerly, 2017). Others, such as Claire Duncanson (2019), argue that women's empowerment and women's rights are complementary and that the approaches should be combined.

Women's Empowerment and Power

At its heart, liberating ideas of empowerment are based on redressing power inequalities, linking empowerment to the etymological root of 'power'.

Batliwala's (1994, p.130) definition of empowerment is hence instructive. She describes it as 'the process of challenging existing power relations, and of gaining greater control over the sources of power'. This gaining of power clearly is not limited to merely including women within pre-existing systems of governance, rather it requires radically changing these systems.

Key to power based definitions of empowerment is understanding different dimensions of power, which Jo Rowlands (1997) outlines as 'power over', 'power with', 'power to' and 'power within'. While 'power over' reflects domineering power, as it has traditionally been conceptualised, the other forms of power are positive and integral components of empowerment. 'Power within' reflects the internal process of change which must occur for empowerment to be realised. Naila Kabeer's work is also important here, illustrating that empowerment is 'the ability to make choices' (Kabeer, 2005, p.13). Kabeer provides important caveats, however, including that one's choices must be made based on a choice of meaningful alternatives. Hence, a choice must be informed and there must be the possibility of making a different choice. Therefore, even within this process of internal empowerment, it is fundamental to understand the surrounding structural constraints and limitations to choices (Kabeer, 2018). This process of 'power within' also needs to be accompanied by 'power to' act and 'power with' others. The role of solidarity, social networks and propensity for collective action is hence another critical component of empowerment (Cornwall, 2016; Kabeer, 2011), which ensures that empowerment is not an entirely individualised process. As such, Kabeer (2016, p.317) reflects that 'collective action by women ... has proven to be the single most important driving force in promoting public action on a range of women's rights'.

It is also important to note that power is not always overt – it is frequently hidden and yet structures every fibre of our societies. Power shapes inequality (Mehta, 2016) and ensures that social norms are upheld, promoting the interests of the powerful. Why don't the oppressed revolt? Or as Akram et al. (2015, p.58) ask: 'How does a social system, despite obvious inequality and disadvantage, survive without depending upon explicit forms of repression or physical coercion to maintain order?'. Because the oppressed, along with the powerful, come to believe that the power inequalities in society are the *norm*. Pierre Bourdieu (1977) explained this idea through the lens of *doxa*. Hierarchical categories of inequality such as race, gender or caste are made to appear normal or natural via a process of 'misrecognition'. As Bourdieu explains: 'the natural and social world appears as self-evident. This experience we shall call doxa' (Bourdieu, 1977, p.164). Social norms and inequalities thus go unquestioned by the majority who view these circumstances as inevitable. Naila Kabeer (2012) and other feminist scholars have drawn on Bourdieu's idea of *doxa* to explain how gender inequality is maintained and patriarchy remains trenchant.

Another important consideration with power is whether the process of gaining power in turn diminishes another person's power. Does an empowered woman weaken her husband's power? One way to describe this consideration is by evaluating whether power is *variable* or *zero* sum. These ideas stem from game theory and are based on the idea that gaining power is either win-win (variable sum power) or win-lose (zero sum power) (Read, 2012). If empowerment is zero-sum it means that as a person gains power, another loses it. Alternately if power is variable sum, one person's empowerment does not take away another's. 'Male backlash models' (Dhanaraj & Mahambare, 2021) which indicate that men are likely to protest against any changes in women's status, adhere with ideas of empowerment being zero-sum. As men feel threatened about losing their power or status, they lash out, sometimes with violence (Kilgallen et al., 2022). Some argue that whether power is zero or variable sum depends on the mindset of individuals involved – for example, a man may see it as win-win if his wife gains new skills as that may help his family. Alternately, he may view his wife's empowerment as a threat as it may mean that he is viewed with less authority or status in the household. Wong et al. (2017) argue that if men have a mindset that power is zero-sum and that they will lose their power if women are empowered, they are more likely to experience negative health outcomes. On the other hand, if programme staff expect only variable sum power and assume that everyone will automatically see another person's empowerment as a 'win' for them, they may be less likely to adequately prepare for any backlash which may occur (Green, 2016).

Women in Development

When examining the history of development programmes aiming to empower women, the 'Women in Development' (WID) movement stands out as a key historical moment. The economist, Esther Boserup's work was highly influential in the adoption of WID by mainstream development actors. Boserup argued in her persuasive work *Woman's Role in Economic Development* (1970), that many development policies were blind to their impact on women and women's contributions. For example, development policies pursued by USAID and others during the 1960s were largely focused on 'modernising' agricultural production. However, these new technologies essentially marginalised women, ignoring women's agricultural expertise and experience (Boserup, 1970). During this time, 'development' was synonymous with 'modernisation' and 'industrialisation', with countries advised to transition their agrarian economies to industrialised economies (Bull & Bøås, 2012). Overall, women were excluded from consideration in this process. Boserup's criticisms were a much needed critique of this process of 'development' which fundamentally overlooked women (Rathgeber, 1990).

Boserup's criticisms informed the development of WID. WID was driven by feminists in the Global North demanding equality within their own societies (Carella & Ackerly, 2017; Miller & Razavi, 1995). WID gained much traction in the US, and was in part aided by the large movement of women campaigning for the Equal Rights Amendment and for women's rights more broadly in the 1970s (Tinker, 1990). There were several 'wins' for women's rights during this era. For example, in 1973, U.S. feminists successfully advocated for a change to the U.S. Foreign Assistance Act, including the provision that the U.S. needed to assist other countries to better 'integrate' women into their economies (Miller & Razavi, 1995). WID thus began to be adopted as policy within USAID and other development aid agencies. From starting out as an 'outside' critique, WID had begun to be accepted within mainstream development circles (Parpart, 1993). WID continued to gain momentum in the 1970s and 80s. For example, the United Nations declared 1976–1985 as the Decade for Women and WID departments were set up at numerous agencies. By the 1980s and 1990s, however, WID was coming under criticism from a number of fronts.

WID had its roots in liberal feminism which emerged as a critical movement in feminism at the time (Beetham & Demetriades, 2007). Liberal feminism focused on women's equal opportunities with men *within* existing societal structures (Wendell, 1987). Liberal feminism was primarily based on ensuring that women were not discriminated against and that they did not have barriers erected to their participation in the economy or public life. WID similarly was focused on the idea of *integrating* women into existing structures – with aid agencies trying to ensure that women were not 'left behind' in a sweeping process of 'modernisation' (Koczberski, 1998). Yet as WID became increasingly integrated within mainstream development departments, Boserup's initial critique of modernisation processes largely went ignored (Brown, 2006). Instead WID largely focused on recommending the inclusion of women within the system of modern 'development' (Moser, 1995). At its heart, WID essentially shied away from confrontation and controversy (Rathgeber, 1990). It did not examine nor rebuke the development architecture which was founded on patriarchal assumptions. Rather, it sought to ensure that women could be included within this system (Moghadam, 1990). As such, Miller and Razavi (1995) argue that WID was primarily based on convincing mainstream development thinkers that focusing on women was both relevant and efficient. In this sense, women's rights became instrumentalised. In needing to make the case for investing in women, WID practitioners had to argue what women's empowerment could do for others.

Further criticisms of WID included that it largely focused on women's role in the labour force, ignoring caring and household responsibilities which largely fell to women (Rathgeber, 1990). WID projects were based on increasing women's earning capacity, i.e. through income generating activities and there was no scope for recognising that men might frequently appropriate income (Rathgeber, 1990). There was also very little focus on women's rights within their households and on their relationships with men. In practice, many WID programmes concentrated on skills needed for women's economic prospects: job skills, training and later access to credit (Sharma,

2008). This focus overlooked the broader structural barriers constraining women, however.

Women and Development

As WID came to be very much based on including women within the larger process of 'development' and 'modernisation', critiques of this movement at the time arose from Marxist feminists. Marxist feminists argued that WID did nothing to criticise colonial structures of subjugation between the 'first' and the 'third' worlds (Bandarage, 1984). Marxist feminists drew from dependency theory, whereby the 'first' world gained its wealth through extraction from the 'third' world. The 'Women and Development' (WAD) movement thus developed out of Marxist feminism and its criticism of capitalism, modernisation theory and relationships of exploitation. WAD argued that women's equality was not going to improve under systems of capitalist production (Koczberski, 1998). Instead, WAD feminists maintained that the overarching system of global capitalism needed to be dismantled for women's rights to be upheld.

Criticisms of WAD, however, focused on the idea that it prioritised class over gender analysis. Rathgeber (1990) for example, critiqued the assumption that gender equality would improve once global capitalism was redressed. Under WAD there seemed to be little analysis of patriarchy as its own system of oppression – patriarchy was subordinate to class as an organising structure. In addition, in common with WID, most attention was given to women's paid employment and labour relations, and not to women's contribution to household and caring labour (Rathgeber, 1990). While WAD did not make a significant imprint on mainstream development policy, it was influential in the shaping of early arguments for a Gender and Development approach (Sharma, 2008).

Gender and Development

Gender and Development (GAD) began to gain traction as a theoretical framework in the 1980s, culminating in influence in the 1990s. GAD theorists argued that WID was too narrow in its focus and that it did not address holistic issues surrounding women's equality (Beetham & Demetriades, 2007). While WID was premised on the idea that women's interests and status could be improved if women were given more attention within development processes, GAD was far more critical of patriarchy and development. For GAD theorists, women's exclusion from mainstream development initiatives was no accident, but a function of women's societal inequality. Inequality was seen as occurring not only in the economic realm, but throughout society – in the home, at school and in the law (Moghadam & Senftova, 2005). GAD theorists thus sought to go beyond focusing only on women's economic status. Instead, much greater attention was given to gender relations at home and how processes of 'development' impacted those relations. By shifting the language from 'women' to that of 'gender', the intention was to focus on *relationships* of power and to emphasise that women's subordinate role in society was not a natural occurrence but a societal construct (Brown, 2006). GAD theorists also criticised WID's emphasis on women's practical needs such as economic opportunities, without addressing what their strategic interests would be (Molyneux, 1985). Under this conception, development programmes should not focus merely on 'including' women or giving women a larger percentage of the 'pie'. Instead projects should be based on redressing power relations.

By going beyond women's economic inclusion, GAD also focused on women's holistic rights. Much activism culminated in the adoption of the Convention on the Elimination of All Forms of Discrimination Against Women (CEDAW) which signalled a new era where women's rights were enshrined in international conventions (Carella & Ackerly, 2017). Collaboration between global networks of women was paramount in the GAD movement. As Gita Sen (2006, p.128) argues, GAD was 'a sterling example of researchers and activists working together to bring about policy change'. Researchers and activists focused on developing an approach which would centre gendered power relations and which would address gender inequality both at home and in public (Rowlands, 1997).

Criticisms of GAD

Despite GAD's seemingly radical calls to redress societal inequality, many have since argued that it has been co-opted by development institutions to satisfy mainstream development objectives and modalities (Calkin, 2015). In particular, a number of scholars have maintained that GAD has been subsumed by the dominant spread of neoliberalism and the promotion of market based solutions (Marchand, 2009). Just as neoliberalism has dominated community development discourse and global government policies for the past thirty to forty years, so too has neoliberalism influenced feminism. Rottenberg (2017) describes how after feminism fell out of fashion in the 1990s, it resurged in combination with neoliberal ideology in the 2000s. Through a revival of feminism via 'girl power' ideals of this era, feminism was framed as the prioritisation of individual choices (Rottenberg, 2017). Neoliberal feminism arguably was able to neatly fit within development institutions which co-opted the language of GAD, particularly the idea of 'empowerment', all while ignoring power inequalities and other structural oppressions (Cornwall & Brock, 2005). Kalpana Wilson summarises this well:

> GAD theorists have in the past two decades increasingly highlighted women's agency...But rather than challenging the racialised power relationships inherent in development, this focus on agency has decisively shifted attention away from both material structures of power and gendered ideologies.
>
> (Wilson, 2011, p.317)

The term 'gender' was adopted by GAD theorists at the time and illustrated a focus on power relations and dynamics between women and men. Yet as GAD was institutionalised within development agencies, GAD became increasingly depoliticised (Marchand, 2009). 'Gender' and 'gender mainstreaming' could hence be viewed as ways of not only focusing on women's rights, but also on the rights of men. Feminist concerns with women's inequality thus were diluted as programme implementers sought to focus on women *and* men. The term 'gender' hence in some instances became disconnected from feminism and was viewed as a 'neutral' way of addressing the differential needs of men and women (Cornwall & Rivas, 2015). Or in other situations, confused development practitioners have used 'gender' as a synonym of 'women', hence losing the power of critiquing gender relations (Baden & Goetz, 1997).

Other criticisms of GAD have included that it has become synonymous with gender 'mainstreaming' whereby 'gender' needed to be incorporated into everything, but essentially was ignored as it was seen as an 'add-on' concern (Cornwall & Rivas, 2015). Menon (2015), for example, argued that 'mainstreaming gender' is useless for women's empowerment, silencing women's criticism of gender inequality, capitalism or the state as they must acquiesce to mainstream 'development'.

In addition, while many GAD theorists maintained the importance of taking an intersectional approach to gender programming, examining the specificity of women's individual context (Beetham & Demetriades, 2007), there have been criticisms that GAD only paid scant attention to issues of race or class (Tripathy, 2010). Others have argued however, that binaries are unhelpful – such as a binary between North and South (Ackerly and True, 2010). Other examples, such as from Lata Narayanaswamy (2016), demonstrate the way in which divisions within feminist movements in the Global South are also based on class and caste distinctions – illustrating the extent to which inequality within feminist movements persists in many forms.

Postcolonial Feminism and Intersectionality

Critiques of GAD as unconcerned with race or colonial legacy draw from postcolonial feminism (Khan et al., 2007). Postcolonial critiques contend that Western feminism has prioritised the voices and perspectives of white women and issues relevant to them, frequently at the expense of women from the Global South (Raj, 2013). Postcolonial feminism indicates that other markers of oppression, such as race and economic exploitation are equally important for defining the experiences of women from the Global South (Chowdhry & Ling, 2010). Rather than focus only on the rights of 'women' as a category, postcolonial feminism illustrates that we should instead be mindful of the 'axes of oppression' and aim to provide space for the viewpoints and perspectives which have historically been sidelined by colonial racism (Khan et al., 2007). Postcolonial feminism therefore not only aims to critique and dismantle patriarchy, but also desires to redress *all* forms of oppression from 'colonialism, nationalism, fundamentalisms, neo-liberalism, neo-colonialism, global feminism' (Deepak, 2012, p.785).

Related to the idea of postcolonial feminism and arising from the struggles of Black feminists, intersectionality has become a leading concept in current feminist thought. Kimberlé Crenshaw's (1989) work was foundational in the development of intersectionality as a key idea which examines multiple forms of oppression – from race, gender, sexuality and class alongside other markers of identity. These forms of oppression inform each other and place individuals and participants in double or triple binds – whereby they experience multiple forms of oppression simultaneously. For example, in the black rights movement, women's rights were deprioritised in favour of racial struggles whereas in the global feminist movement, black women were ignored (Collins & Bilge, 2020).

Power relations are at the heart of gender and other forms of intersectional inequality. As Collins and Bilge (2020) argue, intersectionality must be based on redressing power inequalities and not merely an analytical exercise. Women's empowerment goes beyond gender relations ideally then and also enables a critical questioning of other forms of inequality – for example based on caste or race (Batliwala, 2007). Despite the ubiquity of intersectionality in scholarship, however, it is unclear how much its precepts have been applied in practice – such as in development programming (Mangubhai & Capraro, 2015).

Feminist Pragmatism

Another idea which has helped to guide this research is that of feminist pragmatism, particularly 'black feminist pragmatism'. This movement draws from the philosophical tradition called Pragmatism, popularised by scholars such as Charles Peirce and John Dewey. While the work of the Pragmatists wasn't particularly concerned with feminism, later scholars such as Charlene Seigfried (1991) argued that Pragmatism was a highly useful philosophy for feminists. Pragmatism can be used to guide both feminist philosophy and action by focusing not on the *truth* of a claim but instead addressing the *use* of a claim. Furthermore, this aligns with feminist arguments that all knowledge claims are political (Ackerly & True, 2010). Using feminist pragmatism entreats one to ask the question as to whether a philosophy or action will increase the rights and standing of women (Rorty, 1990). This idea also informs activist forms of research which argue that research *about* women should also be *for* women i.e. in having some practical benefit for women (Olesen, 2005). One must then consider what the practical outcomes will be arising from research. Pragmatism is thus based on future considerations and takes research beyond mere present concerns (James, 2009). It is not a utopian vision, but instead a consideration of the practical next steps which are likely to arise out of research, theory or action (James, 2013). Black feminist pragmatism, such as detailed by V. Denise James (2009) further extends the use of Pragmatism, not only for women but for other historically discriminated groups – particularly those experiencing multiple forms of oppression such as African-American women. Black feminist pragmatism is hence deeply grounded in ideas of social justice and anti-oppressive practice (James, 2009).

Why then is black feminist pragmatism important for theorising women's empowerment and feminist movements? Primarily because there is so much theoretical debate within feminism that one can become lost within epistemic differences. There is also such a diversity of voices and movements within feminism that it can be difficult to make any claims to truth. Rather than focus on truth, however, Black feminist pragmatism encourages us to reflect on whether the theory or hypothesis is useful to women, particularly oppressed women. This will provide an important theory for grounding our considerations of highly contentious topics such as SHG microcredit programmes for women's empowerment.

Gender Transformative Change

Another important way of understanding how to achieve gender equality in community development work is by contrasting the ideas of a programme being either gender-*neutral*, gender-*sensitive* or gender-*transformative* (Dworkin et al., 2013). The research contrasting these models draws significantly from the health literature (in the areas of psychology, public health and health sociology). Many have advocated for gender-transformative approaches which focus on a 'critical examination of gender-related norms and expectations (particularly those related to masculinity) and on increasing gender-equitable attitudes and behaviours' (Casey et al., 2018, p.231).

Gender-neutral programming is essentially gender blind, whereas gender-sensitive programming aims to take into account how a programme may impact gender equality and aims to positively impact women's status. Most gender mainstreaming initiatives would fall within the realm of being gender-sensitive. Gender-transformative programming, by contrast, seeks fundamentally to *transform* gender relations and to redress structural power inequalities (Hillenbrand et al., 2022). Hillenbrand et al. outline key features of gender transformative approaches – including that they work with men, draw from intersectionality, are based on cycles of deliberation and action and examine structural power (Hillenbrand et al., 2022, p.1). Gender transformative approaches also require significant financial investment, a difficult feat when there is repeated emphasis on providing savings and 'value for money' in a variety of sectors (Hillenbrand et al., 2022), including in development programming.

Gender-transformative approaches in health programmes have accelerated since the 1994 International Conference on Population and Development where gender inequality and gender issues were recognised as impacting health and health care (Kågesten & Chandra-Mouli, 2020). Programmes have used the term 'gender-transformative' primarily when they have focused either on reducing violence against women or on reducing HIV/AIDS. Adopters of this approach include larger multilateral organisations such as the United Nations Population Fund (UNFPA) and specific targeted organisations aimed at changing men's behaviour, such as Promundo (Casey et al., 2018). Yet gender-transformative approaches have increasingly been advocated for in various sectors, not just in explicit gender programmes – for example as in WASH (MacArthur et al., 2021) and agricultural programmes (Kantor et al., 2017). Many of these programmes draw from both GAD literature and ideas and from the models used in health programming.

In common with 1970s' ideas of women's empowerment, gender transformative pedagogy also draws significantly from Paulo Freire's critical education (Keddie, 2022). It aims to challenge established norms and develop critical consciousness as to the nature of oppression. A significant component of gender-transformative programming involves working with men. Yet working with men on transforming gender norms is no simple task. Gender-transformative programmes have been criticised when they take too much of an individualistic focus on men's behaviour, without considering the broader social environment (Dworkin et al., 2015). Simply 'involving men' is unlikely to challenge gender hierarchies. As such, Dworkin and Barker (2019) contrast 'male involvement' activities with 'gender-transformative' programming – the latter of which aims to more firmly challenge unequal gender norms. Keddie (2022) also describes how gender transformative approaches will necessitate uncomfortable discussions with boys and men as they may react negatively after being asked to consider their own behaviour. The skills of the educator or community development worker are hence critical here. Dworkin and Barker (2019) also indicate that male backlash is common when men are asked to question their environments, but they note that there are strategies such as working on group collective solidarity amongst men which can mitigate this. They also note that highlighting the negative outcomes of men being limited by gender stereotypes is helpful in promoting behaviour change (Dworkin & Barker, 2019).

There has been a number of promising studies on the impact of gender-transformative programmes, though results vary. Casey et al. (2018) found that seven out of ten gender-transformative programmes involved changes in men's attitudes towards women. Levy et al. (2020) undertook a review of gender-transformative programmes in health and found that three quarters of 59 programmes improved at least one aspect of health. Most programmes targeted youth at the stage of early adolescence, in recognition that this was an important time for behavioural change interventions. Most programmes are reviewed within a short timeframe, however (Dworkin & Barker, 2019; Kågesten & Chandra-Mouli, 2020), illustrating the need for longitudinal studies. The health literature also indicates that an individual transformative approach, while likely beneficial, may only have limited impacts due to broader structural limitations – hence there is a need to also work with governments and with social movements to create more sustainable social change (Kågesten & Chandra-Mouli, 2020).

Despite the prominence of gender-transformative approaches, there has been a number of criticisms of these programmes, both by programme advocates, seeking to improve programming, and by those who are fundamentally opposed to its principles. Dworkin et al. (2015) are seen to be gender-transformative programme advocates but they have criticised the extent to which other markers of inequality outside gender have been ignored in many gender-transformative programmes and they argue that an intersectional approach is needed. The majority of gender-transformative programmes in health do not use intersectional approaches (Kågesten & Chandra-Mouli, 2020). Yet intersectional approaches are also useful as they enable men to empathise with women based on men's experience of different hierarchies i.e. if men were racially discriminated against they may see how gender discrimination is similar (Dworkin & Barker, 2019). Others seek to modify aspects of gender-transformative programming, such as Casey et al. (2018) who argue that the initial outreach to men is highly significant and the strategies used in the outreach stage may significantly change the effectiveness of an intervention, yet this is not studied to the same extent as other stages of implementation.

In a far more critical vein, Brush and Miller (2019) argue that gender-transformative approaches that work with men may entrench gender stereotypes, i.e. that women are vulnerable and that men can be their protectors. They argue that while these programmes may change some violent behaviours, they do not change underlying attitudes. Brush and Miller (2019) highlight that many gender-transformative programmes had mixed outcomes and that there were geographical variations in outcomes. Hollander and Pascoe (2019, p.1682) extend Brush and Miller's critiques and argue that gender-transformative programming is 'not particularly gender transformative at all'. They argue instead that gender-transformative programming is fairly conventional in its application of gender stereotypes and does not give adequate consideration to the threat of male to male violence, particularly if men defy expected social norms.

While the idea of focusing on men's behavioural change has garnered the most controversy, involving men is only one component of gender-transformative change and must be one of many components for successful programming (Casey et al., 2018). Casey et al. (2018) reflect on the dual pressure, of on the one hand, attracting men to engage with gender programming, yet on the other hand, ensuring that the programme does not merely appease men and strengthen existing hierarchies. Casey et al. (2018) argue that while this is difficult, if social norms are *not* addressed then there is unlikely to be changes in intimate partner violence.

Where to From Here?

Women's empowerment is therefore a highly contentious concept and there are numerous movements which have been influential in shaping debates as to the role of women in development programmes. While many aid agencies and NGOs may use the language of GAD today, arguing for 'gender equality', in reality, many programmes still operate along WID principles of 'including' women. In addition, a further focus on women's economic empowerment programming (WEE) and 'smart economics' drives the emphasis away from women's holistic rights and gender relations and more closely to narrowly defined income generating activities. As 'women's empowerment' continues to be the cornerstone of multiple development programmes, including corporate campaigns, it is difficult to resurrect the initial radical interpretation of empowerment, yet those original ideas remain important for meaningful change today.

References

Ackerly, B., & True, J. (2010). Back to the Future: Feminist Theory, Activism, and Doing Feminist Research in an Age of Globalization. *Women's Studies International Forum*, 33(5), 464–472. doi:10.1016/j.wsif.2010.06.004.

Akram, S., Emerson, G., & Marsh, D. (2015). (Re)Conceptualising the Third Face of Power: Insights from Bourdieu and Foucault. *Journal of Political Power*, 8(3), 345–362. doi:10.1080/2158379x.2015.1095845.

Baden, S., & Goetz, A. M. (1997). Who Needs [Sex] When You Can Have [Gender]? Conflicting Discourses on Gender at Beijing. *Feminist review*, 56(1), 3–25. doi:10.1057/fr.1997.13.

Bandarage, A. (1984). Women in Development: Liberalism, Marxism and Marxist-Feminism. *Development and Change*, 15(4), 495–515. doi:10.1111/j.1467-7660.1984.tb00194.x.

Batliwala, S. (1994). The Meaning of Women's Empowerment: New Concepts from Action. In G. Sen, A. Germain, & L. C. Chen (Eds.), *Population Policies Reconsidered: Health, Empowerment and Rights*. Harvard Center for Population and Development Studies.

Batliwala, S. (2007). Taking the Power out of Empowerment – an Experiential Account. *Development in Practice*, 17(4–5),557–565. doi:10.1080/09614520701469559.

Batliwala, S., & Dhanraj, D. (2004). Gender Myths That Instrumentalise Women: A View from the Indian Frontline. *IDS Bulletin*, 35(4), 11–18. doi:10.1111/j.1759-5436.2004.tb00150.x.

Beetham, G., & Demetriades, J. (2007). Feminist Research Methodologies and Development: Overview and Practical Application. *Gender & Development*, 15(2), 199–216. doi:10.1080/13552070701391086.

Boserup, E. (1970). *Woman's Role in Economic Development*. Allen & Unwin.

Bourdieu, P. (1977). *Outline of a Theory of Practice*. Cambridge University Press.

Brown, A. M. (2006). Wid and Gad in Dar Es Salaam, Tanzania: Reappraising Gender Planning Approaches in Theory and Practice. *Journal of Women, Politics & Policy*, 28(2), 57–83. doi:10.1300/J501v28n02_03.

Brush, L. D., & Miller, E. (2019). Trouble in Paradigm: "Gender Transformative" Programming in Violence Prevention. *Violence Against Women*, 25(14), 1635–1656. doi:10.1177/1077801219872551.

Bull, B., & Bøås, M. (2012). Between Ruptures and Continuity: Modernisation, Dependency and the Evolution of Development Theory. *Forum for Development Studies*, 39(3), 319–336. doi:10.1080/08039410.2012.688860.

Calkin, S. (2015). Feminism, Interrupted? Gender and Development in the Era of 'Smart Economics'. *Progress in Development Studies*, 15(4), 295–307. doi:10.1177/1464993415592737.

Carella, A., & Ackerly, B. (2017). Ignoring Rights Is Wrong: Re-Politicizing Gender Equality and Development with the Rights-Based Approach. *International Feminist Journal of Politics*, 19(2), 137–152. doi:10.1080/14616742.2016.1226640.

Casey, E., Carlson, J., Two Bulls, S., & Yager, A. (2018). Gender Transformative Approaches to Engaging Men in Gender-Based Violence Prevention: A Review and Conceptual Model. *Trauma Violence Abuse*, 19(2), 231–246. doi:10.1177/1524838016650191.

Chant, S., & Sweetman, C. (2012). Fixing Women or Fixing the World? 'Smart Economics', Efficiency Approaches, and Gender Equality in Development. *Gender & Development*, 20(3), 517–529. doi:10.1080/13552074.2012.731812.

Chowdhry, G., & Ling, L. H. M. (2010). Race(Ing) International Relations: A Critical Overview of Postcolonial Feminism in International Relations. *Oxford Research Encyclopedia of International Studies*. Oxford University Press.

Collins, P. H., & Bilge, S. (2020). *Intersectionality* (2nd ed.). Polity.

Cornwall, A. (2007a). Buzzwords and Fuzzwords: Deconstructing Development Discourse. *Development in Practice*, 17(4/5), 471–484. http://www.jstor.org/stable/25548244.

Cornwall, A. (2007b). Revisiting the 'Gender Agenda'. *IDS Bulletin*, 38(2), 69–78. doi:10.1111/j.1759-5436.2007.tb00353.x.

Cornwall, A. (2016). Women's Empowerment: What Works? *Journal of International Development*, 28(3), 342–359. doi:10.1002/jid.3210.

Cornwall, A., & Anyidoho, N. A. (2010). Introduction: Women's Empowerment: Contentions and Contestations. *Development*, 53(2), 144–149. doi:10.1057/dev.2010.34.

Cornwall, A., & Brock, K. (2005). What Do Buzzwords Do for Development Policy? A Critical Look at 'Participation', 'Empowerment' and 'Poverty Reduction'. *Third World Quarterly*, 26(7), 1043–1060. doi:10.1080/01436590500235603.

Cornwall, A., & Rivas, A. M. (2015). From 'Gender Equality and 'Women's Empowerment' to Global Justice: Reclaiming a Transformative Agenda for Gender and Development. *Third World Quarterly*, 36(2), 396–415. doi:10.1080/01436597.2015.1013341.

Crenshaw, K. (1989). Demarginalizing the Intersection of Race and Sex: A Black Feminist Critique of Antidiscrimination Doctrine, Feminist Theory and Antiracist Politics. *University of Chicago Legal Forum*, 1(8), 139–167.

Deepak, A. C. (2012). Globalization, Power and Resistance: Postcolonial and Transnational Feminist Perspectives for Social Work Practice. *International Social Work*, 55(6), 779–793. doi:10.1177/0020872811414038.

Dhanaraj, S., & Mahambare, V. (2021). Male Backlash and Female Guilt: Women's Employment and Intimate Partner Violence in Urban India. *Feminist Economics*, 28(1), 170–198. doi:10.1080/13545701.2021.1986226.

Duncanson, C. (2019). Beyond Liberal Vs Liberating: Women's Economic Empowerment in the United Nations' Women, Peace and Security Agenda. *International Feminist Journal of Politics*, 21(1), 111–130. doi:10.1080/14616742.2018.1518725.

Dworkin, S. L., & Barker, G. (2019). Gender-Transformative Approaches to Engaging Men in Reducing Gender-Based Violence: A Response to Brush & Miller's "Trouble in Paradigm". *Violence Against Women*, 25(14), 1657–1671. doi:10.1177/1077801219872555.

Dworkin, S. L., Fleming, P. J., & Colvin, C. J. (2015). The Promises and Limitations of Gender-Transformative Health Programming with Men: Critical Reflections from the Field. *Culture, Health & Sexuality*, 17(sup2), 128–143. doi:10.1080/13691058.2015.1035751.

Dworkin, S. L., Treves-Kagan, S., & Lippman, S. A. (2013). Gender-Transformative Interventions to Reduce Hiv Risks and Violence with Heterosexually-Active Men: A Review of the Global Evidence. *AIDS and Behavior*, 17(9), 2845–2863. doi:10.1007/s10461-013-0565-2.

Eyben, R., & Napier-Moore, R. (2009). Choosing Words with Care? Shifting Meanings of Women's Empowerment in International Development. *Third World Quarterly*, 30(2), 285–300. doi:10.1080/01436590802681066.

Freire, P. (1970). *Pedagogy of the Oppressed*. Herder & Herder.

Green, D. (2016). *How Change Happens*. Oxford University Press.

Hillenbrand, E., Mohanraj, P., Njuki, J., Ntakobakinvuna, D., & Sitotaw, A. T. (2022). 'There Is Still Something Missing': Comparing a Gender-Sensitive and Gender-Transformative Approach in Burundi. *Development in Practice*, 1–12. doi:10.1080/09614524.2022.2107613.

Hollander, J. A., & Pascoe, C. (2019). Comment on Brush and Miller's "Trouble in Paradigm:'Gender Transformative Programming' in Violence Prevention". *Violence Against Women*, 25(14), 1682–1688.

James, V. D. (2009). Theorizing Black Feminist Pragmatism: Forethoughts on the Practice and Purpose of Philosophy as Envisioned by Black Feminists and John Dewey. *The Journal of Speculative Philosophy*, 23(2), 92–99.

James, V. D. (2013). Reading Anna J. Cooper with William James: Black Feminist Visionary Pragmatism, Philosophy's Culture of Justification, and Belief. *the pluralist*, 8(3), 32–45. doi:10.5406/pluralist.8.3.0032.

Kabeer, N. (2005). Gender Equality and Women's Empowerment: A Critical Analysis of the Third Millennium Development Goal 1. *Gender & Development*, 13(1), 13–24. doi:10.1080/13552070512331332273.

Kabeer, N. (2011). Between Affiliation and Autonomy: Navigating Pathways of Women's Empowerment and Gender Justice in Rural Bangladesh. *Development and Change*, 42(2), 499–528. doi:10.1111/j.1467-7660.2011.01703.x.

Kabeer, N. (2012). Empowerment, Citizenship and Gender Justice: A Contribution to Locally Grounded Theories of Change in Women's Lives. *Ethics and Social Welfare*, 6(3), 216–232. doi:10.1080/17496535.2012.704055.

Kabeer, N. (2016). Gender Equality, Economic Growth, and Women's Agency: The "Endless Variety" and "Monotonous Similarity" of Patriarchal Constraints. *Feminist Economics*, 22(1), 295–321. doi:10.1080/13545701.2015.1090009.

Kabeer, N. (2018). Gender, Livelihood Capabilities and Women's Economic Empowerment: Reviewing Evidence over the Life Course. Gender and Adolescence: Global Evidence Report. https://www.gage.odi.org/.

Kågesten, A., & Chandra-Mouli, V. (2020). Gender-Transformative Programmes: Implications for Research and Action. *The Lancet Global Health*, 8(2), e159–e160. doi:10.1016/S2214-109X(19)30528-5.

Kantor, P., Morgan, M., & Choudhury, A. (2017). Amplifying Outcomes by Addressing Inequality: The Role of Gender-Transformative Approaches in Agricultural Research for Development. *Gender, Technology and Development*, 19(3), 292–319. doi:10.1177/0971852415596863.

Keddie, A. (2022). Engaging Boys in Gender Transformative Pedagogy: Navigating Discomfort, Vulnerability and Empathy. *Pedagogy, Culture & Society*, 30(3), 401–414. doi:10.1080/14681366.2021.1977980.

Khan, K. B., McDonald, H., Baumbusch, J. L., Kirkham, S. R., Tan, E., & Anderson, J. M. (2007). Taking up Postcolonial Feminism in the Field: Working through a Method. *Women's Studies International Forum*, 30(3), 228–242. doi:10.1016/j.wsif.2007.03.004.

Kilgallen, J. A., Schaffnit, S. B., Kumogola, Y., Galura, A., Urassa, M., & Lawson, D. W. (2022). Positive Correlation between Women's Status and Intimate Partner Violence Suggests Violence Backlash in Mwanza, Tanzania. *Journal of Interpersonal Violence*, 37(21–22),NP20331–NP20360. doi:10.1177/08862605211050095.

Koczberski, G. (1998). Women in Development: A Critical Analysis. *Third World Quarterly*, 19(3), 395–410. doi:10.1080/01436599814316.

Levy, J. K., Darmstadt, G. L., Ashby, C., Quandt, M., Halsey, E., Nagar, A., & Greene, M. E. (2020). Characteristics of Successful Programmes Targeting Gender Inequality and Restrictive Gender Norms for the Health and Wellbeing of Children, Adolescents, and Young Adults: A Systematic Review. *The Lancet Global Health*, 8(2), e225–e236. doi:10.1016/S2214-109X(19)30495-4.

MacArthur, J., Carrard, N., & Willetts, J. (2021). Exploring Gendered Change: Concepts and Trends in Gender Equality Assessments. *Third World Quarterly*, 42(9), 2189–2208. doi:10.1080/01436597.2021.1911636.

Mangubhai, J., & Capraro, C. (2015). 'Leave No One Behind' and the Challenge of Intersectionality: Christian Aid's Experience of Working with Single and Dalit Women in India. *Gender & Development*, 23, 261–277. doi:10.1080/13552074.2015.1054206.

Marchand, M. H. (2009). The Future of Gender and Development after 9/11: Insights from Postcolonial Feminism and Transnationalism. *Third World Quarterly*, 30(5), 921–935. doi:10.1080/01436590902959149.

Mehta, L. (2016). Why Invisible Power and Structural Violence Persist in the Water Domain. *IDS Bulletin*, 47(5). doi:10.19088/1968-2016.165.

Menon, N. (2015). Is Feminism About 'Women'? A Critical View on Intersectionality from India. *Economic and Political Weekly*, 50(17), 37–44.

Moghadam, V. M. (1990). WID, WAD, GAD: Integration of Women, Women's Concerns, and Gender Issues in the Development Process: *A Review of the Literature and Policy Debates*, 1–30. https://fada.birzeit.edu/bitstream/20.500.11889/2297/1/WID%20WAD%20GAD%20integration%20of%20women%20introduction.pdf.

Moghadam, V. M., & Senftova, L. (2005). Measuring Women's Empowerment: Participation and Rights in Civil, Political, Social, Economic, and Cultural Domains. *International Social Science Journal*, 57(184), 389–412. doi:10.1111/j.1468-2451.2005.00557.x.

Molyneux, M. (1985). Mobilization without Emancipation? Women's Interests, the State, and Revolution in Nicaragua. *Feminist Studies*, 11(2), 227–254.

Moser, C. O. N. (1995). Women, Gender and Urban Development Policy: Challenges for Current and Future Research. *Third World Planning Review*, 17(2), 223.

Narayanaswamy, L. (2016). Whose Feminism Counts? Gender(ed) Knowledge and Professionalisation in Development. *Third World Quarterly*, 37(12), 2156–2175. doi:10.1080/01436597.2016.1173511.

Olesen, V. (2005). Early Millennial Feminist Qualitative Research: Challenges and Contours. In N. K. Denzin & Y. S. Lincoln (Eds.), *The Sage Handbook of Qualitative Research* (3rd ed., pp. 235–278). Sage Publications.

Parpart, J. L. (1993). Who Is the 'Other'?: A Postmodern Feminist Critique of Women and Development Theory and Practice. *Development & Change*, 24(3), 439–464. doi:10.1111/j.1467-7660.1993.tb00492.x.

Raj, K. M. (2013). Postcolonial Feminism: Looking into within-Beyond-to Difference. *International Journal of English and Literature*, 4(4), 129–134. doi:10.5897/IJEL12.165.

Rathgeber, E. M. (1990). WID, WAD, GAD: Trends in Research and Practice. *The Journal of Developing Areas*, 24(4), 489–502.

Razavi, S. & Miller, C. (1995). *From WID to GAD: Conceptual Shifts in the Women and Development Discourse.* UNRISD Occasional Paper No.1 for Fourth World Conference on Women, Beijing. UNRISD, Geneva.

Read, J. H. (2012). Is Power Zero-Sum or Variable-Sum? Old Arguments and New Beginnings. *Journal of Political Power*, 5(1), 5–31. doi:10.1080/2158379x.2012.659865.

Rorty, R. (1990). Feminism and Pragmatism. In *The Tanner Lecture on Human Values.* University of Michigan. https://tannerlectures.utah.edu/_resources/documents/a-to-z/r/rorty92.pdf.

Rottenberg, C. (2017). Neoliberal Feminism and the Future of Human Capital. *Signs: Journal of Women in Culture and Society*, 42(2), 329–348. doi:10.1086/688182.

Rowlands, J. (1997). *Questioning Empowerment: Working with Women in Honduras.* Oxfam GB.

Sardenberg, C. (2008). Liberal Vs. Liberating Empowerment: A Latin American Feminist Perspective on Conceptualising Women's Empowerment. *IDS Bulletin* 39 (6), 18–27. doi:10.1111/j.1759-5436.2008.tb00507.x.

Secretariat UN Secretary-General (2016). Leave No One Behind: A Call to Action for Gender Equality and Women's Economic Empowerment. https://www2.unwomen.org/-/media/hlp%20wee/attachments/reports-toolkits/hlp-wee-report-2016-09-call-to-action-en.pdf?la=en&vs=1028.

Seigfried, C. H. (1991). The Missing Perspective: Feminist Pragmatism. *Transactions of the Charles S. Peirce Society*, 27(4), 405–416.

Sen, G. (2006). The Quest for Gender Equality. In P. Utting (Ed.), *Reclaiming Development Agendas: Knowledge, Power and International Policy Making.* Palgrave Macmillan and UNRISD.

Sharma, A. (2008). *Logics of Empowerment: Development, Gender, and Governance in Neoliberal India*University of Minnesota Press.

Stromquist, N. P. (2014). Freire, Literacy and Emancipatory Gender Learning. *International Review of Education*, 60(4), 545–558. doi:10.1007/s11159-014-9424-2.

Tinker, I. (1990). A Context for the Field and the Book. In I. Tinker (Ed.), *Persistent Inequalities. Women and World Development.* Oxford University Press.

Tripathy, J. (2010). How Gendered Is Gender and Development? Culture, Masculinity, and Gender Difference. *Development in Practice*, 20(1), 113–121. doi:10.1080/09614520903436901.

United States Department of State (2022). Women's Economic Empowerment. https://www.state.gov/womens-economic-empowerment-3.

Wendell, S. (1987). A (Qualified) Defense of Liberal Feminism. *Hypatia*, 2(2), 65–93. doi:10.1111/j.1527-2001.1987.tb01066.x.

Wilson, K. (2011). 'Race', Gender and Neoliberalism: Changing Visual Representations in Development. *Third World Quarterly*, 32(2), 315–331. doi:10.1080/01436597.2011.560471.

Wilson, K. (2015). Towards a Radical Re-Appropriation: Gender, Development and Neoliberal Feminism. *Development and Change*, 46(4), 803–832. doi:10.1111/dech.12176.

Wong, Y. J., Klann, E. M., Bijelić, N., & Aguayo, F. (2017). The Link between Men's Zero-Sum Gender Beliefs and Mental Health: Findings from Chile and Croatia. *Psychology of Men & Masculinity*, 18(1), 12. doi:10.1037/men0000035.

World Bank (2012). World Development Report: Gender Equality and Development.

3 Feminist Movements in India

There is a rich and long tradition of feminist scholarship in India which helps us to better understand both women's empowerment and ways forward for Gender and Development. It is important to note that there is no *one* 'Indian feminism'. Rather, there is a diverse history of feminist movements in India (Banerjee, 2017), from Islamic women's movements (Vatuk, 2008) to secular rights campaigns (Zaman, 2016). It can be helpful to view feminism in India through the 'waves' metaphor (where stronger movements of women's activism were more visible), which has been used to describe key moments in feminism globally (Gupta, 2016; Roy, 2018). In this chapter I elaborate on the different movements within feminism in India, acknowledging that this summary is by no means exhaustive.

The first 'wave' of feminism accounts for the colonial period in India, including the anti-colonial resistance – a large span of time covering the mid-19th century to the mid-20th century. Many Indian feminists were anti-colonial and saw possibilities for women's rights in the 19th century through education and the law. Authors such as Tarabai Shinde (1882) were foundational during this period, including her work: 'A Comparison between Women and Men' and her idea of there being '*stri-jati*', (a caste of women) (Anagol, 2010; Banerjee, 2017). Padma Anagol (2010) details the ground-breaking vocabulary of Shinde and other Marathi-speaking feminists in this period and their use of terms such *bhaginivarg* (sisterhood); *strihak* (women's rights) and *strianubhav* (women's experience) which describe feminist ideals. Renu Pandey (2019) also importantly compares the work of two prominent Indian feminists and writers of the 19th century, Savitribai Phule and Pandita Ramabai, both significant for their contributions to feminism in India. Phule was from a 'low' caste family and worked together with her husband Jotirao Phule for social change and for the education of Dalits. The Phules were engaged in numerous struggles for the rights of women, including protesting against the shaving of widows' heads, developing a shelter home for widows and undertaking extensive humanitarian work. Pandey (2022) compares Phule's work with that of Pandita Ramabai who was born into a high caste family and who was an intellectual in Kolkata. Ramabai rallied against child marriage and the inferior treatment of women and was also a prolific writer at the time. Other significant women in

DOI: 10.4324/9781003356400-3

Bengal include Rokeya Sakhawat Hossain who argued both against male and British domination (Bagchi, 2009). Hossain wrote powerful allegories about feminism, founding a formal school for women and initiating literacy training for poorer women. For Hossain, education was liberation and women's knowledge was fundamental in fighting colonialism (Bagchi, 2009). This focus on education demonstrates the overarching dual focus of feminists at this time – advocating for the rights of women in the law and the rights of girls to an education (John, 2014).

While anti-colonial sentiment shaped early feminist movements in India, it also created an identity problem for Indian feminists as they were seen to collude with Western 'colonial' liberal ideals (Nair, 2020). Many in India have been suspicious of feminism as a 'Western' import (Jackson, 2010). Women during the colonial period sought to align their interests with nationalist struggles, so that they would not be perceived as being complicit with British interests (Dhingra, 2022). Hence many focused on tangible demands such as the right to vote which were not viewed as critical of Indian society (Dhingra, 2022). At the time, idealised versions of Indian womanhood were based on service to the family, self-sacrifice and honour (Nair, 2020). Indian women were ascribed with the symbolism of the nascent state's struggles, as a virtuous, honour-bound figure, willing to give up her life for the country (Komarraju & Raman, 2017). This meant that women's role as a martyr and as a homemaker were valorised, while women's broader needs for societal equality were deemed as less important than the overall struggle for national emancipation (Roy, 2018). Feminism which focused on women's *individual* freedoms was seen in some cases as acting contrary to this self-sacrifice needed for anti-colonial struggles. Tanika Sarkar (1992), for example, documents patriarchal nationalism and the extent to which subjugated Indian males reinforced their patriarchal standing and authority at home under colonialism.

In the 1970s, the 'second wave' of feminism came to the fore in India, with middle class Indian women increasingly becoming politically active for women's rights (Banerjee, 2017). This second wave aligned closely with the second wave of global feminism, commencing during this same period, adjacent to other dominant social movements. Kanjilal (2022) documents how second wave feminists in India were galvanised by a sexual assault case in the 1970s, with feminist movements of the previous decade largely enmeshed with union and other leftist causes. The case that startled women during this period was called the 'Mathura case'. It involved the alleged sexual assault by police officers of an Adivasi girl. The police officers were acquitted, sentenced and acquitted again by the Supreme Court – on highly spurious grounds (Kanjilal, 2022). Four legal scholars wrote an open letter to the Supreme Court, demanding that sexual assault be reframed as a human rights issue. This case brought multiple women to the street who had previously not been active in feminist protests before. It also meant that women had a focus for feminist action – addressing legal injustices and sexual assault (Biswas, 2017).

Another defining feature of this period in India was that feminism was seen as being anti-state (Deo, 2012). After the overreach of state powers during the Emergency period in India, where Sonia Gandhi severely limited activism, anti-state sentiment fermented across the population, including amongst feminists (Deo, 2012). This suspicion of the state was a key component of the second wave of feminism which emerged largely through women's networks, which would later be consolidated as non-governmental organisations (S. Roy, 2015). Roy (2018) argues that the values of radicalism and autonomy were foundational to feminists in the 1970s in India, leading to later criticisms that modern day feminists were too enmeshed with the state.

Indian feminists were also at the forefront of global anti-capitalist feminism during this period. At various UN conferences during this time, women from postcolonial societies argued that capitalist exploitation from Western nations was of greater concern than struggles between women and men (Banerjee, 2017). They argued that the exploitation 'third' world women faced from the 'first' world needed to form the basis of any feminist movement. Indian women were instrumental in shaping the DAWN document in advance of the Nairobi conference, bringing these concerns to the mainstream (Banerjee, 2017). The DAWN document was highly influential in the global spread of postcolonial ideas of feminism (Sen & Grown, 1985). Some, however, such as Arundhati Roy (2015) have criticised Indian feminist movements for their lack of attention to class struggles *within* India, particularly in response to the rights of Adivasi and Dalit women, a criticism which will be explored further later in this chapter.

A 'third wave' of Indian feminism can be seen to arise in India from the 2000s, though in some ways was nascent in the 1990s. Srila Roy (2018) highlights how the 1990s were a period where 'state feminism' came to dominate, with greater opportunities for women in collaboration with the state i.e. through various women's commissions and political reservations. In contrast to radical feminists, liberal feminists have tried to bring about reform through the state and via legislation (Majumdar, 2007). This period also was marked by the 'NGOisation' of feminism, with loosely formed women's movements organising and professionalising as NGOs (Katju, 2022; A. Roy, 2015). Radical feminists have been discontented with this development and have argued that focusing on state and law reforms is meaningless and that feminists instead need to cause a much larger disruption of power dynamics (S. Roy, 2015). Yet this period also saw the development of groundbreaking ideas which were deeply critical of second wave feminism, such as in the rise of intersectional concerns with caste and sexuality (Roy, 2022). Feminism during this period was also highly connected globally and focused on freedom, including sexual freedom (Roy, 2018). As such, conservative critiques continued to argue that feminism in India was a Western import, focused on breaking up the family and increasing divorce rates (Mitra, 2011).

The horrific rape and murder of Jyoti Singh in Delhi in 2012 marked a further turning point for feminism in India. This brutal incident galvanised women (and men) who had previously not been part of any feminist movements. Women and their allies took to the streets to protest how this case was emblematic of the treatment of women across India (Komarraju & Raman, 2017). In addition, the global #metoo movement swept through India shortly after, creating a significant focus on sexual harassment and abuse, particularly in the workplace (Vandana, 2020). This era from 2012 onwards arguably represents a 'fourth wave' of Indian feminism, though in many ways it is highly connected with the 'third wave'.

This current era of Indian feminism is also marked by solidarity and connectedness via social media, online discussions and activism (Bhattacharjya, 2021). For example, Madabhushi et al. (2015, p.39) document the rise of *'largely middle class, urban and individualistic'* feminism through a case study of the online group 'Hyderabad for Feminism'. This digital feminist platform illustrates a key segment of the current Indian feminist movement: middle class women drawn together by experiences of sexual harassment, violence against women and depictions of women in the media (Madabhushi et al., 2015). Twitter has been a particularly powerful platform during this time. Even though it enabled the vicious trolling of feminists, it also brought feminists together and created a sense of unity for common feminist causes (Dehingia & Raj, 2020; Pain, 2022). For example, Titus (2018) documents the #IWillGoOut campaign in India following the sexual assault and harassment of numerous women in Bengaluru during New Year's Eve 2016. Social media galvanised women who were shocked by these events, prompting a tide of women to use the hashtag #IWillGoOut on twitter. This focus on online organising has caused some friction, however, with second wave feminists who were not used to operating in this manner (Bhattacharjya, 2021) and who saw this means of operating as more disparate and disconnected than organising in-person.

#Metoo has been just as powerful in India as it has been in the West. The #metoo movement in India began with a focus on sexual harassment, assault and sexism in both the entertainment and media industries (Goel et al., 2018). The spotlight on sexual violence then moved to other industries, such as academia. Sexual violence is common in India as it is globally and the court system frequently displays the patriarchal attitudes of society, with very narrow ideas of how a woman *should* behave and how she should testify (Pain, 2022). 'Victim blaming' is considerable in India, i.e. the idea that a woman provoked an attack or was somehow deserving of it and this has been perpetuated by the film industry and media which has attempted to show 'both sides' of an attack (Gurman et al., 2018). Prominent cases of sexual assault have continued to motivate feminists in their struggles during this current era. For instance the Tarun Tejpal case received widespread publicity and feminist condemnation. Tejpal, the editor of the magazine *Tehelka*, was alleged to have sexually assaulted a female journalist and was acquitted for it in 2021, with the verdict stating that the survivor did not look 'traumatised' enough after the incident (Pain, 2022, p.2). This case tested the laws for addressing sexual violence which had been revised since 2013 (Pain, 2022), including the Sexual Harassment of Women at Workplace (Prevention, Prohibition and Redressal) Act. This Act sought to redress issues of widespread sexual harassment in the workplace and sparked increased awareness of this issue. Yet cases such as the Tejpal one illustrate how easy it is for alleged perpetrators to escape justice due to the entrenchment of misogyny and patriarchal attitudes.

Despite their limitations, many celebrated the fact that a number of laws were reformed between 2013–2019, including the Criminal Law (Amendment) Act, 2013 (CLA 2013), the Criminal Law (Amendment) Act, 2018 (CLA 2018) and the Protection of Children from Sexual Offences (Amendment) Act, 2019 (POCSO Amendment Act), which make the sexual assault of children under 12 punishable by death (Dash, 2021). Some feminists were more circumspect or disapproving in their stance towards these amendments, however. Dash (2021), for example, illustrates the difficulty of the Indian women's movement in responding to these cases, given many critiques within these movements of both the state and the police. In addition, some argued that by having such a harsh sentence, perpetrators were more likely to be let off on appeals (Dutta & Sircar, 2013), making it further difficult for survivors to seek justice.

During this period, universities have also been significant sites in women's feminist struggles. Vandana (2020) explains how women who have been enrolled in women's studies programmes or who identify as feminists have been mocked and taunted for their beliefs at the university. Universities have also been sites of sexual harassment and assault, particularly impacting Dalit women and other marginalised groups of women (Vandana, 2020). The University as a key locale for feminist struggle was most marked in 2017 when a 'list of sexual harassers in academia' (LoSHA) was produced by Raya Sarkar, a Dalit student based in the United States. This list was released on the internet, naming male academics who were deemed to be 'unsafe'. Within hours of this list appearing, a prominent group of older feminists released a statement in the online magazine *Kafila* saying that the list should be taken down and that due process needed to be followed. This caused much intergenerational tension between feminists, with some likening it to a feminist 'civil war' (Ghosh, 2017). Anasuya (2017) describes how this incident created great hurt amongst marginalised feminists in India. Older feminists argued that they had demonstrated their mettle in fighting for the rights of women to avoid sexual abuse, whereas younger women felt that the statement by older feminists in *Kafila* was condescending and dismissive. Roy (2018) discusses how the established feminist response in *Kafila* was in some quarters seen as ironic, with its focus on 'due process' – given the heinous examples where legal processes had constantly acquitted accused perpetrators. Tensions between feminists were not based solely on generational difference however. Notably, the older critics of the list came from upper caste backgrounds, whereas Raya Sarkar, the woman who released the list was from of Dalit origin. Given the fact that Dalit and other oppressed women were far less likely to receive any 'justice' for crimes committed against them, this insistence on 'due process' by the feminists writing in *Kafila* was particularly problematic. As Roy (2018) argues, this was a powerful evocation of Dalit Bahujan Adivasi feminisms which were able to call into question the legitimacy of mainstream Indian feminism with its caste and class biases. This incident can further be understood through the lens of Dalit feminism which I will expand on in the next section.

Dalit Feminism

Dalit feminism has gained increased prominence in India over the past decade as a unique theoretical strand of feminism. Based on the struggles of Dalit women (from the 'lowest' castes), Dalit feminists have lamented the dual struggles they have had with mainstream Indian feminism which is dominated by upper caste women and with Dalit rights movements which have been controlled by men (Paik, 2018). Dalit feminism thus shares many similarities with 'Black Feminism' and the struggle for black women's voices to be prioritised within either gender or racial equality movements (Crenshaw, 1989). Paik (2018, p.3) describes Dalits living under 'double colonialism' under both British and Brahmin (highest priestly caste) rule. Dalit women have frequently not been represented as active 'agents' in the struggle for gender justice, anti-colonialism or Dalit rights but have often been portrayed as passive 'victims' (Paik, 2018). Furthermore, the majority of the women's movement in India focuses on gender concerns of relevance to upper caste Hindus, while ignoring the pressing needs of Dalit women (Rege, 1998).

Women from Dalit backgrounds additionally face the triple burden of caste, class and gender discrimination in West Bengal, as throughout India. These women are more likely to experience brutal sexual violence (Mangubhai & Capraro, 2015) and there is less likely to be any recourse for the perpetrators' actions (Irudayam et al., 2011). In addition, Dalit women are more likely to be trapped in insecure and exploitative work conditions (Basu, 2012), compounded by lower literacy levels than other women or scheduled caste men (Government of India Census, 2011). The risk of being exploited in child labour is also greater for Dalit women (Chakravarty & Chakravarty, 2008).

The 'Dalit feminist' movement, which is not always termed as such, has connections to Ambedkar's social movement and the 'Dalit Panthers' struggle in the 1970s (Sen, 2019). Sen (2019) documents key female Dalit thinkers at this time, including Baby Kamble (1986) who wrote about the struggles of Dalit women and Urmila Pawar (2003) who details her experience with the feminist movement in Mumbai. Pawar (2003) was aware of the lack of caste-consciousness amongst urban feminists who came from the upper castes and the simultaneous inattention to gender in Dalit-led movements, a point also raised by Gopal (1995). Dalit feminist writing shares similar ideas to that of 'intersectionality', whereby women's multiple oppressions are seen as fundamental to the establishment of an equitable feminism (Rege, 1998).

There has been push back from second wave feminists in India and defensiveness to criticisms that they were not 'intersectional' enough. Nivedita Menon (2015), for example, the leader of the *Kafila* statement, argues that the Indian women's movement has always been 'intersectional'. She contends that involvement in anti-colonial activism gave Indian women a strong awareness of the multiple identity markers women carry. Though not termed 'intersectionality', Menon (2015) argues that Indian women were long concerned with the nexus between religious, caste and class identity and the competing demands of each before Western women became interested. Being engaged with other political movements, especially the anti-colonial struggle, enabled women to understand the multiplicity of oppression. Yet many have contested the extent to which mainstream feminisms in India have been concerned with the plight of Dalit or Adivasi women (Arya & Rathore, 2020).

In the current period, Bhattacharjya (2021) has also described how an increased focus on intersectionality within Indian feminism has further resulted in divisions within feminism, particularly with the rise of Dalit, Islamic and queer feminism. While this may be an era of fragmentation of feminism in India, as Roy (2022) argues, however, rather than seeing these divisions as a threat, they offer hope for a renewal of feminism that addresses the needs and desires of the vast multitude of women, focusing on the most vulnerable.

While Dalit feminism has gained traction in India, there is also scope for it to be recognised more broadly and inform the field of gender and development and feminisms in development globally, with its emphasis on human dignity, awareness of multiple forms of oppression, stress on the exclusionary nature of many mainstream feminist movements and focus on drawing out previously ignored histories.

The Status of Women in West Bengal

Coming to the particulars of women's rights and gender equality in West Bengal, I now describe some of the key trends. Gender inequality is pronounced in West Bengal as it is throughout India and indeed globally. It is based on centuries' long patriarchal customs (Kimuna et al., 2013). Indicators on women's empowerment in West Bengal also fare poorly. For example, women were included in a mere 16% of land titles in West Bengal in 2016 (Government of West Bengal, 2016). The association between poor empowerment and low levels of land ownership has been well documented (Agarwal, 1997), so this is a worrying indicator. In addition, some reports of child marriage indicate that it is most prevalent in West Bengal out of all the states in India (Business Standard 2017), as is female child labour (Chakravarty & Chakravarty, 2008). Sex trafficking is a regular problem also in West Bengal, both with women and children being trafficked within or outside the state and with West Bengal ending up as a location for trafficked victims (Singh, 2015).

Furthermore, while intimate partner violence is a global issue for women, it is noted to have a particularly high prevalence rate in the Eastern states of India. For example, estimates of prevalence rates in India show that there is a 31% lifetime prevalence amongst women in India (Krishnamoorthy et al., 2020). Yet other studies indicate that in the Eastern part of India, the prevalence rate for intimate partner violence is even worse, e.g. Babu and Kar (2010) found that in four Eastern states (including West Bengal) the prevalence rate of intimate partner violence was 50%.

Some indicators for women's empowerment have arguably improved in the past 30 years, for example, women's literacy and access to education (Sarkar, 2017). Quotas for women have also been established at different levels of government in West Bengal and the state is well known for having the influential female Chief Minister, Mamata Banerjee, in power since 2011, the first female Chief Minister of West Bengal. The state government has been quick to deny that there is any widespread violence against women, yet others argue that violence has been increasing in West Bengal and throughout India in the past few decades due to changes in social norms and male backlash (Simon-Kumar, 2014). Some have argued, however, that it is not that there are greater rates of violence but that women feel more comfortable reporting it (Joy et al., 2015). Furthermore, in the highly politicised environment of West Bengal, sexual violence has also been used as a means of reprisal for political opponents (Dasgupta, 2014).

Conclusion

As feminism and feminist movements such as Gender and Development and contemporary feminism in India continue to evolve, there is scope to consider how much attention has been paid to marginalised women and women experiencing intersecting oppressions. While 'intersectionality' is highly ubiquitous within academic debate, the extent to which any real 'intersectional' approach permeates development programming is questionable. Similarly, while Dalit feminism has gained more prominence in recent years in India, it is yet to be fully taken on board in any meaningful programmatic way. How for example, is the concept of marginalisation, of Dalit feminism or of intersectionality represented in microcredit and SHG programming? I will continue to explore these ideas throughout the following chapters, particularly when highlighting examples from the case study in West Bengal. First, however, in the next chapter I will provide a deeper exploration into the debates and situation of microcredit and SHG programming.

References

Agarwal, B. (1997). 'Bargaining' and Gender Relations: Within and Beyond the Household. *Feminist Economics*, 3(1), 1–51. doi:10.1080/135457097338799.

Anagol, P. (2010). Feminist Inheritances and Foremothers: The Beginnings of Feminism in Modern India. *Women's History Review*, 19(4), 523–546. doi:10.1080/09612025.2010.502398.

Anasuya, S. I. (2017, 29 October). Why the Response to a List of Sexual Harassers has Splintered India's Feminist Movement. Daily O. https://www.dailyo.in/politics/sexual-harassment-raya-sarkar-kafila-indian-feminism-20291.

Arya, S., & Rathore, A. S. (2020). Introduction: Theorising Dalit Feminism. In S. Arya & A. Singh Rathore (Eds.), *Dalit Feminist Theory: A Reader*. Routledge.

Babu, B. V., & Kar, S. K. (2010). Domestic Violence in Eastern India: Factors Associated with Victimization and Perpetration. *Public Health*, 124(3), 136–148.

Bagchi, B. (2009). Towards Ladyland: Rokeya Sakhawat Hossain and the Movement for Women's Education in Bengal, C. 1900–C. 1932. *Paedagogica Historica*, 45(6), 743–755. doi:10.1080/00309230903335652.

Banerjee, N. (2017). Feminism at the Crossroads: Where Do We Go from Here? *Indian Journal of Gender Studies*, 24(1), 98–110. doi:10.1177/0971521516678540.

Basu, S. (2012). Gender Knowledge of Female Textile Workers in West Bengal. *Journal of Workplace Rights*, 17(1), 93–111. doi:10.2190/WR.17.1.f.

Bhattacharjya, M. (2021). Chords of Solidarity, Notes of Dissent: The Role of Feminist Conferences in Movement-Building in India. *Gender & Development*, 29(2–3),623–647. doi:10.1080/13552074.2021.2005291.

Biswas, B. (2017). From Mathura to Jyoti: Mapping Public Protests and Anti-Rape Laws in India. In S. Jha & A. Kurian (Eds.), *New Feminisms in South Asia* (pp. 42–59). Routledge.

Business Standard (2017, 12 October). 40% of Country's Child Brides Reside in West Bengal: Supreme Court Survey. *Business Standard*. http://www.business-standard.com/article/current-affairs/40-of-country-s-child-brides-reside-in-west-bengal-supreme-court-survey-117101201187_1.html.

Chakravarty, D., & Chakravarty, I. (2008). Girl Children in the Care Economy: Domestics in West Bengal. *Economic & Political Weekly*, 43(48), 93–100.

Crenshaw, K. (1989). Demarginalizing the Intersection of Race and Sex: A Black Feminist Critique of Antidiscrimination Doctrine, Feminist Theory and Antiracist Politics. *University of Chicago Legal Forum*, 1(8), 139–167.

Dasgupta, S. (2014, 11th July). Why the Concept of 'Bhadralok' in West Bengal's Politics Is Only a Myth. *Saddahaq*. https://www.saddahaq.com/why-the-concept-of-bhadralok-in-west-bengals-politics-is-only-a-myth.

Dash, P. P. (2021). Feminism and Its Discontents: Punishing Sexual Violence in India. *Indian Journal of Gender Studies*, 28(1), 7–28. doi:10.1177/0971521520974843.

Dehingia, N., & Raj, A. (2020). Mining Twitter Data to Identify Topics of Discussion by Indian Feminist Activists. Big Data and Gender in the Age of COVID-19: A Brief Series from UC San Diego. https://data2x.org/wp-content/uploads/2021/01/UCSD-Brief-1_Big-Data-and-Gender-in-Covid-Brief-Series.pdf.

Deo, N. (2012). Running from Elections: Indian Feminism and Electoral Politics. *India Review*, 11(1), 46–64. doi:10.1080/14736489.2012.649126.

Dhingra, A. (2022). Gender Discourses and the Making of the Indian Constitution. *Indian Journal of Gender Studies*, 29(1), 33–54. doi:10.1177/09715215211056794.

Dutta, D., & Sircar, O. (2013). India's Winter of Discontent: Some Feminist Dilemmas in the Wake of a Rape. *Feminist Studies*, 39(1), 293–306.

Ghosh, A. (2017). The Civil War in Indian Feminism – a Critical Glance. *Sabrang*. https://sabrangindia.in/article/civil-war-indian-feminism-%E2%80%93-critical-glance.

Goel, V., Venkataraman, A., & Schultz, K. (2018). After a Long Wait, India's #Metoo Movement Suddenly Takes Off. *The New York Times*. https://www.nytimes.com/2018/10/09/world/asia/india-sexual-harassment-me-too-bollywood.html.

Gopal, G. (1995). Dalit Women Talk Differently. *Economic and Political Weekly*, 30 (41/42), 2548–2550.

Government of India Census (2011). 2011 Census. https://censusindia.gov.in/census.website/.

Government of West Bengal (2016). Women Development and Social Welfare. https://wb.gov.in/portal/web/guest/women-and-social-welfare.

Gupta, H. (2016). Taking Action: The Desiring Subjects of Neoliberal Feminism in India. *Journal of International Women's Studies*, 17(1), 152–168.

Gurman, T. A., Nichols, C., & Greenberg, E. S. (2018). Potential for Social Media to Challenge Gender-Based Violence in India: A Quantitative Analysis of Twitter Use. *Gender & Development*, 26(2), 325–339. doi:0.1080/13552074.2018.1473230.

Irudayam, A., Mangubhai, J. P., & Lee, J. G. (2011). *Dalit Women Speak Out: Caste, Class and Gender Violence in India*. Zubaan Books.

Jackson, E. (2010). *Feminism and Contemporary Indian Women's Writing*. Springer.

John, M. E. (2014). Feminist Vocabularies in Time and Space: Perspectives from India. *Economic and Political Weekly*, 49(22),121–130.

Joy, A., Belk, R., & Bhardwaj, R. (2015). Judith Butler on Performativity and Precarity: Exploratory Thoughts on Gender and Violence in India. *Journal of Marketing Management*, 31(15–16),1739–1745. https://doi.org/10.1080/0267257x.2015.1076873.

Kamble, B. (1986). *The Prisons We Broke* (trans. M. Pandit). Orient Blackswan.

Kanjilal, A. (2022). Narrating Legal Reform: The Open Letter and the Anti-Rape Movement in Perspective. *Indian Journal of Gender Studies*, 29(2), 199–221. doi:10.1177/09715215221082178.

Katju, V. (2022). The Autonomous Women's Movement in India: Beyond the Ngoization Framework. *Asian Journal of Women's Studies*, 28(4), 495–509. https://doi.org/10.1080/12259276.2022.2142361.

Kimuna, S. R., Djamba, Y. K., Ciciurkaite, G., & Cherukuri, S. (2013). Domestic Violence in India: Insights from the 2005–2006 National Family Health Survey. *Journal of Interpersonal Violence*, 28(4), 773–807. doi:10.1177/0886260512455867.

Komarraju, S. A., & Raman, U. (2017). Indian Millennials Define Feminism. *Feminist Media Studies*, 17(5), 892–896. doi:10.1080/14680777.2017.1350519.

Krishnamoorthy, Y., Ganesh, K., & Vijayakumar, K. (2020). Physical, Emotional and Sexual Violence Faced by Spouses in India: Evidence on Determinants and Help-Seeking Behaviour from a Nationally Representative Survey. *Journal of Epidemiology and Community Health*, 74(9), 732–740. doi:10.1136/jech-2019-213266.

Madabhushi, T., Wahlang, M. G. T., & Joshua, G. (2015). Locating 'Hyderabad for Feminism' in the Present Struggle against Violence. *Economic and Political Weekly*, 50(44), 38–46.

Majumdar, R. (2007). Arguments within Indian Feminism. *Social History*, 32(4), 434–445. doi:10.1080/03071020701616803.

Mangubhai, J., & Capraro, C. (2015). 'Leave No One Behind' and the Challenge of Intersectionality: Christian Aid's Experience of Working with Single and Dalit

Women in India. *Gender & Development*, 23, 261–277. doi:10.1080/13552074.2015.1054206.

Menon, N. (2015). Is Feminism About 'Women'? A Critical View on Intersectionality from India. *Economic and Political Weekly*, 50(17), 37–44.

Mitra, A. (2011). To Be or Not to Be a Feminist in India. *Affilia*, 26(2), 182–200. doi:10.1177/0886109911405493.

Nair, S. (2020). Metropolitan Feminisms of Middle-Class India: Multiple Sites, Conflicted Voices. *Indian Journal of Gender Studies*, 27(1), 127–140. doi:10.1177/0971521519891483.

Paik, S. (2018). The Rise of New Dalit Women in Indian Historiography. *History Compass*, 16(10). doi:10.1111/hic3.12491.

Pain, P. (2022). "Will the Law Not Protect Survivors Who Don't Weep": Twitter as a Platform of Feminist Deliberation and Democracy in India. *New Media & Society*, doi:10.1177/14614448221113007.

Pandey, R. (2019). Locating Savitribai Phule's Feminism in the Trajectory of Global Feminist Thought. *Indian Historical Review*, 46(1), 86–105.

Pandey, R. (2022). Two Distant Feminist Standpoints in Nineteenth-Century India: Case Studies of Savitribai Phule and Pandita Ramabai. *Indian Historical Review*, 49(1_suppl), S96–S119. https://doi.org/10.1177/03769836221105796.

Pawar, U. (2003). *Aaydaan*. Granthali Prakshan.

Rege, S. (1998). Dalit Women Talk Differently: A Critique of 'Difference' and Towards a Dalit Feminist Standpoint Position. *Economic and Political Weekly*, 33 (44), WS39–WS46.

Roy, A. (2015). *Capitalism: A Ghost Story*. Verso.

Roy, S. (2015). The Indian Women's Movement: Within and Beyond Ngoization. *Journal of South Asian Development*, 10(1), 96–117. doi:10.1177/0973174114567368.

Roy, S. (2018). Metoo Is a Crucial Moment to Revisit the History of Indian Feminism. *Economic & Political Weekly*, 53(42).

Roy, S. (2022). *Changing the Subject: Feminist and Queer Politics in Neoliberal India*. Duke University Press.

Sarkar, R. (2017). Recent Status of Education, Employment and Empowerment of Women in West Bengal. *International Journal of Scientific and Research Publications*, 7(1), 263–269.

Sarkar, T. (1992). The Hindu Wife and the Hindu Nation: Domesticity and Nationalism in Nineteenth Century Bengal. *Studies in History*, 8(2), 213–235.

Sen, G., & Grown, C. (1985). *Development, Crises, and Alternative Visions: Third World Women's Perspectives*. Monthly Review Press.

Sen, S. (2019). The Village and the City: Dalit Feminism in the Autobiographies of Baby Kamble and Urmila Pawar. *The Journal of Commonwealth Literature*, 54(1), 38–51. doi:10.1177/0021989417720251.

Simon-Kumar, R. (2014). Sexual Violence in India: The Discourses of Rape and the Discourses of Justice. *Indian Journal of Gender Studies*, 21(3), 451–460. doi:10.1177/097152151454071.1.

Singh, S. (2015, 23 August). Bengal Tops the List in Human Trafficking. *The Hindu*. http://www.thehindu.com/todays-paper/tp-national/bengal-tops-the-list-in-human-trafficking/article7570379.ece.

Titus, D. (2018). Social Media as a Gateway for Young Feminists: Lessons from the #Iwillgoout Campaign in India. *Gender & Development*, 26(2), 231–248. doi:10.1080/13552074.2018.1473224.

Vandana. (2020). Dalit Girls and Sexual Harassment in the University. *Indian Journal of Gender Studies*, 27(1), 33–54. doi:10.1177/0971521519891478.

Vatuk, S. (2008). Islamic Feminism in India: Indian Muslim Women Activists and the Reform of Muslim Personal Law. *Modern Asian Studies*, 42(2–3), 489–518. doi:10.1017/s0026749x07003228.

Zaman, N. (2016). From Islamic Feminism to Radical Feminism: Roquiah Sakhawat Hossein to Taslima Nasrin. *Asiatic: IIUM Journal of English Language and Literature*, 10(1), 4–26.

4 The Microcredit Debate

Microcredit has been called a heinous example of exploitation (Bateman, 2019), a groundbreaking revolution (Sengupta & Aubuchon, 2008) and everything in between. Microcredit has been one of the most contentious development initiatives globally, perhaps because of the very large claims made that it would end poverty and empower women (Shetty, 2013). These bold claims continue today, even as the sector has been under intense scrutiny. For example, Rakesh Kumar, the CEO of Light Microfinance, described in India Outlook (2022) how changes in the microfinance sector would lead to 'the future of an India of empowered women'. In this current era, microcredit continues to expand as private capital has found investment 'opportunities' through microcredit. In this chapter I explore the origins of microcredit, its different models, and the evidence thus far for its impact on women's lives.

Does Microcredit Work?

With the rapid expansion of the microcredit industry, many have asked the question: does microcredit work? There are several factors to unpack in this question. First of all, what does it mean to 'work'? Is it the end of poverty or the realisation of women's equality? Or is it more subtle differences – such as a change in income, health status or increased autonomy amongst women? In total, the literature does not indicate that there have been vast improvements in the standard of living or sweeping changes in gender equality, yet there are nuanced results between different types of microcredit initiatives, which I will explore more fully in this chapter.

The other component of the question to consider is what exactly *is* microcredit – the models differ widely. In India, microfinance is defined by the Reserve Bank of India as loans which do not require collateral going to households who earn less than 300,000 Indian Rupees per year. This encompasses a broad range of financial instruments – from loans directly given by banks or for profit entities like non-bank financial companies (NBFCs) to NGO programmes. The aims of each of these implementers is vastly different. For example, many NGOs adopt a 'credit-plus' model

DOI: 10.4324/9781003356400-4

(Develtere & Huybrechts, 2005; Holvoet, 2005) where they connect SHGs with microcredit whilst also undertaking a range of other programmes with the same communities – from helping the SHGs to learn how to manage their loans to conducting health or gender training programmes, for example. By contrast, microcredit loans given by NBFCs, for example, only provide funds. In addition, some microcredit lenders give loans to individuals as opposed to groups. Hence there are vast differences in the types of microcredit implemented and the scale of the programmes, making it difficult to make overarching assessments of microcredit programmes.

Furthermore, in the literature on microcredit we find a broad range of academic studies drawing from quantitative economic research or qualitative ethnographic studies involving in-depth interviews. Frequently these different types of studies are siloed within their disciplines – yet each different school of research provides a better understanding of the multiple dimensions of microcredit and its usefulness. In this chapter I expand on some of these studies and the different viewpoints provided in each. I first detail, however, the scope of the microcredit sector today, particularly in India and trace its origins.

Origins

Mohammed Yunus is well known as the founder of modern microcredit, even though microcredit existed in other forms previously. It is Yunus, however, who took microcredit to the world stage, gaining a Nobel Peace Prize in 2006 for his efforts. Yunus founded the Grameen Bank in 1983 after he experimented with giving small loans to the poor at low interest rates in the town of Jobra in Bangladesh (Yunus, 1999). From this experiment he went on to found the Grameen Bank which issued group loans to poor communities. Groups consisted of between ten and 20 members and they immediately began repaying the loans. Group loans were given on the basis that risk would be shared amongst members and defaults would be less likely. Yunus aimed to assist poor communities by freeing them from the grips of predatory moneylenders who charged usurious interest rates. He also saw microcredit as a means by which individuals would have increased agency, could start their own businesses and have more control in shaping their lives (Yunus, 2005).

While Yunus' ideas were gaining traction around the world, many saw how microcredit aligned with market based ideas of poverty alleviation, such as through the financial systems approach promoted by the Harvard Institute for International Development (Robinson, 1997), for example. These ideas were further promulgated by the rise of neoliberalism – an ideology which proposes that the free market should not be hampered by government intervention (Weber, 2002). For market advocates, microcredit was appealing as it promised to solve poverty through 'including' the poor in the market, so that they could have access to capital (Gerard and Johnston, 2019). In addition, global corporations, such as Citibank and Deutsche World began to see how microcredit to poor communities could be profitable (Knowledge at Wharton, 2005). Moreover, a number of not for profit organisations also transformed into for profit enterprises during this period, with the for profit enterprises usually charging higher rates of interest. For example, the Grameen Bank began as a not for profit organisation but was converted into a corporate entity in 2002 and was renamed Grameen II.

The State of the Sector Today

Even though microcredit has been the subject of much substantial criticism in the past decade, the sector has continued to grow and public funding for microcredit increased during the height of the Covid-19 pandemic (Tolzmann, 2022). For example, it is estimated that $160 billion was expended in loans in 2020 – roughly twice the total of loans disbursed in 2009 (Finch & Kocieniewski, 2022). Many talk of the market being 'untapped' – hence there has been interest from private equity and venture capital firms globally (Reuters, 2022). In 2021 the microfinance industry in India demonstrated 17% annual growth and it is estimated that this market will grow by more than 40% in 2025 (NABARD, 2021).

There are numerous different types of lenders involved in the sector today, including NGOs, non-banking financial institutions, commercial banks and cooperative banks. In addition, there are a range of different bodies who fund these lenders – from governments to private equity and investment firms, bilateral overseas development agencies, the World Bank and other development banks. Private international investors have markedly increased their interest in microfinance in the past twenty years, e.g. Citigroup lent one billion dollars to MFIs as of January 2020 (Finch & Kocieniewski, 2022). With such a wide variety of lenders, there are multiple microcredit models in existence. Most microcredit programmes in the past were based on providing loans for income generating projects but many examples of microfinance today illustrate that loans are used for daily consumption, and worryingly even to pay off other loans (Shakya & Rankin, 2008).

The ballooning of the industry has seen the rise of unscrupulous lenders also, who have pressured clients at their homes and places of work, demanding repayments (Mader, 2015). There have been global examples of these predatory lenders and one of the most publicised cases was in Andhra Pradesh in India in 2010, which I will detail later in this chapter. Unfortunately this example from Andhra Pradesh is not a one off occurrence, and similar examples of predatory lending and borrower despair have been reported across numerous countries, from Mexico, to Sri Lanka and Cambodia – to name some prominent instances (Heller, 2021). By way of example, Finch and Kocieniewski (2022) detail the situation in Sri Lanka where two hundred women died by suicide between 2019–2022 over the pressure to repay loans. They tell the story of Madhuka Kumari in Sri Lanka who borrowed $425 from the private LOLC Finance to start a business. After falling behind on payments, loan officers came to her home and started shouting at her – threatening her with police action. She felt such despair and shame that she tried to die by suicide. When she ended up in hospital, the loan officers further followed her there (Finch & Kocieniewski, 2022). This example of predatory lending and client despair has been witnessed in other countries also. Yunus himself has been highly critical of this privatised version of microcredit, arguing that development banks have encouraged loan shark behaviour amongst for profit microfinance institutions. Yunus has maintained that rates should not be set too high or the loans would become predatory. He has hence argued that this new model of private lending is fundamentally different from the microcredit programme he developed (Yunus, 2011).

Microcredit in India

India makes for an important case study in microcredit. The country has a long history of microcredit programming and it supports the largest microcredit programme globally (NABARD, 2022a). In 2021, microfinance was estimated to equal a massive $29.52 billion in India (Reuters, 2022). In addition, interest in microcredit only seems to be increasing, as programmes set to expand to cover populations which had not accessed microcredit previously (Garg, 2022).

Regarding the history of microcredit in India, there were two key developments to note. First, the Self Employed Women's Association (SEWA) Bank started a small programme of loans to its members, linking them with banks. SEWA Bank was founded by 4,000 women in 1974 who had been part of SEWA which had been registered as a trade union two years prior. SEWA Bank began by linking women with loans from nationalised banks and then extended loan coverage from its own funds. The second large significant development in the history of microcredit in India was in 1992 with the National Bank for Agriculture and Rural Development (NABARD). In 1992, NABARD undertook a pilot programme linking 500 SHGs to financial institutions (NABARD, 2022a). SHGs typically included up to twenty members which were usually all women. Out of this pilot project, NABARD developed the SHG-Bank Linkage Program (SHG-BLP). It was estimated that in 2021, 138 million households accessed microcredit through over 11 million SHGs in this programme (NABARD, 2021). Importantly, they estimate that 84% of the SHGs they fund are women-only groups (NABARD, 2021).

NABRAD has partnered with many institutions including NGOs, farmers' clubs and SHG federations. The SHG-BLP connects SHGs with financial institutions, including with commercial banks, regional rural banks and cooperative banks. Many NGOs work as 'Self Help Group Promoting Institutions' (SHPIs), helping community members in SHGs to form linkages with the banks. The SHG-BLP operates via group lending. The group saves and distributes loans within the group and then they apply for a loan with a registered bank. The Bank gives one loan to the group who then determine how to distribute it amongst members. The group is all responsible for the loan. Either SHGs connect directly with banks, or they are supported by a government department or NGO to be linked to the bank (Sarkar & Chattopadhyay, 2021).

Both national and state governments have supported funding for SHGs in India. SHGs gained support from the central government from 1999 and the Government of India initiated a number of schemes including 'Swarnajayanti Gram Swarozgar Yojna' (SGSY) for groups below the poverty line. In 2011 this programme was revamped into the National Rural Livelihood Mission (NRLM) and in 2016 the NRLM was renamed Deendayal Antyodaya Yojana–National Rural Livelihoods Mission (DAY-NRLM). In addition, many state governments themselves have funded SHG programmes – including: the Podupulakshmi and Indira Kranti Patham programme (Andhra Pradesh), Jeevika (Bihar), Mahalir Thittam (Tamil Nadu), Kudumbashree (Kerala) and TRIPTI/ Mission Shakti projects (Odisha) (NABARD, 2021).

A significant crisis occurred in the microcredit industry in India in 2010. SKS Microfinance became the largest lender in Andhra Pradesh and was funded by international finance conglomerates. Their practices were highly problematic as they regularly hounded borrowers who were unable to pay their loans. They also enabled borrowers to become over indebted (Picherit, 2015). This led to a spate of borrowers dying by suicide in 2010 which then prompted the state government to temporarily suspend microcredit in the state while the Reserve Bank of India held an enquiry and subsequently tightened restrictions. The Reserve Bank of India's Department of Regulation attributes the crisis in Andhra Pradesh to the 'irrational exuberance of some MFIs who, in their eagerness to grow business, had given a go by to the conventional wisdom and good practices such as due diligence in lending and ethical recovery practices' (NABARD, 2021, p.4), meaning that any failure in due diligence was caused only by the sheer enthusiasm of lenders. Rather than 'irrational exuberance', however, it was more likely to be predatory unscrupulousness which led to this crisis. During the crisis, SKS in fact reported a revenue of over Rupees 10 billion in FY11 (Mistry, 2022).

While this crisis dampened enthusiasm for lending for a period of time, before long, private Microfinance Institutions (MFIs) began to rapidly expand in India (Biswas & Gupta, 2022). Today there is a broad range of actors working in microcredit in India. Microcredit is distributed through: scheduled commercial banks (SCBs) who lend directly to SHGs and businesses; cooperative banks, non-banking financial companies (NBFCs) and microfinance institutions (MFIs) (some of which are registered as NBFCs). Not for profit institutions have decreased in their share of the microcredit market. The NABARD Status of Microfinance in India Report (NABARD,

2022b) indicated that only 1.24% of the microfinance market was with not for profit MFIs. While microcredit has continued to expand throughout the private sector, critics have argued that instead of being a commercial enterprise, microcredit should be distributed via Public Sector Banks (PSBs), Regional Rural Banks (RRBs) or Cooperative Banks at interest rates of between 4 and 9% (Krishnan, 2022). Yet despite criticisms, there seems to be no signs of growth abating in the private market for microcredit.

Deregulation has further aided the growth of the private microcredit sector. In April 2022, the RBI loosened some of the regulations in the sector which had been tightened following the crisis in Andhra Pradesh. The regulations in 2011 had focused heavily on NBFC-MFIs, capping their interest rates. Under the new RBI Guidelines, however, interest rates are no longer capped. In addition, microfinance has been broadened to include loans to households with an annual income up to 300,000 Indian Rupees per annum (the previous cap was at an annual income of 240,000 Indian Rupees). Some think that this may broaden the scope of clients, making microcredit more attractive to urban residents (Dey, 2022). Some limitations remain in place under the new guidelines, however, including that clients may only borrow up to the extent that their maximum repayment does not exceed 50% of their monthly income. Borrowers may also make early repayments. The RBI argues that the new guidelines were developed to try to create a consistent framework across microcredit lenders and to not single out NBFC-MFIs. Concerningly, however, there is a provision in the new guidelines where lenders may go to a borrower's home or workplace if the borrower has not met with the lender's representative at the agreed time and location at least twice. Some have argued that this can result in harassment which contributed to suicides in the past (Krishnan, 2022).

Interestingly, private MFIs have generally viewed the revised guidelines favourably, for example, Rakesh Kumar, CEO of Light Microfinance stated:

> There is still a huge market to capture and the December 2011 rules were becoming 'stumbling blocks' for the sector to sustain its growth.
>
> (Kumar, 2022)

Jigar Mistry, co-founder of Buoyant Capital took a similar view in writing for the *Economic Times in India*:

> If collections (i.e. repayment rates) hold, MFIs will start focusing on growth again, and there is a big untapped opportunity still awaiting.
>
> (Mistry, 2022)

Given deregulation in the market and the desire of corporations to constantly find 'new' ways of making profit, there are estimates that the microfinance market will expand rapidly over the coming decade (NABARD, 2021).

Measuring the Effect on Poverty and the Rise of the RCTs

Most studies on the impact of microcredit on poverty are quantitative and come from the field of economics. Early studies held much enthusiasm for the ability of microcredit to improve the economic conditions of the poor. For example, Mark Pitt and Shahid Khandker's (1998) well-cited study argued that microcredit was effectively lifting women out of poverty in Bangladesh. In recent years, there has been more criticism of these early studies (Roodman & Morduch, 2014), however. There has also been a flourishing in the past decade of Random Controlled Trials (RCTs) on microcredit interventions. In 2015, the American Economic Journal published the results of six RCTs from around the world and Banerjee et al.'s (2015) combined review of these RCTs. This issue included analysis of data from Banerjee et al.'s (2015) RCT in India of the for profit lender Spandana. Reviewing the six studies, Banerjee et al. (2015, p.1) argue that the previous enthusiasm for microcredit was unfounded and that these programmes have had 'modestly positive, but not transformative effects'. Their studies found that microcredit increased business activity but that there was no statistically significant increase in household income nor household consumption (Banerjee, Karlan, et al., 2015). However, the finding that microcredit households received a greater percentage of income from business vs wages than the control group could indicate that microcredit borrowers had greater autonomy and self-reliance as they may be less likely to be trapped within poor jobs. They also indicated that there were no changes in children's schooling nor in women's empowerment except in the study in Mexico. While Banerjee et al. (2015) did not find sweeping changes in the lives of microcredit borrowers, they also did not see evidence of harmful effects, despite individual borrowing in two studies and a high interest rate in one study (in Mexico). Banerjee et al. (2015, p.3) conclude 'if microcredit's promise were increasing freedom of choice it would be closer to delivering on it'.

Other recent economic studies include Meager's (2019) examination of the datasets of seven RCT microcredit studies across seven different countries using Bayesian statistical analysis. In common with Banerjee et al.'s (2015) study, Meager found that belonging to a microcredit intervention resulted in little impact or changes in income or consumption, but then neither did she find evidence of over-indebtedness or exploitation. Focused on South Asia, Gopalaswamy, Babu and Dash (2015) also undertook a study of 69 microcredit programmes. They indicated that there was no statistically significant impact on income or consumption across the programmes, however there was an increase in assets owned by households participating in microcredit in studies where that information was available. In a different kind of study, Breza and Kinnan (2021) examined the dataset of 25 micro lenders in addition to household data from the National Sample Survey to determine what the impact was of microcredit being halted in Andhra Pradesh and they found that its cessation had had a negative effect on the economy.

While RCTs have flourished in recent years, RCTs are not without their criticisms. Morduch (2020), for example, has argued that RCTs should be only one of many methods for evaluating the impact of microcredit. He argues that the RCT studies of 2015 focus on marginal borrowers in marginal areas and hence the results cannot be generalised widely. Non-marginal borrowers who have long been accessing microcredit may well be more motivated and have a different profile which enables them to gain better outcomes from receiving microcredit (Morduch, 2020; Rajbanshi et al., 2015). Naila Kabeer (2019) has also criticised RCTs for their lack of transparency about what went wrong and for the way that results are skewed by those who join the programme and by those who do not wish to join the programme – one example she cites is of Muslim minorities choosing not to be part of the microcredit programme in West Bengal and how that skewed the results of the study. By essentially ignoring prior studies and knowledge on microcredit, RCTs provide little understanding of the contextual factors around microcredit programming and its vast nuances. It is also very difficult to generalise past the very specific example which RCTs provide. For instance, Banerjee et al. (2015) argue that their microcredit interventions studied showed no signs of exploitation or negative effects, yet the lenders they study are a small percentage of the whole. Even if *some* lenders are scrupulous, that does not mean that the entirety of lenders behave well. There certainly are well documented instances of lenders hounding potential borrowers to take out loans and then continuing to harass the borrowers to repay their loans (Mader, 2013).

In addition, the RCTs generally focused on microcredit interventions which were purely loans with no credit-*plus* dimensions. This was in many cases intentional, so that they could analyse the impact of 'pure' microcredit, however these results then say little about what the outcomes of a credit-plus model may be. Indeed, many studies also do not differentiate between different practices within organisations (see Kabeer (2017) for criticisms). Banerjee et al. (2015) have indicated that they recognise this and state that their results could have been different if they had studied a Grameen type model.

Women's Empowerment

While previous studies have not illustrated any widespread changes to community poverty levels from belonging to a microcredit intervention, what does the research say as to microcredit's impact on women's empowerment? Again, the results are conflicting and studies have used an array of qualitative and quantitative methodologies to try to answer this question.

First, there are largely qualitative critical studies which argue that women are essentially exploited through belonging to a microcredit programme, becoming entrapped by debt (Keating et al., 2010; Paprocki, 2016; Reboul et al., 2021). As women have taken out loans and in many cases have been unable to repay these loans, they have had to either borrow additional funds, or work in increasingly exploitative roles to repay their debt. This process of becoming trapped by debt also has led to feelings of shame and despair, where women see no options out of their current circumstances and feel afraid of being harassed by the microcredit lenders at their workplace and in public (Engel & Pedersen, 2019). Critical scholars argue that women and the community at large are tricked through promises of 'women's empowerment' and that targeting women is merely a means for expanding the financialisation of private capital (Federici, 2014). Many of these criticisms focus on programmes which are microcredit-only and distributed through for profit providers, yet there are also some criticisms of NGO run credit-plus models, particularly that they still operate on the principles of shaming women in a group (Karim, 2008). These critical studies have also built on earlier research which has argued that microcredit funds were extracted by the husbands of female SHG members and used by the men to control women (Karim & Law, 2015; Singh et al., 2016). In a similar vein, other research has argued that microcredit programming was disempowering for women because it substantively increased women's workload (Geleta, 2016; Sengupta, 2013).

For each critical study, however, there is also a positive example provided by other authors. For example, Naila Kabeer's work on microcredit found that while it was no 'magic bullet' (Kabeer, 2005), there were several highly positive examples arising from credit-plus microcredit interventions. Other studies also found that belonging to a microcredit programme increased a number of aspects of wellbeing which could fall under the category of 'empowerment'. For instance, Swain and Wallentin (2009) indicated that women who belonged to a microcredit programme had more decision making authority within their homes, similar to Browning and Chiappori's (1998) stance that microcredit users had improved bargaining power in the household. Crucially, also, a number of studies have indicated that the social gains made from belonging to a microcredit programme were often more significant than any financial gains (Davidson & Sanyal, 2017; Garikipati, 2008; Holvoet, 2005). Paromita Sanyal (2014, 2015) and Naila Kabeer (2011) both especially make strong arguments for the connections which belonging to an SHG enabled women to make. Deshpande and Khanna (2021) also indicate that belonging to an SHG improves women's social capital even when there is no increase in income. They also found that belonging to an SHG increased women's propensity for collective action, similar to Kabeer (2017) and Sanyal's (2009) results.

In recent years there has also been a spate of quantitative studies and overarching literature reviews which have aimed to measure the extent to which microcredit empowers women. These studies have used a number of proxy indicators for empowerment, from women's control of income, to their mobility outside the house, measured levels of confidence and incidents of reported domestic violence (United States Government Accountability Office, 2021). These studies indicated a range of results. From the recent review studies, Brody et al. (2017) examined 34 qualitative and quantitative studies of self-help groups and found that belonging to an SHG improved mobility, decision making and control of finances but that it did not result in any changes to psychological empowerment. Gopalaswamy and Dash (2015) reviewed 26 studies in South Asia and indicated that belonging to a microcredit programme improved the extent to which women controlled finances in their household. Gichuru et al. (2019) reviewed 27 global studies on microcredit and found that accessing credit either had no impact or mixed outcomes on domestic violence, women's freedom of movement or decision making. Duvendack and Mader (2020), in addition, reviewed 11 studies focused on financial services and argued that empowerment effects largely resulted from training programmes not necessarily from access to finance itself. Reboul et al. (2021) collected survey data from 1,610 people in rural areas of Tamil Nadu and found that men were more likely to take out loans for entrepreneurial purposes than women (who took out loans largely for consumption). Kumar et al. (2021) examined the impact of belonging to an SHG on women's empowerment using the A-WEAI and the Pro-WEAI to analyse survey data. They drew on data from 1,470 rural Indian women from across five states and found that SHG membership had a positive effect on the following indicators for women's empowerment: control over household expenditure, increased decision making at home and greater mobility. They did not find that belonging to an SHG, however, resulted in any changes to intimate partner violence, workload or shifts in the level of respect they gained at home. Through analysing the Jeevika SHG-BLP project in Bihar, Datta (2015) indicated that belonging to an SHG improved women's mobility, decision making and scope for collective action.

Conclusion

How then to account for this wide range of conclusions as to the value of microcredit? It is important to remember that each microcredit borrower is unique, as is each lender, and what works for one woman may not work for another. In summary, it seems that sole microcredit programmes (without any credit-plus components) may only benefit some women and the results are modest. Credit-plus programmes showed more promise but also demonstrated mixed results and the specifics of the model of microcredit are particularly important. In the following chapters I will show the nuances of microcredit interventions, even within one overarching programme. In the next chapter I will illustrate the extent to which 'smart economics' and more feminist holistic models of microcredit may be contrasted and how this continuum may explain some of the differences in the results of microcredit programming.

References

Ahmed, S. M. (2005). Intimate Partner Violence against Women: Experiences from a Woman-Focused Development Programme in Matlab, Bangladesh. *Journal of Health, Population and Nutrition*, 95–101.

Bajracharya, A., & Amin, S. (2013). Microcredit and Domestic Violence in Bangladesh: An Exploration of Selection Bias Influences. *Demography*, 50(5), 1819–1843. doi:10.1007/s13524-013-0226-0.

Banerjee, A., Duflo, E., Glennerster, R., & Kinnan, C. (2015). The Miracle of Microfinance? Evidence from a Randomized Evaluation. *American Economic Journal: Applied Economics*, 7(1), 22–53. doi:10.1257/app.20130533.

Banerjee, A., Karlan, D., & Zinman, J. (2015). Six Randomized Evaluations of Microcredit: Introduction and Further Steps. *American Economic Journal: Applied Economics*, 7(1), 1–21. doi:10.1257/app.20140287.

Bateman, M. (2019). South Africa's Post-Apartheid Microcredit Experiment: Moving from State-Enforced to Market-Enforced Exploitation. *Forum for Social Economics*, 48(1), 69–97. doi:10.1080/07360932.2015.1056202.

Bhuiya, A., Sharmin, T., & Hanifi, S. (2003). Nature of Domestic Violence against Women in a Rural Area of Bangladesh: Implication for Preventive Interventions. *Journal of Health, Population and Nutrition*, 48–54.

Biswas, B., & Gupta, R. P. (2022). Role of Microfinance Institutions in Social Inclusion: A Study with Reference to India. In R. C. Das (Ed.), *Microfinance to Combat Global Recession and Social Exclusion* (pp. 229–247). Springer.

Breza, E., & Kinnan, C. (2021). Measuring the Equilibrium Impacts of Credit: Evidence from the Indian Microfinance Crisis. *The Quarterly Journal of Economics*, 136(3), 1447–1497. doi:10.1093/qje/qjab016.

Brody, C., de Hoop, T., Vojtkova, M., Warnock, R., Dunbar, M., Murthy, P., & Dworkin, S. L. (2017). Can Self-Help Group Programs Improve Women's Empowerment? A Systematic Review. *Journal of Development Effectiveness*, 9(1), 15–40. doi:10.1080/19439342.2016.1206607.

Browning, M., & Chiappori, P. A. (1998). Efficient Intra-Household Allocations: A General Characterization and Empirical Tests. *Econometrica*, 66(6), 1241–1278.

Datta, U. (2015). Socio-Economic Impacts of Jeevika: A Large-Scale Self-Help Group Project in Bihar, India. *World Development*, 68, 1–18. doi:10.1016/j.worlddev.2014.11.013.

Davidson, T., & Sanyal, P. (2017). Associational Participation and Network Expansion: Microcredit Self-Help Groups and Poor Women's Social Ties in Rural India. *Social Forces*, 95(4), 1695–1724. doi:10.1093/sf/sox021.

Deshpande, A., & Khanna, S. (2021). Can Weak Ties Create Social Capital? Evidence from Self-Help Groups in Rural India. *World Development*, 146. doi:10.1016/j.worlddev.2021.105534.

Develtere, P., & Huybrechts, A. (2005). The Impact of Microcredit on the Poor in Bangladesh. *Alternatives*, 30(2), 165–189. doi:10.1177/030437540503000203.

Dey, P. (2022, 20 April). New RBI Rules May Change Customer Focus of Microfinance Lenders, Say Experts. *Money Control*. https://www.moneycontrol.com/news/business/banks/new-rbi-rules-may-change-customer-focus-of-microfinance-lenders-say-experts-8385521.html.

Duvendack, M., & Mader, P. (2020). Impact of Financial Inclusion in Low-and Middle-Income Countries: A Systematic Review of Reviews. *Journal of Economic Surveys*, 34(3), 594–629.

Duvendack, M., & Palmer-Jones, R. (2016). Micro-Finance, Women's Empowerment and Fertility Decline in Bangladesh: How Important Was Women's Agency? *The Journal of Development Studies*, 53(5), 664–683. https://doi.org/10.1080/00220388.2016.1205731.

Engel, S., & Pedersen, D. (2019). Microfinance as Poverty-Shame Debt. *Emotions and Society*, 1(2), 181–196. doi:10.1332/263168919X15653391247919.

Federici, S. (2014). From Commoning to Debt: Financialization, Microcredit, and the Changing Architecture of Capital Accumulation. *South Atlantic Quarterly*, 113(2), 231–244. doi:10.1215/00382876-2643585.

Finch, G., & Kocieniewski, D. (2022, 3 May). Big Money Backs Tiny Loans That Lead to Debt, Despair and Even Suicide. *Bloomberg*. https://www.bloomberg.com/graphics/2022-microfinance-banks-profit-off-developing-world/?leadSource=uverify%20wall.

Garg, R. (2022, 9 December). As Microfinance Takes Off in India, Attention to Detail Is the Need of the Hour. *Times of India*. https://timesofindia.indiatimes.com/blogs/voices/as-microfinance-takes-off-in-india-attention-to-detail-is-the-need-of-the-hour/.

Garikipati, S. (2008). The Impact of Lending to Women on Household Vulnerability and Women's Empowerment: Evidence from India. *World Development*, 36(12), 2620–2642. doi:10.1016/j.worlddev.2007.11.008.

Geleta, E. B. (2016). *The Microfinance Mirage: The Politics of Poverty, Social Capital and Women's Empowerment in Ethiopia*. Routledge.

Gerard, K., & Johnston, M. (2019). Explaining Microfinance's Resilience: the case of Microfinance in Australia. *Globalizations*, 16(6), 876–893. doi:10.1080/14747731.2018.1560188.

Gichuru, W., Ojha, S., Smith, S., Smyth, A. R., & Szatkowski, L. (2019). Is Microfinance Associated with Changes in Women's Well-Being and Children's Nutrition? A Systematic Review and Meta-Analysis. *BMJ Open*, 9(1), e023658. doi:10.1136/bmjopen-2018-023658.

Gopalaswamy, A. K., Babu, M., & Dash, U. (2015). Systematic Review of Quantitative Evidence on the Impact of Microfinance on the Poor in South Asia. *EPPI-Centre, Social Science Research Unit, Institute of Education, University College London*. https://eppi.ioe.ac.uk/cms/Portals/0/PDF%20reviews%20and%20summaries/Microfinance%20impact%202015%20Gopalawamy%20protocol.pdf?ver=2015-06-24-111207-627.

Heller, P. W. (2021). The Lessons of Microcredit. In K. Wendt (Ed.), *Theories of Change: Change Leadership Tools, Models and Applications for Investing in Sustainable Development* (pp. 153–168). Springer.

Holvoet, N. (2005). The Impact of Microfinance on Decision-Making Agency: Evidence from South India. *Development and Change*, 36(1), 75–102. doi:10.1111/j.0012-155X.2005.00403.x.

Kabeer, N. (2001). Conflicts over Credit: Re-Evaluating the Empowerment Potential of Loans to Women in Rural Bangladesh. *World Development*, 29(1), 63–84. doi:10.1016/S0305-750X(00)00081-4.

Kabeer, N. (2005). Is Microfinance a 'Magic Bullet' for Women's Empowerment? Analysis of Findings from South Asia. *Economic and Political Weekly*, 40(44/45), 4709–4718.

Kabeer, N. (2011). Between Affiliation and Autonomy: Navigating Pathways of Women's Empowerment and Gender Justice in Rural Bangladesh. *Development and Change*, 42(2), 499–528. doi:10.1111/j.1467-7660.2011.01703.x.

Kabeer, N. (2017). Economic Pathways to Women's Empowerment and Active Citizenship: What Does the Evidence from Bangladesh Tell Us? *The Journal of Development Studies*, 53(5), 649–663. doi:10.1080/00220388.2016.1205730.

Kabeer, N. (2019). Randomized Control Trials and Qualitative Evaluations of a Multifaceted Programme for Women in Extreme Poverty: Empirical Findings and Methodological Reflections. *Journal of Human Development and Capabilities*, 20(2), 197–217. doi:10.1080/19452829.2018.1536696.

Karim, K. M. R., & Law, C. K. (2015). Microcredit and Marital Violence: Moderating Effects of Husbands' Gender Ideology. *Journal of Family Violence*, 31(2), 227–238. doi:10.1007/s10896-015-9763-1.

Karim, L. (2008). Demystifying Micro-Credit: The Grameen Bank, NGOs, and Neoliberalism in Bangladesh. *Cultural Dynamics*, 20(1), 5–29. doi:10.1177/092137400708.

Keating, C., Rasmussen, C., & Rishi, P. (2010). The Rationality of Empowerment: Microcredit, Accumulation by Dispossession, and the Gendered Economy. *Signs: Journal of Women in Culture and Society*, 36(1), 153–176. doi:10.1086/652911.

Knowledge at Wharton (2005). Microcredit Is Becoming Profitable, Which Means New Players and New Problems. University of Pennsylvania. School of Wharton. https://knowledge.wharton.upenn.edu/article/microcredit-is-becoming-profitable-which-means-new-players-and-new-problems/.

Krishnan, C. P. (2022, 27 March). Withdraw RBI Guidelines on Microfinance Loans. *People's Democracy.* https://peoplesdemocracy.in/2022/0327_pd/withdraw-rbi-guidelines-microfinance-loans.

Kumar, N., Raghunathan, K., Arrieta, A., Jilani, A., & Pandey, S. (2021). The Power of the Collective Empowers Women: Evidence from Self-Help Groups in India. *World Development*, 146. doi:10.1016/j.worlddev.2021.105579.

Kumar, R. (2022, 8 April). Microfinance Is Evolving, So Should the Rules. Outlook India. https://www.outlookindia.com/business/microfinance-is-evolving-so-should-the-rules-news-190538.

Mader, P. (2013). Rise and Fall of Microfinance in India: The Andhra Pradesh Crisis in Perspective. *Strategic Change*, 22(1–2),47–66. doi:10.1002/jsc.1921.

Mader, P. (2015). *The Political Economy of Microfinance: Financializing Poverty.* Springer.

Meager, R. (2019). Understanding the Average Impact of Microcredit Expansions: A Bayesian Hierarchical Analysis of Seven Randomized Experiments. *American Economic Journal: Applied Economics*, 11(1), 57–91. doi:10.1257/app.20170299.

Mistry, J. (2022, 4 April). RBI's New Guidelines to Make Microfinance Stronger. *The Economic Times.* https://economictimes.indiatimes.com/markets/stocks/news/rbis-new-guidelines-to-make-microfinance-stronger/articleshow/90639257.cms?from=mdr.

Morduch, J. (2020). Why RCTs Failed to Answer the Biggest Questions About Microcredit Impact. *World Development*, 127. doi:10.1016/j.worlddev.2019.104818.

NABARD. (2021). Women Are the Best Borrowers and the Best Repayers. National Bank for Agriculture and Rural Development. https://www.nabard.org/news-article.aspx?id=25&cid=552&NID=435.

NABARD. (2022a). Microcredit Innovation. National Bank for Agriculture and Rural Development. https://www.nabard.org/contentsearch.aspx?AID=225&Key=shg+bank+linkage+programme#:~:text=Self%20Help%20Group%20%E2%80%93%20Bank%20Linkage%20Programme%20(SHG%2DBLP)&text=What%20started%20as%20a%20pilot,which%20follow%20%27Panchsutras%27%20viz.

NABARD. (2022b). Status of Microfinance in India. National Bank for Agriculture and Rural Development. https://www.nabard.org/auth/writereaddata/tender/2707225843somfi-2021-22-final-english.pdf.

Paprocki, K. (2016). 'Selling Our Own Skin:' Social Dispossession through Microcredit in Rural Bangladesh. *Geoforum*, 74, 29–38. doi:10.1016/j.geoforum.2016.05.008.

Picherit, D. (2015). When Microfinance Collapses: Development and Politics in Andhra Pradesh. In I. Guérin, M. Labie, & J.-M. Servet (Eds.), *The Crises of Microcredit* (pp. 170–186). Zed Books.

Pitt, M. M., & Khandker, S. R. (1998). The Impact of Group-Based Credit Programs on Poor Households in Bangladesh: Does the Gender of Participants Matter? *Journal of Political Economy*, 106(5), 958–996.

Rajbanshi, R., Huang, M., & Wydick, B. (2015). Measuring Microfinance: Assessing the Conflict between Practitioners and Researchers with Evidence from Nepal. *World Development*, 68, 30–47. doi:10.1016/j.worlddev.2014.11.011.

Reboul, E., Guérin, I., & Nordman, C. J. (2021). The Gender of Debt and Credit: Insights from Rural Tamil Nadu. *World Development*, 142. doi:10.1016/j.worlddev.2020.105363.

Reuters (2022, 14 March). India Central Bank Removes Pricing Curbs on Micro-Finance Loans. https://www.reuters.com/markets/funds/india-central-bank-removes-pricing-curbs-micro-finance-loans-2022-03-14/.

Robinson, M. S. (1997). Sustainable Microfinance. In D. H. Perkins, R. Pagett, M. Roemer, D. R. Snodgrass & J. J. Stern (Eds.), *Assisting Development in a Changing World: The Harvard Institute for International Development* (pp. 1980–1995). Harvard Institute for International Development.

Roodman, D., & Morduch, J. (2014). The Impact of Microcredit on the Poor in Bangladesh: Revisiting the Evidence. *Journal of Development Studies*, 50(4), 583–604. doi:10.1080/00220388.2013.858122.

Sanyal, P. (2009). From Credit to Collective Action: The Role of Microfinance in Promoting Women's Social Capital and Normative Influence. *American Sociological Review*, 74(4), 529–550. doi:10.1177/000312240907400402.

Sanyal, P. (2014). *Credit to Capabilities: A Sociological Study of Microcredit Groups in India*. Cambridge University Press.

Sanyal, P. (2015). Group-Based Microcredit & Emergent Inequality in Social Capital: Why Socio-Religious Composition Matters. *Qualitative Sociology*, 38(2), 103–137. doi:10.1007/s11133-015-9301-8.

Sarkar, S., & Chattopadhyay, S. (2021). Significance of the Microcredit Delivery Models for Livelihood Upgradation: A Comparison between Shgs–Bank Linkage Model and Micro Finance Institutions Model with Case Studies from Rural West Bengal, India. *Small Enterprises Development, Management and Extension Journal*, 48(2), 192–202. doi:10.1177/09708464211068085.

Sato, N., Shimamura, Y., & Lastarria-Cornhiel, S. (2022). The Effects of Women's Self-Help Group Participation on Domestic Violence in Andhra Pradesh, India. *Feminist Economics*, 28(1), 29–55. doi:10.1080/13545701.2021.1987499.

Schuler, S. R., & Nazneen, S. (2018). Does Intimate Partner Violence Decline as Women's Empowerment Becomes Normative? Perspectives of Bangladeshi Women. *World Development*, 101, 284–292. doi:10.1016/j.worlddev.2017.09.005.

Sengupta, N. (2013). Poor Women's Empowerment: The Discursive Space of Microfinance. *Indian Journal of Gender Studies*, 20(2), 279–304. doi:10.1177/0971521513482220.

Sengupta, R., & Aubuchon, C. P. (2008). The Microfinance Revolution: An Overview. *Federal Reserve Bank of St. Louis Review*, 90(1), 9–30.

Shakya, Y. B., & Rankin, K. N. (2008). The Politics of Subversion in Development Practice: An Exploration of Microfinance in Nepal and Vietnam. *The Journal of Development Studies*, 44(8), 1214–1235. doi:10.1080/00220380802242461.

Shetty, S. (2013). Microcredit, Poverty, and Empowerment: Exploring the Connections. In *The Credibility of Microcredit* (pp. 163–198). Brill.

Singh, R. N., Hurley, D., & Singh, D. (2016). Towards Identifying and Ranking Selected Types of Violence against Women in North India. *International Journal of Comparative and Applied Criminal Justice*, 41(1–2),19–29. doi:10.1080/01924036.2016.1212246.

Swain, R. B., & Wallentin, F. Y. (2009). Does Microfinance Empower Women? Evidence from Self-Help Groups in India. *International Review of Applied Economics*, 23(5), 541–556. doi:10.1080/02692170903007540.

Tolzmann, M. (2022). Cgap Funder Survey 2020: Trends in International Funding for Financial Inclusion. https://www.cgap.org/sites/default/files/publications/2022_01_Focus_Note_2020_Funder_Survey.pdf.

United States Government Accountability Office (2021). Microenterprise and Related Development Assistance: Challenges in Evaluating Lasting Benefits for Women and the Poor. GAO: Report to Congressional Committees. https://www.gao.gov/assets/gao-21-328.pdf.

Weber, H. (2002). The Imposition of a Global Development Architecture: The Example of Microcredit. *Review of International Studies*, 28(3), 537–555.

Yunus, M. (1999). The Grameen Bank. *Scientific American*, 281(5), 114–119.

Yunus, M. (2005). Microcredit Changes Lives. *Appropriate Technology*, 32(1), 6.

Yunus, M. (2011, 14 January). Sacrificing Microcredit for Megaprofits. *The New York Times*. https://www.nytimes.com/2011/01/15/opinion/15yunus.html.

5 Contrasting Models of Microcredit

From Credit Plus to 'Smart Economics'[1]

In the past decade, 'smart economics' has been volubly promoted by numerous government and multilateral aid agencies (Chant, 2016a). 'Smart economics' refers to the notion that empowering women is smart because it is seen to be good for both women and the economy. The logic is that by focusing on women's empowerment, especially women's economic empowerment, development programmes can also boost economic growth and productivity (United States Agency for International Development, 2012). Microcredit programmes can easily fit within a 'smart economic' rubric: they aim to empower women economically, and by improving women's access to loans, they may also boost economic productivity in a given area. It is arguable that the microcredit 'explosion' has been assisted by the growth of 'smart economics' approaches in aid agencies and government

My analysis of 'smart economics' and microcredit builds on scholarship addressing the influence of neoliberalism on microcredit (Alawattage, Graham, & Wickramasinghe, 2019; Faraizi, Rahman, & McAllister, 2011; Guérin & Kumar, 2017; Maclean, 2010), but takes a different approach. While these studies describe the general impact of neoliberal policies on microcredit, they do not specifically address the 'smart economics' phenomenon. The few studies which do link microcredit and 'smart economics' (Byatt, 2018; Chant, 2016b, Price, 2019) are largely theoretical, do not detail the lived experience of microcredit users and do not examine how 'smart economics' differs from other approaches such as Women in Development (WID).

In this chapter I demonstrate how 'smart economics' operates in practice, by focusing on the lived experience and perspectives of female microcredit users. I further illustrate how 'smart economics' microcredit programming differs from more holistic approaches to microcredit which are based on gender and development (GAD) principles. By comparing these differing types of approaches, this chapter further provides insights into why there is so much contention about microcredit programming and illustrates which models of programming may be more beneficial for women's empowerment. This chapter further shows the limitations of microcredit programming in

DOI: 10.4324/9781003356400-5

achieving women's empowerment and illustrates the need for governments to continue to invest in other plans for women, including increasing job creation and social security strategies.

The NGO involved in this research, Swadhinata Program Team (SPT),[2] employed a 'credit-plus approach, implementing a broader model of SHG programming, including training, educational and agricultural activities as part of their model. By contrast, government run SHGs were focused on linking participants with credit only. By drawing together these examples, this chapter argues that 'smart economic' models of microcredit programming, focused only on economic outcomes, are inadequate for improving the lives of women and empowering them. In 'smart economics' we see that women's lives are exploited as a means to the promised end of economic growth (Chant, 2012; Roberts & Soederberg, 2012; Gerard, 2019). Ultimately this does little to empower women holistically. The idea of 'smart economics' being an easy solution which benefits women and the economy simultaneously (Woetzel et al., 2015) appears to be undeserved hype.

In this chapter I instead argue that by taking a broader approach, SHG programming can benefit women and contribute to empowerment. If we view microcredit on a spectrum, we are better able to understand why research on microcredit produces such contrasting results, either emphasising the benefits (Finnis, 2017; Weber & Ahmad, 2014) or fundamental issues (Geleta, 2016). We are also better able to allow for the fact that one programme will vary in implementation style and can be simultaneously empowering and disempowering.

Women's Economic Empowerment, Feminist Development Strategies and 'Smart Economics'

'Smart economics' is essentially an argument for increasing women's economic 'empowerment' on the basis that it stimulates the economy while also supposedly benefiting women (Commonwealth of Australia, 2017; United States Agency for International Development, 2012). Widespread donor interest in 'smart economics' emerged following the publication of the World Bank's Gender Action Plan 2007–2010 and 2012 World Development Report (Chant, 2016a). 'Smart economic' programming generally focuses on increasing women's incomes and access to finance. Some scholars argue that microcredit projects are examples of 'smart economic' programming, as many concentrate on women's economic empowerment and increase women's integration into the mainstream economy (Roberts & Soederberg, 2012). 'Smart economics' has been criticised on a number of fronts, particularly for using women at the service of the economy (Calkin, 2015a) and for its assumed causality between promoting women's access to the market and the overall empowerment of women (Chant, 2016b). Improving the lives of women is not viewed as an end in itself; rather, women's lives become conduits to achieving the promised end of economic growth (Calkin, 2018).

Even for social goals, such as the reduction of fertility or the achievement of higher levels of children's education, women's positions are subordinated for the good of society at large (Chant, 2012).

Enthusiasm from government and multilateral agencies for 'smart economics' certainly indicates that it is a fresh innovation which neither feminists nor development actors had thought of (Commonwealth of Australia, 2017; Woetzel et al., 2015). Despite the hype, 'smart economics' borrows heavily from previous approaches, such as from Women in Development (WID) (Chant & Sweetman, 2012), which I have detailed in Chapter 2. As I argued, it is possible to interpret the last 50 years of feminist development scholarship as divided into two dominant approaches that either promote economic strategies for women's empowerment, or alternatively advocate for more critical and holistic visions of women's empowerment which go beyond economic objectives (Sardenberg, 2008). However, while it may appear that there are two different schools of thought regarding women's empowerment, many programmes will use feminist language while actually following the logic of 'smart economics' (Cornwall and Edwards, 2014).

'Smart Economics' and Self-Help Groups in West Bengal

Self-Help Groups (SHGs) have continued to expand in West Bengal and they are frequently described as a key strategy for economic development (Department of Self-Help Group & Self Employment, n.d.). While the language of 'smart economics' is not explicitly used, the same principle of promoting women's financial empowerment as a means to enhance the economy underlies this enthusiasm (Ministry of Rural Development, 2014b). For example, proponents have argued that lending to SHGs is an 'opportunity' to be 'tapped by banks by looking at this "bottom of the pyramid" as not a social obligation or mandated lending but as a viable commercial opportunity' (Adikesavan, 2021). Both the Indian and West Bengal state government frequently use the language of reaching untouched populations. The idea promoted is that of 'inclusive economic growth' (Ministry of Rural Development, 2014a, p.11) and of helping in 'unleashing this entrepreneurial capability' of 'the poor' (Ministry of Rural Development, n.d.). To try to reach women who were not already part of SHGs, the West Bengal government introduced the 'Jaago' programme in 2019 which trains women who have no access to credit on financial management and links them to loans with low interest rates from banks or cooperative societies (Chaudhuri, 2018).

'Smart Economics' or Holistic Approaches

NGO models of operating SHGs vary greatly, but generally they run much broader SHG programmes than government agencies, encompassing a wide variety of activities. This was the approach taken by SPT and other NGOs during this research. Women belonging to the NGO run SHGs whom I interviewed indicated that they highly valued broader activities than just receiving access to microcredit. Across the SHGs, women expressed that they found it very important that they had gained 'awareness'. Women said that this 'awareness' contrasted to their previous feelings of lacking knowledge. 'Awareness' constituted awareness of one's rights, awareness of gender norms, awareness of the worth of education and how to keep healthy and awareness of skills such as going to the bank.

Participants were asked in all focus group discussions what they saw as the most significant changes after belonging to the SHG programme, as illustrated in Table 5.1 below. Women were encouraged to list as many changes as they felt were significant. Importantly, many of the changes identified by women focused on gender related issues. While arguably every change has a dimension relating to gender equality, reported improvements such as that they 'feel they can leave the house', 'increased awareness of gender equality', 'family planning' and 'decreased domestic violence' are distinctly gendered. It is also important to note that the broader benefits of belonging to an SHG, outside of any financial benefits, were more commonly indicated as highly significant to participants, as evidenced in the table below.

Table 5.1 Most significant changes identified by women in SHGs

	B	*B*	*B*	*SP*	*SP*	*SP*	*SP*	*SP*	*K*	*K*
	#1	*#2*	*#3*	*#4*	*#5*	*#6*	*#7*	*#8*	*#9*	*#10*
Learned new skills (life and employment)	X			X					X	X
Increased income					X				X	X
Children receiving more education	X		X		X		X			X
Family planning	X									
Improved sanitation	X					X	X			
Improved roads				X	X					
Feel they can leave the house	X	X	X	X	X					X
Increased confidence		X	X	X		X	X		X	X
Better agricultural production				X						
Better health				X	X					
Increased awareness of gender equality						X	X	X	X	
Decreased domestic violence							X			

Villages/settlements in each location
B = Birbhum
SP = South 24 Parganas
K = Kolkata

Women interviewed also described the differences between government run SHGs and NGO run SHGs, the former of which they argued only offered money, and did not result in many changes for communities. Women in focus group discussions detailed the way government-run SHGs operated and the lack of support they provided on gender issues, healthcare or confidence building. Women indicated that all government run SHGs did was link women with credit, leaving participants no better off. Women contrasted their own 'awareness' with that of government-run SHG members. For example, a quotation from *Bipasha*[3], a female focus group participant in South 24 Parganas, illustrates this point:

> Money is not everything, awareness is everything. If awareness levels are not high, they don't spend money in the right way. Education is the main thing – both school and informal education.

NGO staff emphasised that it was essential that front line workers repeat the messages of the gender trainings through regular discussions with communities. Women noted that they valued the open discussions that they had had with staff members and that they learned a good deal from them about women's rights and equitable gender relations.

In my interviews with women, I discussed changes in gender equality and respect at home. While the SPT SHG programme certainly did not overturn patriarchal structures of inequality, there was evidence that women were better consulted in the household by men and a number of women had an increased voice in their communities. For example, I asked 'Were there any changes in household relations following your involvement with the SHG?' Women responded with similar sentiments to a young woman called *Tuhina* who was part of a focus group discussion in Birbhum:

> There was no respect before. Ugly words and beatings were a regular feature of life, now it is decreasing day by day.

Similarly, in Kolkata, women felt much more consulted in the household, illustrated by *Padma*, a woman from a local SHG who explained:

> Respect for women has increased. Before husbands used to make all the decisions, now women also have decision-making power.

Women raised issues with their husbands about their children's education and early marriage. Women interviewed remarked that these changes occurred due to their increased 'awareness' after being part of the SHG programme. In my observational notes, I made frequent mention of the differences with which women in the SPT programmes carried themselves and spoke, illustrating high levels of confidence, compared with the generally shy and quiet women who I had interviewed in other SHGs.

When asked about significant changes which had occurred in their lives, women also indicated that they were much more mobile than before and that they felt more confident and their families were less restrictive about them leaving the house. For example, women indicated that they felt confident to go to a much greater variety of places than they were able to before. Previously women described being relatively confined to their homes and indicated that it was generally deemed unacceptable for them to go places outside of their home (unless they were working in a particular location).

In contrast to the SHG programme, when I interviewed women from a government-run SHG, they said that the government only provided them with linkages to the banks and some training on bookkeeping. When I discussed the issue of gender equality, they indicated they had not broached this subject before and they said that men were the unquestioned leaders of the household and that they had to follow them in every decision.

In the SPT-run SHGs, women said that having access to funds enabled them to start small businesses in some cases or to spend money on their children's weddings. Their income, however, was supplementary to other work they did (in Kolkata they frequently worked as domestic servants, in Bibrhum and South 24 Parganas they worked on the land or sometimes in exploitative industries, like with stone crushers). Any funds which they raised from the SHG weren't enough to create significant changes in their working life nor change the fact that they needed to remain in insecure work. One benefit they mentioned, however, was that they were better able to access government schemes. Even though they were eligible for various schemes before, they had not been able to access them due to the inordinate amount of paperwork and bureaucracy required. Being part of the SHG programme meant that NGO staff could link women directly with government services. Women were also trained by SPT in human rights and were assisted by programme staff to advocate for government services.

The Spectrum of Microcredit Programming

This chapter builds on feminist critiques of 'smart economics' as an approach which fundamentally uses women for some 'greater' good, whether that be for economic gains, community development or for children's well-being (Calkin, 2015a, 2015b, 2018; Chant, 2012, 2016b; Chant & Sweetman, 2012; Roberts & Soederberg, 2012). The examples from this case study illustrate the limitations of 'smart economics' models in government-run SHGs and the benefits of more holistic approaches. We can see from the examples, such as women's descriptions of the most significant changes which had occurred in their lives, that the non-financial benefits of SHGs outweighed any financial gains.

There is furthermore clearly a difference between 'smart economic', 'women in development' (WID) and 'gender and development' (GAD) programming. While it may be somewhat self-evident how 'smart economics' –

focused only on economic outcomes – differs from a broader more holistic feminist approach found in GAD programming (Batliwala, 2007; Cornwall, 2016), it is not as clear how 'smart economics' differs from WID. The discourse of smart economics goes a step further than WID, however, by instrumentalising women for economic outcomes and by viewing women as 'the bottom of the pyramid' (Ministry of Rural Development, 2014b) to be reached for profit (Adikesavan, 2021). In 'smart economics' we see that women's lives are used as a means to the promised end of economic growth (Chant, 2012; Roberts & Soederberg, 2012). The unscrupulous strategies of MFIs, desperate for new customers, wishing to gain clientele from women who may not be able to repay debts (Bateman, 2019), is but one example. While government run SHGs may be less directly exploitative than MFIs, by focusing only on linking women with credit without creating necessary enabling environments, they frequently set women up to fail – either because women did not have the skills to continue to maintain SHGs or because patriarchal constraints meant they had no autonomy over their activities related to the SHG.

By way of contrast, the examples from NGO-run programmes indicate a number of non-financial benefits which were important to the women interviewed. It is hence necessary to interrogate which model of microcredit each study is analysing and important to recognise that microcredit programmes exist along a continuum; from financial to credit-plus models. The SPT run SHGs were examples of this broader, more holistic approach to microcredit programming than government operated SHGs, though SPT's programming also varied.

This case example hence affirms the need for programme implementers to adopt a holistic credit-plus approach, supporting previous studies which argue that credit-plus models of microcredit are distinct from financial models (Davidson & Sanyal, 2017; Holvoet, 2005; Jitha, 2013; Mayoux, 2000; Schuler, Lenzi, Badal, & Nazneen, 2018; Sengupta, 2013). SHGs and microcredit programmes are not therefore intrinsically good or bad (Sanyal, 2014). Instead this study demonstrates that microcredit programming needs to be coupled with activities which assist women to address patriarchal norms in their communities. The wider issue remains, however, that while microcredit may not be fundamentally disempowering, it is problematic if it gives the state the excuse to minimise welfare or if lenders remain unregulated. As this case study details, many women benefited if the SHG linked their members to state services and state welfare schemes. Without welfare, women were still trapped in exploitative work. This counters Yunus' idea that microcredit is a meaningful replacement of welfare (Nelson, 2018). While women were better able to challenge gender norms and make improvements in their communities, by being trapped in insecure, casual employment in sometimes exploitative industries, women were again vulnerable to exploitative moneylenders and MFIs once the NGO programme had finished.

Conclusion

'Smart economics' hence needs to be viewed critically, rather than be seen as an overarching solution to economic growth and women's empowerment. In this chapter I have illustrated that microcredit programming exists along a continuum from 'smart economics' to more feminist informed GAD approaches. These differing models of programme implementation help to explain why there is such a diversity of opinion as to the value of microcredit programming. Therefore, rather than focus on rapidly expanding SHGs, governments and NGOs should instead assess the quality of SHG and microcredit programmes, advocating for *credit-plus* models which include components promoting health, education and gender equality. In addition, instead of seeing the rollout of SHGs as an alternative to welfare or job creation for women, SHGs should be viewed as complimentary to broader structural reform for women's empowerment.

Notes

1 This chapter has been modified from an earlier article which appeared as 'The Microcredit Continuum: From 'Smart Economics' to Holistic Programming' (2022) by Annabel Dulhunty, *Journal of International Development, 34*(6), 1213–1226. DOI: 10.1002/jid.3625. This work was licensed under a Creative Commons Attribution-NonCommercial 4.0 International License Creative Commons – Attribution-NonCommercial 4.0 International – CC BY-NC 4.0.
2 As noted previously, SPT is an alias. All NGOs and locations have been given aliases in this book.
3 Pseudonyms are used for all participants in this book.

References

Adams, J., Raymond, F. (2008). Did Yunus Deserve the Nobel Peace Prize: Microfinance or Macrofarce? *Journal of Economic Issues*, 42(2), 435–443. doi:10.1080/00213624.2008.11507152.

Adikesavan, S. (2021, 16 February). Micro Loans to Women Improve Livelihoods. *The Hindu*. https://www.thehindubusinessline.com/opinion/micro-loans-to-women-improve-livelihoods/article33835979.ece.

Alawattage, C., Graham, C., & Wickramasinghe, D. (2019). Microaccountability and Biopolitics: Microfinance in a Sri Lankan village. *Accounting, Organizations and Society*, 72, 38–60. doi:10.1016/j.aos.2018.05.008.

Bali Swain, R. & Wallentin, F.Y. (2017). The Impact of Microfinance on Factors Empowering Women: Differences in Regional and Delivery Mechanisms in India's SHG Programme. *The Journal of Development Studies*, 53(5), 684–699. doi:10.1080/00220388.2016.1205732.

Bateman, M. (2012). The Role of Microfinance in Contemporary Rural Development Finance Policy and Practice: Imposing Neoliberalism as 'Best Practice'. *Journal of Agrarian Change*, 12 (4), 587–600. doi:10.1111/j.1471-0366.2012.00376.x.

Bateman, M. (2019). Microcredit and Development. In M. Bateman, S. Blankenburg & R. Kozul-Wright (Eds.), *The Rise and Fall of Global Microcredit: Development, Debt and Disillusion* (pp. 42–68). Routledge.

Batliwala, S. (2007). Taking the Power out of Empowerment – an Experiential Account. *Development in Practice*, 17(4–5),557–565. doi:10.1080/09614520701469559.

Beetham, G. & Demetriades, J. (2007). Feminist Research Methodologies and Development: Overview and Practical Application. *Gender & Development*, 15(2), 199–216. doi:10.1080/13552070701391086.

Boserup, E. (1970). *Woman's Role in Economic Development*. Earthscan.

Brown, A.M. (2006). WID and GAD in Dar es Salaam, Tanzania: Reappraising Gender Planning Approaches in Theory and Practice. *Journal of Women, Politics & Policy* 28(2), 57–83. doi:10.1300/J501v28n02_03.

Buvinić, M. & Furst-Nichols, R. (2016). Promoting Women's Economic Empowerment: What Works? *The World Bank Research Observer*, 31(1), 59–101. doi:10.1093/wbro/lku013.

Byatt, B. (2018). The Case of Kiva and Grameen: towards a Marxist Feminist Critique of 'Smart Economics'. *Capital & Class*, 42(3), 403–409. doi:10.1177/0309816818799702.

Calkin, S. (2015a). Feminism, Interrupted? Gender and Development in the Era of 'Smart Economics'. *Progress in Development Studies*, 15(4), 295–307. doi:10.1177/1464993415592737.

Calkin, S. (2015b). "Tapping" Women for Post-Crisis Capitalism. *International Feminist Journal of Politics* 17(4), 611–629. doi:10.1080/14616742.2015.1071994.

Calkin, S. (2018). *Human Capital in Gender and Development*. Routledge.

Chakravarty, D. (2018). Lack of Economic Opportunities and Persistence of Child Marriage in West Bengal. *Indian Journal of Gender Studies*, 25(2), 180–204.

Chambers, R. (1994). The Origins and Practice of Participatory Rural Appraisal. *World Development*, 22(7), 953–969.

Chant, S. (2012). The Disappearing of 'Smart Economics'? The World Development Report 2012 on Gender Equality: Some Concerns about the Preparatory Process and the Prospects for Paradigm Change. *Global Social Policy: An Interdisciplinary Journal of Public Policy and Social Development*, 12(2), 198–218. doi:10.1177/0971521518761430.

Chant, S. (2016a). Galvanizing Girls for Development? Critiquing the Shift from 'Smart' to 'Smarter Economics. *Progress in Development Studies*, 16(4), 314–328. doi:10.1177/1464993416657209.

Chant, S. (2016b). Women, Girls and World Poverty: Empowerment, Equality or Essentialism? *International Development Planning Review*, 38(1), 1–24. doi:10.3828/idpr.2016.1.

Chant, S. & Sweetman, C. (2012). Fixing Women or Fixing the World? 'Smart Economics', Efficiency Approaches, and Gender Equality in Development. *Gender & Development*, 20(3), 517–529. doi:10.1080/13552074.2012.731812.

Chaudhuri, S.R. (2018, 11 March). West Bengal Govt Targets Rural Woman with Rs 700 Crore SHG Scheme. *Hindustan Times*. https://www.hindustantimes.com/india-news/west-bengal-govt-targets-rural-woman-with-rs-700-crore-shg-scheme/story-xzsAREo0aBPtOfa4mBTYvJ.html.

Commonwealth of Australia. (2017). Australia Advancing Women's Economic Empowerment through Aid, Trade and Economic Diplomacy. Department of Foreign Affairs and Trade. https://dfat.gov.au/about-us/publications/Documents/australia-advancing-womens-economic-empowerment-aid-trade-economic-diplomacy.pdf.

Cons. J. & Paprocki, K. (2010). Contested Credit Landscapes: Microcredit, Self-Help and Self-Determination in Rural Bangladesh. *Third World Quarterly*, 31(4), 637–654. doi:10.1080/01436591003701141.

Cornwall, A. (2016). Women's Empowerment: What Works? *Journal of International Development*, 28(3), 342–359. doi:10.1002/jid.3210.

Cornwall, A. & Brock, K. (2005). What do Buzzwords do for Development Policy? A Critical look at 'Participation', 'Empowerment' and 'Poverty Reduction'. *Third World Quarterly*, 26(7), 1043–1060. doi:10.1080/01436590500235603.

Cornwall, A. & Edwards, J. (2014). *Feminisms, Empowerment and Development: Changing Women's Lives.* Zed Books.

Davidson, T. & Sanyal, P. (2017). Associational Participation and Network Expansion: Microcredit Self-Help Groups and Poor Women's Social Ties in Rural India. *Social Forces*, 95(4), 1695–1724. doi:10.1093/sf/sox021.

Department of Panchayats and Rural Development, Government of West Bengal (n.d.) Department of Panchayats and Rural Development, Government of West Bengal. http://www.wbprd.gov.in/index.aspx.

Department of Self-Help Group and & Self Employment, Government of West Bengal (n.d.) Department of Self-Help Group and & Self Employment, Government of West Bengal. https://www.shgsewb.gov.in/.

Devika, J. (2017). Surviving in Contemporary Kerala: Reflections from Recent Research in a Fisher Village. *Development and Change*, 48(2), 364–386. doi:10.1111/dech.12299.

Eisenstein, H. (2005). A Dangerous Liaison? Feminism and Corporate Globalization. *Science and Society*, 69(3), 487–518.

Faraizi, A., Rahman, T. & McAllister, J. (2011). *Microcredit and Women's Empowerment*. Routledge.

Finnis, E. (2017). Collective Action, Envisioning the Future and Women's Self-Help Groups: A Case Study from South India. *Indian Journal of Gender Studies*, 24(1), 1–23. doi:10.1177/0971521516678529.

Fraser, N. (2009). *Scales of Justice: Reimagining Political Space in a Globalizing World.* Columbia University Press.

Garikipati, S. (2008). The Impact of Lending to Women on Household Vulnerability and Women's Empowerment: Evidence from India. *World Development*, 36(12), 2620–2642. doi:10.1016/j.worlddev.2007.11.008.

Garikipati, S., Johnson, S., Guérin, I. & Szafarz A. (2017). Microfinance and Gender: Issues, Challenges and the Road Ahead. *The Journal of Development Studies*, 53(5), 641–648. doi:10.1080/00220388.2016.1205736.

Geleta, E.B. (2016). Microfinance and Women's Empowerment: An Ethnographic Inquiry. *Development in Practice*, 26(1), 91–101. doi:10.1080/09614524.2016.1114071.

Gerard, K. (2019). Rationalizing 'Gender-Wash': Empowerment, Efficiency and Knowledge Construction. *Review of International Political Economy*, 26(5), 1022–1042. doi:10.1080/09692290.2019.1625423.

Ghosh, A.K., Banerjee, S., & Naaz, F. (2018). Adapting to Climate Change-Induced Migration: Women in Indian Bengal Delta. *Economic and Political Weekly*, 53(17).

González, F. (2020). Micro-credit and the Financialization of Low-Income Households. In P. Mader, D. Mertens & N. van der Zwan (Eds.), *The Routledge International Handbook of Financialization* (pp. 229–247). Routledge.

Goswami, D. (2019). Low and Declining Female Work Participation: The Case of Rural West Bengal. *Journal of Labor and Society*, 22(3), 325–343. doi:10.1111/wusa.12411.

Guérin, I. & Kumar, S. (2017). Market, Freedom and the Illusions of Microcredit. Patronage, Caste, Class and Patriarchy in Rural South India. *The Journal of Development Studies*, 53(5), 741–754. doi:10.1080/00220388.2016.1205735.

Holvoet, N. (2005). The Impact of Microfinance on Decision-Making Agency: Evidence from South India. *Development and Change*, 36(1), 75–102. doi:10.1111/j.0012-155X.2005.00403.x.

Husain, Z., Mukherjee, D. & Dutta, M. (2014). Self Help Groups and Empowerment of Women: Self-Selection or Actual Benefits? *Journal of International Development*, 26(4), 422–437. doi:10.1002/jid.2815.

Jiang. M., Paudel, K., & Zou, F. (2020). Do Microcredit Loans do what they are Intended to do? A Case Study of the Credit Village Microcredit Programme in China. *Journal of International Development*, 32, 73–792. doi:10.1002/jid.3477.

Jitha, T. J. (2013). Mediating Production, Re-powering Patriarchy: The Case of Microcredit. *Indian Journal of Gender Studies*, 20(2), 253–278. doi:10.1177/0971521513482219.

Keating, C., Rasmussen, C., & Rishi, P. (2010). The Rationality of Empowerment: Microcredit, Accumulation by Dispossession, and the Gendered Economy. *Signs*, 36(1), 153–176. doi:10.1086/652911.

Kingra, K. J. & Singh, S. (2021, 31 January). Pandemic and the Gender Divide. *The Indian Express*. https://indianexpress.com/article/opinion/pandemic-and-the-gender-divide-7169012/.

Maclean, K. (2010). Capitalizing on Women's Social Capital? Women-Targeted Microfinance in Bolivia. *Development and Change*, 41(3), 495–515. doi:10.1111/j.1467-7660.2010.01649.x.

Mader, P. (2018). The Instability of Commercial Microfinance: Understanding the Indian crisis with Minsky. In M. Bateman, S. Blankenburg & R. Kozul-Wright (Eds.) *The Rise and Fall of Global Microcredit: Development, Debt and Disillusion* (pp. 194–215). Routledge.

Marchand, M.H. (2009). The Future of Gender and Development after 9/11: Insights from Postcolonial Feminism and Transnationalism. *Third World Quarterly*, 30(5), 921–935. doi:10.1080/01436590902959149.

Mayoux, L. (1999). Questioning Virtuous Spirals: Micro-finance and Women's Empowerment in Africa. *Journal of International Development*, 11(7), 957–984. doi:10.1002/(SICI)1099–1328(199911/12)11:7<957:AID-JID623>3.0.CO;2-#.

Mayoux, L. (2000). Micro-finance and the Empowerment of Women: A Review of the Key Issues. *ILO Working Papers*. International Labour Organization. https://econpapers.repec.org/RePEc:ilo:ilowps:993441343402676.

McKinnon, K., Carnegie, M., Gibson, K. & Rowland, C. (2016). Gender Equality and Economic Empowerment in the Solomon Islands and Fiji: A Place-Based Approach. *Gender, Place & Culture*, 23(10), 1376–1391. doi:10.1080/0966369x.2016.1160036.

Ministry of Rural Development, Government of India (2014a). Report of the Expert Group on Setting up a Developmental Financial Institution for Women SHGs. https://aajeevika.gov.in/sites/default/files/nrlp_repository/Report%20of%20the%20Expert%20group%20-%20Final-PMO.pdf.

Ministry of Rural Development, Government of India (2014b). NRLM National Rural Livelihoods Mission Programme Implementation Plan. https://aajeevika.gov.in/en/content/programme-implementation-plan-nrlm.

Ministry of Rural Development, Government of India (n.d.) Deendayal Antyodaya Yojana. https://aajeevika.gov.in/en/content/faq.

Narayanaswamy, L. (2016). Whose Feminism Counts? Gender(ed) Knowledge and Professionalisation in Development. *Third World Quarterly*, 37(12), 2156–2175. doi:10.1080/01436597.2016.1173511.

Nelson, E. (2018, 8 October). Nobel Winner Muhammed Yunus Wants Two Financial Systems One for the Rich and One for the Poor. *Quartz*. https://qz.com/1430076/nobel-winner-muhammad-yunus-wants-two-financial-systems-one-for-the-rich-and-one-for-the-poor.

Price, S. (2019). The Risks and Incentives of Disciplinary Neoliberal Feminism: The Case of Microfinance. *International Feminist Journal of Politics*, 21(1), 67–88. doi:10.1080/14616742.2018.1454843.

Rahman, S., Junankar, P. N., & Mallik, G. (2009). Factors Influencing Women's Empowerment on Microcredit Borrowers: A Case Study in Bangladesh. *Journal of the Asia Pacific Economy*, 14(3), 287–303. doi:10.1080/13547860902975648.

Roberts, A. & Soederberg, S. (2012). Gender Equality as Smart Economics? A Critique of the 2012 World Development Report. *Third World Quarterly*, 33(5), 949–968. doi:10.1080/01436597.2012.677310.

Sanyal, P. (2014). *Credit to Capabilities: A Sociological Study of Microcredit Groups in India*. Cambridge University Press.

Sardenberg, C. M. B. (2008). Liberal vs. Liberating Empowerment: A Latin American Feminist Perspective on Conceptualising Women's Empowerment. *IDS Bulletin* 39 (6), 18–27. doi:10.1111/j.1759-5436.2008.tb00507.x.

Schuler, S. R., Lenzi, R., Badal, S. H., & Nazneen, S. (2018). Men's Perspectives on Women's Empowerment and Intimate Partner Violence in Rural Bangladesh. *Culture, Health & Sexuality*, 20(1), 113–127. doi:10.1080/13691058.2017.1332391.

Schuler, S. R. & Nazneen, S. (2018). Does Intimate Partner Violence Decline as Women's Empowerment becomes Normative? Perspectives of Bangladeshi Women. *World Development*, 101, 284–292. doi:10.1016/j.worlddev.2017.09.005.

Seng, K. (2018). Revisiting Microcredit's Poverty-reducing Promise: Evidence from Cambodia: Microcredit's Poverty-reducing Promise. *Journal of International Development*, 30, 615–642. doi:10.1002/jid.3336.

Sengupta, N. (2013). Poor Women's Empowerment: The Discursive Space of Microfinance. *Indian Journal of Gender Studies*, 20(2), 279–304. doi:10.1177/0971521513482220.

Sengupta, R. & Aubuchon CP. (2008). The Microfinance Revolution: An Overview. *Federal Reserve Bank of St. Louis Review*, 90(1), 9–30.

Shankar, K. (2011). Defects in Self-Help Groups. *Economic and Political Weekly*, 46(11), 5.

Sharma, A. (2008). *Logics of Empowerment: Development, Gender, and Governance in Neoliberal India*. University of Minnesota Press.

Singh, H.R. & Singh, N.D. (2014). An Impact Assessment of Microfinance: A Case Study of Socio-economic Empowerment of SHG Members in Manipur (India). *Paripex - Indian Journal of Research* 3(1), 141–147. doi:10.15373/22501991.

Tambe, S., Patnaik, S., Bisaria, J., Pandey, A., Kumar Sarma, U. & Vadivelu, G.A. (2017). How does Government Microfinance Impact the Rural Poor?: Evidence from Madhya Pradesh. *Economic and Political Weekly*, 52(30).

United Nations (2004). International Year of Microcredit 2005: Building Inclusive Financial Sectors to Achieve the Millennium Development Goals. https://www.un.org/en/events/pastevents/microcredit_2005/.

United Nations Secretary General Secretariat (2017). Leave No one Behind: Taking Action for Transformational Change on Women's Economic Empowerment. http://

hlp-wee.unwomen.org/-/media/hlpwee/attachments/reports-toolkits/hlp-wee-report-2017–2003-taking-action-en.pdf?la=en.

United States Agency for International Development (2012). *Gender Equality and Female Empowerment Policy.* USAID.

Weber, O., & Ahmad, A. (2014). Empowerment through Microfinance: The Relation between Loan Cycle and Level of Empowerment. *World Development*, 62, 75–87. doi:10.1016/j.worlddev.2014.05.012.

Wilson, K. (2015). Towards a Radical Re-appropriation: Gender, Development and Neoliberal Feminism. *Development and Change*, 46 (4), 803–832. doi:10.1111/dech.12176.

Woetzel, J., Madgavkar, A., Ellingrud, K., Labaye, E., Devillard, S., Kutcher, E. & Krishnan, M. (2015). The Power of Parity: How Advancing Women's Equality can add $12 trillion to Global Growth. https://www.mckinsey.com/featured-insights/employment-and-growth/how-advancing-womens-equality-can-add-12-trillion-to-global-growth.

World Bank. (2012). *World Development Report: Gender Equality and Development.* World Bank Group.

Year of Microcredit (2014). International Year of Microcredit 2005: Building Inclusive Financial Sectors to Achieve the Millennium Development Goals. https://www.yearofmicrocredit.org/.

Yunus, M. (2011, 14 January). Sacrificing Microcredit for Megaprofits. *The New York Times.* https://www.nytimes.com/2011/01/15/opinion/15yunus.html?_r=1&hp.

6 Community Development Frameworks

Just as the previous chapter illustrated the importance of understanding the different models of microcredit used, from 'smart economics' to more holistic gender-transformative approaches, so too does the model of *community development* adopted by the implementing organisation matter. Certainly as was evidenced in the previous chapter, MFIs, governments and NGOs have very different models of operating but even within NGOs there is a multitude of ways that an NGO may view their role in community development, even if they adopt a credit-plus approach. The extent to which NGOs collaborate with the government, spend time establishing and maintaining SHGs and supporting frontline staff, all create nuanced differences which produce different results in empowerment. In this chapter I explore these ideas through providing a contextual understanding of the literature on different models of community development and then by analysing the experience of NGOs in establishing SHGs.

Neoliberalism

As the previous chapters have indicated, we live in an era defined by neoliberalism, which shapes both international and local community development projects (Kuol, 2016; Sahoo, 2016). How can neoliberalism be understood? Gary Gerstle's (2022, p.5) definition here is useful: 'Neoliberalism is a creed that prizes free trade and the free movement of capital, goods, and people. It celebrates deregulation as an economic good that results when governments can no longer interfere with the operation of markets'. Neoliberalism draws from the ideals of liberalism with its focus on freedom, individuality and choice, yet it particularly fixates on markets and market based approaches. Gerstle (2022) argues that advocates for neoliberalism sought to reclaim liberalism from what they saw as an enmeshment with socialism, in policies such as the New Deal in the USA, for example. Neoliberalism was based on the idea that neoclassical economics needed to be revitalised, influenced by thinkers such as Milton Friedman and the Chicago School and the British Institute of Economic Affairs (Peet & Hartwick, 2015). These ideas pitted themselves against the influence of Keynesianism at the time which emphasised the role of government in managing markets and in trying to minimise

DOI: 10.4324/9781003356400-6

the worst excesses of capitalism (Fine, 2009; Routray, 2015). Deepak Lal (1983) for example, argued that Keynesianism subverted the 'logic' of the market and limited economic growth. According to advocates for neoliberalism, the state needed to absent itself from interfering with markets and global capitalism (Colclough, 2016). Instead, communities could rely on non-governmental organisations and charities and businesses would create sustainable solutions to 'development' (Mosse, 2013). The sweeping belief in neoliberalism in the 1990s and early 2000s was overwhelming, particularly with the collapse of the Soviet Union (Gerstle, 2022). It meant that some, such as Francis Fukuyama (1992) declared this period 'the end of history'. The free market was seen as having been victorious over state socialism and everywhere economies were liberalising, with governments removing regulations on a large variety of industries.

Neoliberalism further became entrenched in the development of the 'Washington Consensus' whereby the World Bank, the International Monetary Fund and the Government of the United States forged an agreement focused on market liberalisation (Peet & Hartwick, 2015). This substantially influenced the landscape of global 'development' and impacted countries such as India, who were forced to liberalise their economies (Nayyar, 2017). Many have hence argued that neoliberalism has been enmeshed with modern ideas of colonialism (Venn, 2009).

Neoliberalism in Community Development

How then have these large scale process of neoliberalism influenced SHGs and microcredit programming? As the previous chapter outlined, neoliberalism has clearly allowed the global flourishing of Microfinance Institutions and other Non-Bank Financial Companies (NBFCs). Yet neoliberalism has impacted SHG programming in other ways as well and has influenced both government and non-government ideologies. First of all, neoliberalism emphasises the role of the individual and transfers the responsibility of 'development' and wellbeing firmly from the state to the individual. This is regardless of the power or resources of the individual, and poverty is frequently viewed as a moral or intellectual failure (Sweet, 2018).

Under neoliberalism, NGOs are meant to take the role of state services and are particularly valuable if they encourage individuals to 'help' themselves. It is hence easy to see how Self-Help Groups could be seen as aligned with neoliberalism in this form (Jakimow & Kilby, 2006). SHG microcredit programmes provide an opportunity for individuals to connect with global capitalism, without relying on state intervention (Batliwala & Dhanraj, 2004). SHGs are therefore seen as requiring minimum state resources (Desai & Joshi, 2014) while being conduits for maximising economic growth. SHGs then provide a means for the state to withdraw from social services as poor individuals are given an 'opportunity' to advance themselves through a self-help group model (Bateman, 2012).

Partnership Models of Community Development

Geoghegan and Powell (2009) helpfully contrast three different models of community development which help us to better understand contrasting models of SHG microcredit programming. First, they outline a 'neoliberal' model of community development which is premised on the aforementioned ideas. Their second model of community development programming is a 'partnership' model of community development, based on 'service delivery' (Geoghegan & Powell, 2009). This second model is founded on principles of 'collaboration', often between government, businesses and NGOs (DeFilippis, 2008). On a larger scale this can be seen in examples such as Public Private Partnerships (PPPs) which frequently outsource services which were once run by governments. Similar examples include the contractualisation of community services to local companies (Martinez-Cosio & Bussell, 2012). Partnership models of community development aim to be non-confrontational and are premised on the idea of 'win-win' solutions. While these models aim to draw the private sector into community development concerns, ultimately they do not directly challenge inequality (DeFilippis, 2008). Instead this model focuses on establishing networks and relationships. Influential in partnership models is the idea of enabling 'social capital' (Putnam, 1995). Advocates for 'social capital' argue that many poor communities not only lack financial resources, but also important connections and linkages with others, which they term 'social capital' (Putnam, 1995). While not all aspects of social capital theories align with neoliberalism, ideas such as emphasising 'voluntary' associations and apolitical approaches to community development have also been promoted by neoliberal advocates (Mowbray, 2010). Geoghegan and Powell (2009) criticise the assumptions made by advocates for social capital who advocate for it as a magical solution to all community based problems. Conveniently while relying on voluntary organisations, the role of the welfare state is reduced. Also the very process of building social capital requires no redistribution of resources, it is simply a matter of 'connecting' individuals with each other. As such, no meaningful changes in structural inequality are likely to result from these initiatives. Partnership models of development also focus on 'managerial' approaches to community development, based on principles of programme organising from the private sector (DeFilippis, 2008).

When we view SHGs and microcredit from a partnership model of community development we see how it draws together the private sector, NGOs and government, ostensibly with the aim of 'empowering' poor communities. In this essentially apolitical ideal of community development, communities are meant to be 'connected' via SHGs with corporations and other actors. In this model which focuses on trying to achieve broad 'consensus' amongst communities, businesses and other organisations, it is easy to see how any activist inclinations of community organising would become lost.

Transformative Approaches

In contrast to both neoliberal and partnership models of community development, 'transformative' or 'activist' approaches, follow a different set of principles. Geoghegan and Powell (2009) outline how an activist model draws from the radical history of community development which arose from protest movements and principles of social justice. Similarly, Popple and Quinney (2002, p. 71) argue that the foundations of community development arose from 'radical community action' against oppression. In this conception, SHGs can be liberating and enable community transformation (Finnis, 2017). Transformative approaches to SHG programming may or may not involve microcredit. Ultimately they are much more focused on the social good of bringing women together for collective change, then they are based on providing access to credit. Numerous examples of SHG programmes (Finnis, 2017; Jakimow & Kilby, 2006; Newransky et al., 2014) provide evidence that transformative approaches are possible. In addition, some argue that neoliberal objectives of microcredit providers can in some instances be subverted into a more transformational approach (Chaudhuri & Chakravarty, 2012; Sengupta, 2013).

Transformative approaches draw on a range of social justice theories and frameworks which I shall now outline. A social justice approach focuses on redressing power relations and on upholding the rights of the most marginalised (Ife, 2009). A human-rights based approach or a rights based approach is one example of a transformative approach to community development. It is also based on redressing inequality and promoting social justice (Kindornay et al., 2012). A rights based approach draws on international human rights conventions such as the Universal Declaration of Human Rights. It is founded on the idea that development programmes should promote human rights by ensuring that communities, governments and other stakeholders are aware of the inalienable and indivisible rights which individuals have. A rights based approach advocates that each individual has inherent human rights and hence are 'rights-holders' and that governments and the international community are 'duty bearers', whereby they are responsible for upholding the rights of communities (United Nations Sustainable Development Group, 2023). Rights Based Approaches further focus on participatory principles so that the voices and perspectives of the marginalised shape the design of a programme. Key features of a Rights Based Approach include 'participation, accountability, equality and non-discrimination, transparency, and empowerment' (Gready, 2008, p.735). A rights based approach aims to address structural inequality and to go beyond charity based approaches to community development (Uvin, 2007). Similar to gender and development frameworks, however, rights based approaches in action have frequently used the *language* of rights without necessarily demanding much of the state (Uvin, 2007). Rights based approaches have also been criticised as being a 'Western' imposition, adopted and promoted by the unfair global United

Nations system (Deepak, 2012; Noh, 2017). Yet others have argued that rights based approaches align also with Eastern religions and cultural traditions (Berween, 2002; Ibrahim, 2016). Finally, proponents advocate that rights based approaches are the best means for *re*-politicising development (Uvin, 2007), demanding that the state and international community take responsibility for the rights of all citizens, not just the rich and powerful.

Another related model is the 'capabilities' approach devised by Amartya Sen (1997) and Martha Nussbaum (2000). This approach is based on the idea that development is not just about economic growth or economic ends, but is more fundamentally based on the flourishing of human capabilities (Sen, 1997). Adequate health, education and gender status are all important and are not merely components of achieving higher levels of economic growth (Sen, 1999). Sen (1999) argues that individual agency is paramount, and that any processes of 'development' should enable 'the expansion of the "capabilities" of people to lead the kind of lives they value - and have reason to value' (Sen, 1999, p.18).

As I have described in Chapter 2, critical education is another important approach which has influenced transformative community development practice. Developed by Paulo Freire (1970) in Brazil, it was based on his concern that the educational methods of the country were ultimately methods of indoctrination, whereby poor communities were taught via rote learning and were not facilitated to be able to critically question their environments. Freire's model was primarily a method of adult education which acknowledged the vast life experience of adults and sought their opinions. Rather than being a top-down method of education, it sought to draw participants together in 'learning circles' and to enable students to critically question their environment and their taken for granted assumptions.

There are, of course, numerous constraints to transformational approaches. As Robert Chambers (1994) argued some 30 years ago, effective transformational community development is based on active and meaningful participation and yet in reality, most NGO projects are shaped by donor demands. Chambers (1995, p.210) further describes:

> Northern staff on mission are impatient and insistent. The incentives are to spend, and for uppers to pressurise lowers to spend more and faster... rushing reinforces dominance. Participation takes time, but time is always short.

Little has arguably changed in the past thirty years, indeed with the growth of neoliberal expectations of minimised community development, the environment seems to have become worse for transformational programming. Whether the donors are from northern international development institutions or whether they are from local government, the pressures are usually to spend and to spend fast. The ability to spend time with communities is limited by both time pressures and by a desire to show 'value for money'.

The Role of Frontline Workers

The role of front-line workers (sometimes called 'field workers') is frequently overlooked in theories of change. Many assume that transformational change will merely occur if trainings are scheduled or if the right 'activities' are developed. The role of frontline staff, however, in catalysing this change is undervalued. Recent scholarly literature has helped to draw out this issue and argue that any community transformation must be predicated on front-line workers' skills and ability. This is true not only from NGOs but from within a large variety of sectors which rely on the emotional labour of front-line workers (Baines, 2011). Emotional labour is not merely a simple endeavour but a highly skilled and frequently exhausting and under-remunerated expectation in the workplace (Baines et al., 2022). While significant attention has been given to the demands of front-line workers in the Global North, far less attention has been paid to NGO frontline staff in community development projects in the Global South (O'Reilly, 2011). Ahmad (2010) documents the extensive issues met by frontline staff in Bangladesh, facing precarious work conditions, poor treatment at work and poor opportunities for promotion. Similar issues of exploitatively low wages being paid and lack of access to health care and insurance have been documented in India, exacerbated by a culture of 'volunteerism' (Vasan, 2004). As Roy (2019) argues, there is surplus labour in India, as in many countries in the Global South, resulting in employers viewing workers as expendable. Many NGOs rely on volunteers, drawing from poorer scheduled caste communities, yet the benefits these women receive from being volunteers is highly mixed (Roy, 2019). Women employed as frontline staff are particularly disadvantaged and have little recourse over their 'superiors', illustrating how sexual harassment and assault are easily able to become tacitly accepted within organisations without repurcussions (Vasan, 2004). Yet despite their poor conditions, much of the success of any 'transformational' programme rests with frontline staff, including their ability to listen (Jacobs & Wilford, 2010), to think critically (Foley, 2008) and to promote critical consciousness amongst communities.

Case Study Examples

Difficulty in Establishing SHGs

For NGOs not directly connected with the government, it was difficult in many cases to build trust amongst the community and to establish SHGs, particularly without eliciting significant male backlash. Moreover, given the situation in West Bengal where a number of women have been scammed into believing that there are job or marital opportunities and then have been trafficked, it is even more difficult for an independent NGO to establish credibility. For example, one woman, *Aarna*, an SHG member in South 24 Parganas, said that there was significant doubt in her community as to what the intentions were of the NGO which had begun to set up SHGs in the area. Men in the community were particularly doubtful and she described the discussions they had had in their community:

> When we were starting they were saying the NGO folk will sell you to another country, don't go through the development process.

The NGO staff member working in this area also explained the difficulty in establishing SHGs in the area:

> For one whole year we tried to set up the SHG, but then we connected to an ex-panchayat (local council) member and we discussed with her and she conducted a meeting in the community as to how the NGO worked.

Even though the NGO had wished to remain independent of the government, this was not always possible, and they had had to rely on the legitimacy with which government representatives could bring.

Maintaining SHGs

For this research I interviewed staff and SHG members who belonged to a range of NGO initiatives. SPT very kindly facilitated my meeting with an SHG which had fallen apart. I provide more detail of this in Chapter 9. For the most part, however, NGOs understandably introduced me to SHGs which were still in existence. Hence research participants largely had at least somewhat successful experiences of sustained involvement with SHGs. Interviews with staff, however and a review of project documents revealed that many SHGs had disbanded and were difficult to sustain. For example, in Birbhum, staff indicated that *only* between 15–23% of SHGs were functioning well, 10% had dissolved and the remainder were struggling.

Staff outlined the key reasons they thought that SHGs were difficult to maintain. They believed that the number one reason why many SHGs fell apart was due to political interference or tensions between members of different political parties. The second reason they gave was that there was nepotism and problematic leadership amongst the appointed heads of SHGs. Staff then outlined that top-down pressure from within their NGO (and also donor pressure) meant that the establishment of many SHGs was rushed. This meant that many SHG members were not provided with adequate training or support in the initial phases. Staff also detailed that lack of skills amongst SHG members, such as skills in bookkeeping or literacy, meant that it was difficult for SHGs to stay well organised and maintain their operations. Staff then finally cited problematic relationships and disputes amongst SHG members and a lack of linkages with government schemes as reasons for SHGs becoming defunct. SHGs were noted to be less likely to struggle if they were well connected with government bodies, there were strong relationships between group members, meetings were regularly scheduled and SHG members had confidence in the leader of their group.

Example from North 24 Parganas

In addition to time spent with SPT, as detailed in the previous chapter, I also conducted research with the NGOs Shiksha and Sochetana in North 24 Parganas. I interviewed and spent time with both the staff and the SHG participants. In talking with the SHG members, it was evident that they were highly pleased with the benefits which being part of the SHG had enabled. The women were confident and were exceedingly happy about changes in their community. They also showed me their joint projects – from banana plantations to sewing activities. While these women were adamant about changes which had occurred in their lives, it is important to note that conducting this research through NGOs meant that they were most likely to grant access to SHGs which were well functioning. SHG members which had been part of a disbanded SHG were much less likely to be willing to speak and additionally the NGO staff may feel that it reflected badly on them if I was to interview unsuccessful SHGs. Thankfully, as mentioned, in Birbhum, staff did take me to interview members of a highly struggling SHG. Many staff were also candid about the extent to which SHGs were difficult to maintain, as I detailed in the section above. Yet the NGO in North Parganas was keen for me to spend time with an SHG which was clearly thriving. While I cannot say how representative this SHG was of their whole programme, it provides an example of SHGs in their best case scenario – how an SHG may work if the conditions and inputs are right.

I spent time with the project team who described their point of difference with government agencies running SHGs. One enthusiastic young man, *Dulal*, a Project Coordinator explained:

> We are different from other organisations, other organisations form SHGs for the sake of business, ours is not. We form groups and disseminate information. We give continuous input, without continuous input it is not easy to make them aware. All activities are implemented by and through the group.

The Project Coordinator continued, describing the way that the government established their SHGs:

> There is a flood of SHGs and government departments trying to implement SHGs. Sometimes they hijack our SHGs.

The Coordinator described how the government departments had strict targets as to the number of SHGs established which they had to meet. Rather than provide the SHGs with substantial training, they were known to create them and then move on to setting up the next SHG, leaving the SHGs with very little support.

A senior staff member of the NGO, a woman in her early 60s, who had been part of the organisation for a long time further explained:

> The government program is quite good but there are corrupt people, sometimes there is fault in the delivery system. The most important opportunity under the NRLM is bank loans of lower interest at 7%. Banks will provide loans at 11% interest to SHGs so this is a 4% government subsidy.

Connecting with the government run SHGs hence meant that women were better able to access these lower interest rates. There was thus benefits in not excluding government entirely and in adopting a partnership model of programming.

The Project Coordinator, *Dulal*, continued to describe their model of SHGs, indicating that their support to SHGs was holistic and not merely focused on distributing loans. He enthused:

> We give them legal support, a legal literacy camp. They are more aware than before!

This term 'awareness' (সচেতনতা sochetana), as described in the previous chapter, was commonly used by both project staff and communities across locations to discuss how belonging to a holistic SHG had benefited them. For NGOs running a credit-plus model, connecting members with micro-credit was only one component of the overall programme.

Another Project Coordinator in this area, *Indroneel*, also described how belonging to an SHG was transformational for gender attitudes, not only amongst women but with staff also. He explained:

> We thought that women are vulnerable, they are not vulnerable. Women are told they should not go out…It is a customary attitude that women are inferior to men. They are always obstructed. Things have improved a lot now that the groups are running.

The senior leader further elaborated that SHGs allowed for strength in numbers, particularly when women were challenging violence in their communities or asking for government services, for example. She elucidated:

> For grassroots people, the SHG is very important. It is very difficult for one poor woman to fight.

Staff at this NGO also described how their model aimed to bring SHGs together amongst 3–4 tiers, from the village level to the level of a Block

Federation to create a 'revolution' which the Project Coordinator had described:

> We gather different SHGs together for an annual meeting. Sometimes there is competition between groups. We promote 10,000 SHGs and microfinance every day.

Frontline Staff

As stated, NGO staff also agreed that 'awareness' (সচতেনতা sochetana) was a highly important component of the SHG programme. The strategies which NGOs used, however, to elicit 'awareness' varied considerably. The underlying philosophy of this 'awareness' correlated with Freirean philosophy which was based on informal community education. Though they didn't discuss Freire, there was a similar sentiment of empowering communities through making them 'aware' of their environments – through learning about health, education, gender and legal rights. At times though, some of the NGOs involved in this study used more didactic methods of imparting information, i.e. through large community gatherings where the community would listen to long speeches by the project staff. It seems unlikely that community members would have retained much of these lectures, compared to when project staff would discuss topics conversationally in small groups. In some locations, staff members did spend significant time with small groups of women. Yet in other instances, staff were too stretched between visiting multiple SHGs that they couldn't visit with the frequency that they wished.

Within SPT, as well, female frontline workers were not well supported. While they did employ some female frontline workers, they were not given any 'special treatment', as it was described to me. Managers acknowledged that it was frequently dangerous for women travelling at night and in remote locations, but the added cost of paying someone to accompany the female frontline worker or of providing better transport for the female frontline worker was deemed too expensive. Yet without providing additional support, without the so called 'special treatment', it was difficult to attract female frontline workers. In addition, employing female frontline workers was viewed as something of an organisational risk. Given the desire to promote transformational gender change, both female and male frontline workers should be supported to provide intensive support to SHGs, particularly in respect to 'awareness' activities. As was the case with the majority of NGOs, however, frontline workers were at the bottom of the hierarchy in terms of both status and remuneration.

Discussion

The rise of neoliberalism has resulted in the manifestation of philosophies such as 'smart economics', as detailed in the previous chapter. This has aided in the deregulation of the microcredit sector and the exponential rise of

Microfinance Institutions and private capital investing in microcredit. This solely economic model has been challenged by numerous scholars and practitioners and on a macro level, we see that a Capabilities Approach tries to go beyond this narrow realm (Sen, 1999). Yet it is tough to constantly go against the tide and with constant pressure and focus on women's *economic* empowerment (Secretariat, UN Secretary-General, 2016), it is difficult to maintain a holistic approach.

Within NGOs there are also different options for operating, based on contrasting underlying philosophies. As Geoghegan and Powell (2009) argue, many community development projects can be seen to either take a neoliberal, partnership or transformative approach. The staff members of NGOs which participated in this research certainly maintained that they were adopting a 'transformative' approach and to varying degrees this was true. Yet, while many NGOs might contrast their work with that of the government, arguing that government run SHGs are hampered by corruption or lack of support, in reality, many NGOs need to broker some form of partnership with the state. An idealised 'transformative' approach as within Geoghegan and Powell's (2009) model may not then be possible in its purest form. Instead the state cannot be entirely ignored, particularly in the need to enable SHG members to access government programmes, schemes and interest rates, in addition to supporting NGOs with the establishment of their legitimacy in communities.

While a programme may still need to be enmeshed with government, to more closely resemble transformational programming, it would be helpful to look at Freirean methods which require a probing of critical consciousness (Freire, 1970). It is not merely a matter of imparting information to communities, but also of engaging them in critical questioning and an understanding of their environments, ensuring that they are aware of what is the established social order or *doxa* (Bourdieu, 1977) and then being able to question that. To take this approach, also aligned with a 'gender-transformative approach' as adopted by many health programmes (as detailed in Chapter 2), significant investment in frontline staff is also necessary. Gender-transformative or Freirean style programmes which provoke changes in critical consciousness cannot be delivered with only a 'light touch' of staffing. In addition, creating poor working environments for frontline workers is first of all, exploitative and secondly, will only hamper the success of the programme. Rather, it is especially important to make special provisions for the safety of frontline workers, particularly women. Furthermore, it is crucial that organisations provide decent standards of pay and access to benefits. Unfortunately the critical role of frontline workers is overlooked in many assumptions as to what enables the success of women's empowerment programming (Ahmad, 2010).

Conclusion

In summary, in this chapter I have further described various models of community development and different components of transformative approaches. While many NGOs may wish to separate themselves from the state, in many instances they will need to adopt some form of a partnership approach and connect with the state to enable communities to access government benefits. While neoliberalism continues to dominate, there is space, however, for NGOs to adopt more transformational styles of working, which focus on promoting the critical consciousness of communities. To do this, significant investment is needed in frontline staffing to ensure that they are not overstretched and that they are provided with decent and safe conditions. In this environment, in the best cases, SHGs can provide meaningful spaces for women to form networks of solidarity and to feel confident to challenge hegemonic practices within their communities. Yet despite these positive examples, there are many instances of SHGs which are difficult to maintain and which disband without adequate support and investment.

References

Ahmad, M. M. (2010). Who Cares? The Personal and Professional Problems of Ngo Fieldworkers in Bangladesh. *Development in Practice*, 12(2), 177–191. doi:10.1080/09614520220127694.

Baines, D. (2011). Resistance as Emotional Work: The Australian and Canadian Non-Profit Social Services. *Industrial Relations Journal*, 42(2), 139–156. doi:10.1111/j.1468-2338.2011.00616.x.

Baines, D., Dulhunty, A., & Charlesworth, S. (2022). Relationship-Based Care Work, Austerity and Aged Care. *Work, Employment and Society*, 36(1), 139–155. doi:10.1177/09500170209809.

Bateman, M. (2012). The Role of Microfinance in Contemporary Rural Development Finance Policy and Practice: Imposing Neoliberalism as 'Best Practice'. *Journal of Agrarian Change*, 12(4), 587–600. doi:10.1111/j.1471-0366.2012.00376.x.

Batliwala, S., & Dhanraj, D. (2004). Gender Myths That Instrumentalise Women: A View from the Indian Frontline. *IDS Bulletin*, 35(4), 11–18. doi:10.1111/j.1759-5436.2004.tb00150.x.

Berween, M. (2002). The Fundamental Human Rights: An Islamic Perspective. *The International Journal of Human Rights*, 6(1), 61–79. doi:10.1080/714003742.

Bourdieu, P. (1977). *Outline of a Theory of Practice.* Cambridge University Press.

Chambers, R. (1994). The Origins and Practice of Participatory Rural Appraisal. *World Development*, 22(7), 953–969.

Chambers, R. (1995). The Primacy of the Personal. In M. Edwards & D. Hulme (Eds.), *Non-Governmental Organisations - Performance and Accountability: Beyond the Magic Bullet* (pp. 207–217). Routledge.

Chaudhuri, S., & Chakravarty, A. (2012). Strategic Framing Work(S): How Microcredit Loans Facilitate Anti-Witch-Hunt Movements. *Mobilization: An International Quarterly*, 17(2), 175–194. doi:10.17813/maiq.17.2.f54x1h0622750028.

Colclough, C. (2016). States or Markets–Twenty-Five Years On. *IDS Bulletin*, 47(2A). doi:10.19088/1968-2016.182.

Deepak, A. C. (2012). Globalization, Power and Resistance: Postcolonial and Transnational Feminist Perspectives for Social Work Practice. *International Social Work*, 55(6), 779–793. doi:10.1177/0020872811414038.

DeFilippis, J. (2008). Paradoxes of Community-Building: Community Control in the Global Economy. *International Social Science Journal*, 59(192), 223–234. doi:10.1111/j.1468-2451.2009.00694.x.

Desai, R. M., & Joshi, S. (2014). Collective Action and Community Development: Evidence from Self-Help Groups in Rural India. *The World Bank Economic Review*, 28(3), 492–524. doi:10.1093/wber/lht024.

Fine, B. (2009). Development as Zombieconomics in the Age of Neoliberalism. *Third World Quarterly*, 30(5), 885–904. doi:10.1080/01436590902959073.

Finnis, E. (2017). Collective Action, Envisioning the Future and Women's Self-Help Groups: A Case Study from South India. *Indian Journal of Gender Studies*, 24(1), 1–23. doi:10.1177/0971521516678529.

Foley, C. (2008). Developing Critical Thinking in Ngo Field Staff. *Development in Practice*, 18(6), 774–778. doi:10.1080/09614520802386827.

Freire, P. (1970). *Pedagogy of the Oppressed*. Herder & Herder.

Fukuyama, F. (1992). *The End of History and the Last Man*. Penguin Adult.

Geoghegan, M., & Powell, F. (2009). Community Development and the Contested Politics of the Late Modern Agora: Of, Alongside or against Neoliberalism? *Community Development Journal*, 44(4), 430–447. doi:10.1093/cdj/bsn020.

Gerstle, G. (2022). *The Rise and Fall of the Neoliberal Order: America and the World in the Free Market Era*. Oxford University Press.

Gready, P. (2008). Rights-Based Approaches to Development: What Is the Value-Added? *Development in Practice*, 18(6), 735–747. http://www.jstor.org/stable/27751980.

Ibrahim, A. M. (2016). A Not-So-Radical Approach to Human Rights in Islam. *The Journal of Religion*, 96(3), 346–377. doi:10.1086/686568.

Ife, J. (2009). *Human Rights from Below: Achieving Rights through Community Development*. Cambridge University Press.

Jacobs, A., & Wilford, R. (2010). Listen First: A Pilot System for Managing Downward Accountability in NGOs. *Development in Practice*, 20(7), 797–811. doi:10.1080/09614524.2010.508113.

Jakimow, T., & Kilby, P. (2006). Empowering Women:A Critique of the Blueprint for Self-Help Groups in India. *Indian Journal of Gender Studies*, 13(3), 375–400. doi:10.1177/097152150601300303.

Kindornay, S., Ron, J., & Carpenter, C. (2012). Rights-Based Approaches to Development: Implications for NGOs. *Human Rights Quarterly*, 34(2), 472–506. doi:10.1353/hrq.2012.0036.

Kuol, L. B. D. (2016). State, Market and Society Relations: The Roaring Last Fifty Years. *IDS Bulletin*, 47(2A).

Lal, D. (1983). *The Poverty of Development Economics*. Institute of Economic Affairs.

Martinez-Cosio, M., & Bussell, M. R. (2012). Private Foundations and Community Development: Differing Approaches to Community Empowerment. *Community Development*, 43(4), 416–429. doi:10.1080/15575330.2012.705869.

Mosse, D. (2013). The Anthropology of International Development. *Annual Review of Anthropology*, 42, 227–246. doi:10.1146/annurev-anthro-092412-155553.

Mowbray, M. (2010). What Became of the Local State? Neo-Liberalism, Community Development and Local Government. *Community Development Journal*, 46(Supplement 1), i132–i153. doi:10.1093/cdj/bsq051.

Nayyar, D. (2017). Economic Liberalisation in India. *Economic & Political Weekly*, 52 (2), 41.

Newransky, C., Kayser, K., & Lombe, M. (2014). The Development of Self-Efficacy Beliefs of Widowed and Abandoned Women through Microcredit Self-Help Groups: The Case of Rural South India. *Journal of Social Service Research*, 40(2), 201–214. doi:10.1080/01488376.2013.865579.

Noh, J. E. (2017). Contextualisation of Human Rights Discourse by Ngo Workers in the Context of Bangladesh. *Journal of International Development*, 29(8), 1106–1122. doi:10.1002/jid.3274.

Nussbaum, M. (2000). Women's Capabilities and Social Justice. *Journal of Human Development*, 1(2), 219–247. doi:10.1080/713678045.

O'Reilly, K. (2011). "We Are Not Contractors": Professionalizing the Interactive Service Work of NGOs in Rajasthan, India. *Economic Geography*, 87(2), 207–226. doi:10.1111/j.1944-8287.2011.01106.x.

Peet, R., & Hartwick, E. R. (2015). *Theories of Development* (3rd ed.). Guilford Press.

Popple, K., & Quinney, A. (2002). Theory and Practice of Community Development: A Case Study from the United Kingdom. *Community Development*, 33(1), 71–85. doi:10.1080/15575330209490143.

Putnam, R. D. (1995). Bowling Alone: America's Declining Social Capital. *Journal of Democracy*, 6(1), 64–78.

Routray, S. (2015). The Post-Development Impasse and the State in India. *Third World Quarterly*, 36(10), 1906–1921. doi:10.1080/01436597.2015.1070665.

Roy, S. (2019). Precarity, Aspiration and Neoliberal Development: Women Empowerment Workers in West Bengal. *Contributions to Indian Sociology*, 53(3), 392–421. doi:10.1177/0069966719861758.

Sahoo, S. (2016). Market Liberalism, Marginalised Citizens and Countermovements in India. *Asian Studies Review*, 41(1), 1–19. doi:10.1080/10357823.2016.1263887.

Secretariat, UN Secretary-General (2016). Leave No One Behind: A Call to Action for Gender Equality and Women's Economic Empowerment. https://www2.unwomen.org/-/media/hlp%20wee/attachments/reports-toolkits/hlp-wee-report-2016-09-call-to-action-en.pdf?la=en&vs=1028.

Sen, A. (1999). *Development as Freedom*. Alfred A Knopf.

Sen, G. (1997). Empowerment as an Approach to Poverty. *Human Development Report*, 97.

Sengupta, N. (2013). Poor Women's Empowerment: The Discursive Space of Microfinance. *Indian Journal of Gender Studies*, 20(2), 279–304. doi:10.1177/0971521513482220.

Sweet, E. (2018). 'Like You Failed at Life': Debt, Health and Neoliberal Subjectivity. *Social Science & Medicine*, 212, 86–93. doi:10.1016/j.socscimed.2018.07.017.

United Nations Sustainable Development Group (2023). Human Rights-Based Approach. https://unsdg.un.org/2030-agenda/universal-values/human-rights-based-approach#:~:text=The%20human%20rights%2Dbased%20approach,promoting%20and%20protecting%20human%20rights.

Uvin, P. (2007). From the Right to Development to the Rights-Based Approach: How 'Human Rights' Entered Development. *Development in Practice*, 17(4–5),597–606. doi:10.1080/09614520701469617.

Vasan, S. (2004). NGOs as Employers: Need for Accountability. *Economic and Political Weekly*, 39(22), 2197–2198.

Venn, C. (2009). Neoliberal Political Economy, Biopolitics and Colonialism: A Transcolonial Genealogy of Inequality. *Theory, Culture & Society*, 26(6), 206–233. doi:10.1177/0263276409352194.

7 The Role of Dignity[1]

In this chapter I provide new theoretical insights into microcredit programming by using a framework of feminist dignity to assess the value of these programmes. As the previous chapters have shown, feminist scholarship has been critical of the co-option of women's development programmes for other ends: arguing that programmes instrumentalise women (Calkin, 2015a; Chant, 2016), view women as a resource to be exploited (Calkin, 2015b) and perniciously extend the global reach of neoliberalism into previously unchartered territories (Roberts, 2015). Most criticisms draw from Marxist (Byatt, 2018; Price, 2019; Roberts, 2015) or poststructuralist philosophies (Calkin, 2015b, 2018) to critique the neoliberal spread of global markets.

While the idea of dignity is relevant to poststructuralist and Marxist criticisms, it is also a crucial concept for broader philosophical and political traditions, heavily influencing liberalism, democratic constitutionalism and Rights Based Approaches (Bayefsky, 2013). Having dignity can be defined as being an 'end' in oneself and believing oneself to have intrinsic worth as a human being (Kant, 2012/1785). By drawing on feminist dimensions of dignity, I provide in this chapter a framework for designing and evaluating programmes so that they can best promote women's empowerment.

A Framework for Feminist Dignity

Despite numerous studies existing on the topic of microcredit and women's empowerment, scholars have not explicitly used the conceptual framework of dignity to analyse these programmes. Indeed, the idea of dignity has been frequently overlooked in development theory, outside of the capabilities approach (Nussbaum, 2011b; Sen, 1992, 1999) and the work of Indrajit Roy (2013) and Tony Castleman (2016).The definition of dignity I employ here draws from the women interviewed in SHGs, the work of Immanuel Kant and from feminist and Dalit writers in India. Having dignity can be defined as being 'an end' in oneself and not merely being a 'means' to an end (Kant, 2012/1785). A human being is therefore intrinsically valuable, their worth has no price. We cannot sacrifice one human being for the good of the whole community (contrasting with utilitarianism which gives greater weight to the overall happiness of a

DOI: 10.4324/9781003356400-7

society than any individual's wellbeing) (Ferry, 2013). It is thus imperative for us to treat others as worthy and to not use or deceive people (Kant, 2012/1785).

In concrete terms, being an 'end' in oneself means that an individual should be viewed (and view themselves) with respect because they are a human being, not because they can deliver some service or skill. Elaborating on a slightly different example from Kant (2012/1785): imagine you treated a 'friend' with respect only because you wanted to borrow money from them. This would not be treating one's friend with dignity. A further example of using someone as a 'means' to an 'end' is if we treat a woman with respect only because she cares for children. If we say we must respect women because they are mothers, we are not valuing them as an 'end' in themselves, they are merely of 'use' in caring for children.

Despite Kant's work on dignity, there is an inherent sexism in much of his writing (Hay, 2013), which has carried through to modern ideas of human liberty which emphasise the dignity of '*white, Western, male and able-bodied*' subjects (Miller, 2017, p.110). Kant's understanding of dignity also focuses on rationality as a precondition for dignity (Hay, 2013; Nussbaum, 2006). This emphasis on rationality is problematic as it excludes those who do not function with the highest level of self-autonomy, such as young children or those with severe disabilities (Kittay, 1999). Despite these criticisms, the idea of individuals being an end in themselves and not a means to an end has remained a cornerstone in modern conceptions of dignity (Bayefsky, 2013). Feminist philosophers such as Nussbaum (2011a), Cornell (2014) and Hay (2013) have drawn from this basic tenet of Kant's while remaining critical of other aspects of Kant's work.

Feminist philosophers and political scientists have therefore reclaimed the concept of dignity and argued that it is a core concern for women's emancipation and empowerment. Eva Kittay (1999, 2002) for example, advocates for a different conception of dignity. She criticises the liberal emphasis on relationships between 'equal' public citizens which ignores the 'private' sphere, overlooks issues of dependency and the role of both the carer and the cared for. Kittay (2002) instead argues that the public and private spheres are drawn together. Martha Nussbaum has also comprehensively critiqued the traditional notion of dignity and advanced the idea from a feminist perspective. Nussbaum developed her idea of dignity in her work on a Capabilities approach (Nussbaum, 2000, 2006, 2011b) which she created in conjunction with Amartya Sen (1999). Like Kittay (2002), Nussbaum is highly critical of the way that the liberal concept of dignity is founded on the idea of a social contract between men which consistently overlooks women and the 'private' sphere (Nussbaum, 2006). Not only have women been excluded from arguments about dignity, Nussbaum illustrates that women have frequently been viewed as a means to achieving the ends of men, not as ends in themselves (2006, p.71). For Nussbaum, the equality of humans is a foundational component of human dignity and gender equality is an essential precondition of dignity (Nussbaum, 2011b).

There is also an expansive history of scholarship on dignity in India, with crucial insights from feminists and Dalit activists. In West Bengal, there has been a long lineage of women working for women's rights, including Begum Rokeya Sakhawat Hossain who I have briefly mentioned in Chapter 3. Begum Rokeya produced a number of written works and speeches which outlined her ideas on women's dignity (Bagchi, 2009). Rokeya argued for women's equality with men, stating that women had been tricked by men into being '*their domesticated animals, or some kind of a prized property*', yet treated even worse than animals (Quayam 2013, p.23). For Rokeya, education was fundamental to women's liberation – not only for reading and writing, but for women 'to earn their rights as citizens' (Quayam, 2013, p.137), harnessing the 'inner faculties of the individual' (Quayam, 2013, p.29). Rokeya was both anti-patriarchy and anti-colonialist (Bagchi, 2009), reflecting the multiple simultaneous struggles which Bengali feminists have had to contend with.

The idea of dignity has also been especially important in the Dalit rights movement, emphasising the notions of self-respect, education and agency (Biswas, 2012; Guru, 2009; Rawat, 2013; Roy, 2019). Arya and Rathore (2020) argue that Dalit women's lives are marked by a denial of human dignity and that the caste system maintains unequal dignity. Dalit women must contend with others' perceptions of themselves as undeserving of dignity, as the objects of lust and disgust (Arya & Rathore, 2020). Rather than being perceived as an 'end' in themselves, Dalit women have been degraded to be viewed as inhuman, frequently subjugated in sexual servitude (Paik, 2014; Sonalkar, 2020). In defiance of this denigration, many Dalit feminists refer to the importance of 'self-respect' (Paik, 2020), indeed there was a 'Self-Respect Movement' within Dalit activism led by E.V. Ramaswamy 'Periyar' (Sonalkar, 2020). Dalit writers have further emphasised the notion of 'selfhood' – the idea that an individual's life, desires and self is important (Rao, 2015). Having dignity thus means having a strong sense of self, acting as an agent and not being treated as passive victims (Paik, 2020).

Drawing from these ideas, I outline a Framework for Feminist Dignity (Table 7.1) to design and evaluate women's empowerment programmes. This

Table 7.1 A Framework for Feminist Dignity

Guiding Principle: Individuals are ends in themselves	
Perception	*Situation*
Does the programme encourage **inner dignity**?	Does the programme promote **holistic dignity**, beyond masculinist notions of 'public' dignity?
Does the programme enable **dignity from others**?	Does the programme enhance **equality of dignity** through redressing power imbalances?

framework is based on the idea that women are 'ends' in themselves. To better understand how a programme may enhance or limit dignity, the framework asks four key questions which relate to different components of dignity. This framework differentiates between our perception of dignity (e.g. how do we view ourselves and others) and the concrete situation which affords or limits dignity (e.g. does the individual have agency and opportunities).

Inner Dignity

The first question we ask is whether a programme encourages inner dignity – for example does it enable a person to have a resilient sense of themselves as an important individual, do they view themselves as an 'end' in themselves? The ideas of 'self-esteem, self-confidence, determinacy and daring' help us to better understand 'inner dignity' from Paik's (2020, p.65) description of the aims of Dalit educational reformers. The concept of 'inner dignity' also draws in part from Jacobson's (2007) notion of 'dignity-of-self' which is based on self-confidence and self-worth. The idea of 'inner dignity' however also emphasises that individuals must view themselves as ends in themselves. Even if individuals feel confident and worthy, this feeling should not be contingent on anything (i.e. the capacity to earn an income).

This notion of inner dignity is also based on self-respect, which is so prominent in the work of Dalit activists and Indian feminists (Rao, 2015). One must believe in their inner dignity and reject others' notions that they are unequal or meant to be subjugated, as Begum Rokeya (Quayum, 2013) argues.

Dignity from others

Certainly, our own individual sense of dignity is easily threatened by others' ideas of our worth. 'Dignity from others' is based on others' perception. This concept also draws from Jacobson's (2007, p.294) idea of 'dignity-in-relation' where one's sense of self-respect mirrors the opinions of others and is either elevated or denigrated based on others' viewpoints (Jacobson, 2007). We should also ask whether an individual is respected by others as a whole person, or as a source of money or labour only. Roy further elaborates on this idea in Dalit scholarship, describing how each individual has inherent dignity but this remains frequently unacknowledged by others: 'dignity belongs to all, but is only recognised by some. It is this lack of recognition which claims of dignity challenge' (Roy, 2019, p.351). It is therefore in others' perceptions that we frequently see that dignity is affronted (Arya & Rathore, 2020) as illustrated in the disrespect shown towards many Dalit women. A crucial part of indignity is thus the state of being rejected and disrespected by others, causing shame and humiliation (Zavaleta Reyles, 2007).

Holistic Dignity

I define holistic dignity here as dignity of both the public and private spheres. It stems from a feminist critique of masculinist and liberal conceptions of dignity which focus mainly on the dignity of 'rational' men in the public sphere (Nussbaum, 2006; Kittay, 1999, 2002). It addresses the fact that women have frequently been viewed as a means to achieving the ends of men, not as ends in themselves (Nussbaum, 2006, p. 70). It also redresses the neglect of issues of dependency and the dignity of both the carer and the cared for (Kittay, 1999). This idea also draws from Bengali and Indian feminists who have criticised the constant devaluing of women's work, whether paid or unpaid (Banerjee, 2017; Jain, 2018). When we address holistic dignity in a women's empowerment programme we evaluate whether women doing care work are respected and whether both paid and unpaid work are valued.

Equality of Dignity

The framework also asks whether there is equality of dignity i.e. do women have the same opportunities and freedom from constraints as men. This draws from human rights based frameworks which promote universal equality amongst humans as a precondition for dignity (Siegert & Ward, 2010). These frameworks are based on the principle that all individuals possess fundamental human rights, as outlined in human rights charters (Miller, 2017). Furthermore, in addressing equality of dignity, we must redress power imbalances and challenge discriminatory gender norms (Batliwala, 2007). Gender equality is a part of 'equality of dignity' but so too is caste and class equality, reflecting the broad range of concerns of Dalit and Indian feminists (Arya & Rathore, 2020).

Using the Framework for Feminist Dignity

Does the Programme Encourage Inner Dignity?

There are many layers and complexities when investigating whether belonging to a microcredit programme enhances one's sense of inner dignity and dignity from others. Crucially, women interviewed from SHGs (largely from scheduled caste backgrounds) discussed the idea of dignity in terms of 'respect' and 'self-respect'. Other elements of dignity which were important to women interviewed were that they had 'courage', 'independence' and 'confidence'. Confidence was listed by women as a most significant change in seven out of ten locations. Women interviewed overwhelmingly stated that they had very poor confidence prior to belonging to the SHG programme. Common themes emerged amongst women from all ten locations: that they did not believe they had any worthy skills prior to joining the SHG and they were previously wary of strangers. For example, in one focus group in Birbhum participants agreed with one woman, *Malati*, who said:

> If people like you had come in the past, we would have run into our houses but now we can talk – this is a big change: we are courageous now, we are not scared anymore.

Women described that they felt 'courageous', 'unafraid' and that they deserved 'respect'. Women repeatedly stated that they felt more confident, and this was demonstrated through: their expressions and body language in most focus group discussions; the lively way they spoke, making direct eye contact, speaking loudly and clearly; and through their general ease in discussion. Staff also made similar comments and the donor evaluations highlighted the increased confidence with which women spoke following the trajectory of the project. These impressions contrasted starkly with observations of the government run-SHGs and in previous experience with other SHGs in West Bengal.

Women interviewed indicated that belonging to the SHG had changed theirs and the community's perceptions around norms of respectability for women. Women said that prior to the programme, women were viewed as dishonourable if they talked openly and loudly with other women and appeared confident. They indicated that after joining the SHGs, women *had* to meet regularly and talk in meetings if their SHG operations and their projects such as a study centre were to succeed. Participants also expressed that they had greater confidence because they had an increased income which they earned through savings collected as being part of the SHG or through setting up small micro-enterprises (such as jewellery making) with loans from the SHG.

Does the Programme Enable Dignity From Others?

On the surface, women's contentment with gaining extra access to finance and increased self-confidence may appear unproblematic. Deeper investigation, however, indicates several issues, particularly with how women were perceived by men. In all locations, women and men stated that men in the community better respected women after being part of the SHG programme. Men and women indicated that this change was significantly influenced by women earning an increased income from the SHG programme, with both women and men emphasising that women now 'contributed' to the household. Troublingly, many women indicated that they had come to judge their self-worth on the basis of their financial contribution, expressing that they could demand respect since they were 'now working' and that this financial bargaining power offered women the right to confer with men. This was particularly evident in Birbhum and Kolkata. The quotation below from a female focus group participant, *Mithai*, best illustrates the strength of this idea:

> The more income you generate the more respect you have.

By way of further example, in Kolkata, one woman, *Priya*, said that women were consulted to a greater extent in decision-making because:

> Men used to earn – he was the boss, he was the king, if you disobey you get a good beating from me. Now both are earning and both are running the family. Need to make them understand you have to value me.

A further quotation from a different SHG member, *Kalpana*, also illustrates this linkage between respect and paid work:

> Why is there more respect? Women are also now a part of development. Previously husbands were working in the family, now both husbands and wives are working.

These quotations are emblematic of longer focus group and interview discussions with SHG members. Women for the most part expressed significant happiness about the increased level of respect from their husbands which they felt had in part resulted from earning an income. These changes, however, indicate a clear correlation between respect and one's financial usefulness.

Does the Programme Promote Holistic Dignity, Beyond Masculinist Notions of 'Public' Dignity?

The perception of care work and the dignity and value of women's work in the private sphere did not seem to radically change following membership of the SHG. Involvement in the SHG increased women's labour burden in most locations, ensuring that they spent a far greater time working than men. Significantly, women's descriptions of their workload were imbued with value judgements about their self-worth. Women reported that after being involved in the SHG, they were much busier and more 'productive' working. Women noted that after the creation of SHGs, men would do some household chores if women were sick or breastfeeding, which pleased women. However, this involvement from men was irregular, and did not substantively change the day-to-day gendered division of labour.

While being proud of their wives' achievements and income generating activities, men did not appear to value the high levels of household and care work which women performed. Instead, men indicated that women were either idle or incompetent before. The private sphere was taken-for-granted and deemed as irrelevant. For example, numerous examples in the data mirror sentiments expressed by one male focus group participant, *Swapan*:

> Earlier the women had nothing to do except the household work but now women have joined the SHG for the development of the community and the family. They are working in everything, now it is better. I appreciate that.

NGO workers from both SPT and other NGOs welcomed men's attitudes about women working, as previously men had forbidden women from accessing the programme. However, positive attitudes were based on a cost-benefit analysis by men who judged that it would be favourable to them to support women's access to finance. One male NGO worker from an NGO in North 24 Parganas noted that men appreciated the double labour of women:

> The husbands are very clever, they analyse the situation; they see that these ladies are not doing badly for the family, they are contributing something for the family. She is giving full labour as well as earning money.

In this way, women's hard and unequal labour was the price paid for enabling women to access SHG programmes or move beyond their houses. This directly challenged women's holistic dignity and their equality of dignity with men. NGO workers were not keen to challenge men in these instances, as men could withdraw their support for the programmes. Other NGO workers portrayed women's long hours of work (completing combined care, household, SHG and paid work) as illustrative of women's 'virtue' and the extent to which they were dedicated to the programme.

Does the Programme Enhance Equality of Dignity Through Redressing Power Imbalances?

Across all locations, women expressed that the SPT SHG programme resulted in better holistic outcomes for themselves than the purely monetary based government-run SHGs. Women's equality of dignity with men was only improved when the programme did more than provide funds – challenging gender inequality was critical in these instances. The SPT programme engaged participants in a broad range of non-financial activities, including but not limited to: training on gender equality, human rights, agricultural techniques, the importance of education and how to operate an effective SHG. SPT staff emphasised the importance of enabling critical 'awareness' amongst women, of their situation and opportunities.

Significantly, women from the five SPT communities in South 24 Parganas appeared to experience greater changes in equality of dignity with men following their involvement in the programme than women from Birbhum or Kolkata. In South 24 Parganas, program staff engaged with men more in critically challenging gender norms. Women were poorer and less educated in South 24 Parganas than in Kolkata, so these improvements did not appear to be based on socio-economic status.

In South 24 Parganas, women were reflective on the differences between the SPT SHGs which included activities such as gender trainings and government-run SHGs which their mothers or sisters were a part of. For example, the quotation from a female SHG member in South 24 Parganas, illustrates the differences:

> The Government level SHG is only monetary. There is no awareness, they don't know what is wrong or right, they know only the money. My mother now has income but no awareness; she is not part of any women's programs.

Discussion

In using a framework of feminist dignity to review the case study, I have shown that the programme promoted the dignity of women to a varied extent, resulting in mixed outcomes as to the effectiveness of the programme in improving women's empowerment. By using a framework of feminist dignity we better understand how the one programme may have ambivalent results (Garikipati et al., 2017), demonstrating the importance of the implementation model and mechanisms of programme delivery used (Kabeer, 2017; Sanyal 2014).

At the core of the framework on feminist dignity (Table 7.1) is the idea that women are 'ends' in themselves as important individuals. In these examples, we see that without the wider challenging of gender norms, women's value was equated with their economic contribution, not their intrinsic worth. This was reflected in participants' assessment that: 'The more income you generate the more respect you have'. This demonstrates how a 'smart economics' approach focusing mainly on women's economic empowerment dehumanises and instrumentalises women (Chant, 2012), as a 'resource' to be mined (Calkin, 2015b) and does not treat women as an 'end' in themselves (Kant, 2012/1785; Nussbaum, 2011b). We see from the examples given, how staff portraying women in communities as 'virtuous' for using extra hours of the day to work on their micro-enterprises or on SHG activities demonstrates an acceptance that women sacrifice themselves for the wellbeing of the whole community. In this way, 'smart economics' programming relies on a utilitarian sacrifice of the individual for the 'good' of the whole (Chant, 2016; Ferry, 2013).

Women's sense of inner dignity on the one hand was bolstered by a feeling of improved confidence and courageousness. As illustrated, women across the different programme locations indicated that improved confidence was one of the most important changes which had occurred after they joined the microcredit programme. Women felt emboldened to move beyond the house, interact with others and do things they had never done before. While this confidence was highly significant to women interviewed, their inner dignity was affected when they viewed themselves as worthy only based on their earning capacity. This was illustrated by the numerous times women discussed their self-worth in relation to their improved incomes, describing themselves as inadequate and ignorant before becoming involved in the SHG. This problematic self-image reflected the dominant normative attitudes of men (Jacobson, 2007) who portrayed them as previously 'idle'. These examples illustrate the fragility of self-worth and a sense of inner dignity. It further demonstrates the issue with reported self-confidence. An individual may report increased confidence but it is important to examine what this is based on, and if it goes beyond one one's assessment of one's economic worth. It is therefore essential that an individual has self-respect, based on an enduring resilient sense of self (Paik, 2020; Arya & Rathore, 2020). This must go beyond valuing oneself contingent upon skills gained or income earned, as I have demonstrated in this case study.

For the women interviewed, respect and self-respect were fundamental in their understanding of dignity and their own wellbeing. They felt happy with themselves when they felt valued by their husbands and the community. This is represented in the idea of 'dignity from others' in the Feminist Dignity Framework (Table 7.1). 'Dignity from others', based on respect and recognition of one's humanity, is crucial for forming one's sense of self (Castleman, 2016; Roy, 2019). 'Dignity from others' can be hampered by the prejudices of the powerful – whether that be caste, class or gender based (Sonalkar, 2020), as illustrated by the perceptions of men in communities as to women's worth. An important counterpoint, however, is that 'dignity from others' can also be expanded through solidarity and alliances with others (Kabeer, 2017).

Furthermore, in using a feminist framework of dignity to determine whether the programme promotes holistic dignity, we see how 'smart economics' prioritises income generation and paid work over unpaid labour and care work (Chant & Sweetman, 2012), leading to the demand for women to work longer hours in addition to already exhausting workloads (Chopra & Sweetman, 2014). Women's 'private' work was marginalised and only women's 'public' economic contributions were valued (Kittay, 1999, 2002; Nussbaum, 2006). These attitudes were reflected by programme staff and men and women in the community. Care work was not discussed with any real worth, as compared to paid work. Care work and household labour were largely treated as invisible in consideration of women's time to engage in SHG activities or microenterprises. This emphasis on paid employment further ignores feminist research into the real financial contribution and value of care work (Reid et al., 2012; Ward, 2017).

The last issue with 'smart economics' approaches when addressed through the lens of feminist dignity is that they do not emphasise *equality* of dignity as reflected in human rights discourses (Nussbaum, 2011a). Instead 'smart economics' ignores power imbalances and hierarchies and in turn, reproduces them (Roberts, 2015). For example, participants in the government run

SHGs in West Bengal which were purely financial, did not question gender or caste hierarchies at all and simply accepted them. While SPT and other NGOs made much more of an effort to discuss gender issues than government-run SHGs, it would be useful if all implementing organisations made use of explicit learnings from Dalit feminism (such as focusing on respect, self-respect and dignity) and interrogated more fully the maintenance of patriarchy in programmes, reassessing attitudes about care work and women's worth.

By contrast, 'equality of dignity' can be enhanced through including critical education as a component of microcredit programming and by challenging social norms through critical thinking, as emphasised by Bengali feminists like Begum Rokeya (Quayam) and Dalit leaders (Paik, 2020). These activities should challenge gender norms (Garikipati, 2008; Holvoet, 2005; Mayoux, 1999) and caste inequality. Skills development should be based on ideas of human flourishing (Gooptu & Chakravarty, 2018), enhancing dignity, not just economic gains. It is these activities which can better promote a stronger sense of independence and autonomy, based on a resilient sense of self (Rao, 2015), not just financial earnings.

In addition, while scholarship on dignity and the Gender and Development literature for the most part do not appear to overlap (outside of the capabilities approach) (Nussbaum, 2011b; Sen, 2004), there are important synergies and ways in which the idea of dignity can inform Gender and Development frameworks. Three important ideas in Gender and Development frameworks relate closely to the idea of dignity: first, the emphasis on women's strategic interests over practical needs (Hillenbrand et al., 2014; Molyneux, 1985); second, the recognition of women's unpaid work and criticism of a binary distinction between the public and private spheres (Esquivel, 2014; Rowlands, 1997; Sepúlveda Carmona & Donald, 2014); and third, the focus on redressing power inequalities and hierarchies for the attainment of gender equality (Batliwala, 2007; Cornwall, 2016; Jakimow & Kilby, 2006).

Conclusion

In this chapter I have provided a framework for determining how to support human dignity in community development programming. I have further illustrated how human dignity is complex and multifaceted and requires self-confidence and self-respect. Moreover, when others do not respect us, this does not diminish our dignity but it hurts our self-esteem and belief in ourselves. Any programme aiming to improve women's empowerment must fundamentally ensure that it uplifts our sense of self. In addition, by adopting a *feminist* framework of dignity, I have outlined how programmes must focus on holistic notions of dignity, whereby an individual is valued in both the private and public spheres. Finally, a programme must focus on equality of dignity – aiming to ensure that it is not only the powerful who are afforded with dignity.

Note

1 An earlier version of this chapter appeared as 'Examining microcredit self-help groups through the lens of feminist dignity' by Annabel Dulhunty in Oxford Development Studies, 50:4, 307–320. Copyright © 2022. Oxford Department of International Development, reprinted by permission of Taylor & Francis Ltd, http://www.tandfonline.com on behalf of Oxford Department of International Development.

References

Arya, S., & Rathore, A. S. (2020). Introduction: Theorising Dalit Feminism. In S. Arya & A. Singh Rathore (Eds.), *Dalit Feminist Theory: A Reader* (pp. 1–22). Routledge.

Bagchi, B. (2009). Towards Ladyland: Rokeya Sakhawat Hossain and the Movement for Women's Education in Bengal,C. 1900–C. 1932. *Paedagogica Historica*, 45(6), 743–755. doi:10.1080/00309230903335652.

Banerjee, N. (2017). Feminism at the Crossroads: Where do we go from here? *Indian Journal of Gender Studies*, 24(1), 98–110. doi:10.1177/0971521516678540.

Batliwala, S. (2007). Taking the Power out of Empowerment – an Experiential Account. *Development in Practice*, 17(4–5),557–565. doi:10.1080/09614520701469559.

Bayefsky, R. (2013). Dignity, Honour, and Human Rights. *Political Theory*, 41(6), 809–837. doi:10.1177/0090591713499762.

Biswas, M. M. (2012). Bengali Dalit Literature and Culture: A Dignity Discourse. *Contemporary Voice of Dalit*, 5(1), 131–137. doi:10.1177/0974354520120109.

Byatt, B. (2018). The Case of Kiva and Grameen: Towards a Marxist Feminist Critique of 'Smart Economics'. *Capital & Class*, 42(3), 403–409. doi:10.1177/0309816818799702.

Calkin, S. (2015a). Feminism, Interrupted? Gender and Development in the Era of 'Smart Economics'. *Progress in Development Studies*, 15(4), 295–307. doi:10.1177/1464993415592737.

Calkin, S. (2015b). "Tapping" Women for Post-Crisis Capitalism. *International Feminist Journal of Politics*, 17(4), 611–629. doi:10.1080/14616742.2015.1071994.

Calkin, S. (2018). *Human Capital in Gender and Development*. Routledge.

Castleman, T. (2016). The Role of Human Recognition in Development. *Oxford Development Studies*, 44(2), 135–151. doi:10.1080/13600818.2015.1109615.

Chant, S. (2012). The Disappearing of 'Smart Economics'? The World Development Report 2012 on Gender Equality: Some Concerns About the Preparatory Process and the Prospects for Paradigm Change. *Global Social Policy: An Interdisciplinary Journal of Public Policy and Social Development*, 12(2), 198–218. doi:10.1177/1468018112443674.

Chant, S. (2016). Women, Girls and World Poverty: Empowerment, Equality or Essentialism? *International Development Planning Review*, 38(1), 1–24. doi:10.3828/idpr.2016.1.

Chant, S., & Sweetman, C. (2012). Fixing Women or Fixing the World? 'Smart Economics', Efficiency Approaches, and Gender Equality in Development. *Gender & Development*, 20(3), 517–529. doi:10.1080/13552074.2012.731812.

Chopra, D., & Sweetman, C. (2014). Introduction to Gender, Development and Care. *Gender & Development*, 22(3), 409–421. doi:10.1080/13552074.2014.975486.

Cornell, D. (2014). *Law and Revolution in South Africa: uBuntu, Dignity, and the Struggle for Constitutional Transformation*. Fordham University Press.

Cornwall, A. (2016). Women's Empowerment: What Works? *Journal of International Development*, 28(3), 342–359. doi:10.1002/jid.3210.

Esquivel, V. (2014). What Is a Transformative Approach to Care, and Why Do We Need It? *Gender & Development*, 22(3), 423–439. doi:10.1080/13552074.2014.963303.

Ferry, M. (2013). Does Morality Demand Our Very Best? On Moral Prescriptions and the Line of Duty. *Philosophical Studies*, 165, 573–589. doi:10.1007/s11098-012-9968-6.

Garikipati, S. (2008). The Impact of Lending to Women on Household Vulnerability and Women's Empowerment: Evidence from India. *World Development*, 36(12), 2620–2642. doi:10.1016/j.worlddev.2007.11.008.

Garikipati, S., Johnson, S., Guérin, I., & Szafarz, A. (2017). Microfinance and Gender: Issues, Challenges and the Road Ahead. *The Journal of Development Studies*, 53(5), 641–648. doi:10.1080/00220388.2016.1205736.

Gooptu, N., & Chakravarty, R. (2018). Skill, Work and Gendered Identity in Contemporary India: The Business of Delivering Home-Cooked Food for Domestic Consumption. *Journal of South Asian Development*, 13(3), 293–314. doi:10.1177/0973174118804448.

Guru, G. (2009). *Humiliation: Claims and Context*. Oxford University Press.

Hay, C. (2013). *Kantianism, Liberalism, and Feminism*. Palgrave Macmillan.

Hillenbrand, E., Lakzadeh, P., Sokhoin, L., Talukder, Z., Green, T., & McLean, J. (2014). Using the Social Relations Approach to Capture Complexity in Women's Empowerment: Using Gender Analysis in the Fish on Farms Project in Cambodia. *Gender & Development*, 22(2), 351–368. doi:10.1080/13552074.2014.920992.

Holvoet, N. (2005). The Impact of Microfinance on Decision-Making Agency: Evidence from South India. *Development and Change*, 36(1), 75–102. doi:10.1111/j.0012-155X.2005.00403.x.

Jacobson, N. (2007). Dignity and Health: A Review. *Social Science and Medicine*, 64 (2), 292–302. doi:10.1016/j.socscimed.2006.08.039.

Jain, D. (2018). *The Journey of a Southern Feminist*. SAGE Publications.

Jakimow, T., & Kilby, P. (2006). Empowering Women:A Critique of the Blueprint for Self-Help Groups in India. *Indian Journal of Gender Studies*, 13(3), 375–400. doi:10.1177/097152150601300303.

Kabeer, N. (2017). Economic Pathways to Women's Empowerment and Active Citizenship: What Does the Evidence from Bangladesh Tell Us? *The Journal of Development Studies*, 53(5), 649–663. doi:10.1080/00220388.2016.1205730.

Kant, I. (2012/1785). Groundwork of the Metaphysics of Morals. In M. Gregor & J. Timmermann (Eds.), *Immanuel Kant: Groundwork of the Metaphysics of Morals*. Cambridge University Press.

Kittay, E. F. (1999). *Love's Labor: Essays on Women, Equality, and Dependency*. Routledge.

Kittay, E. F. (2002). Love's Labor Revisited. *Hypatia*, 17(3), 237–250.

Mayoux, L. (1999). Questioning Virtuous Spirals: Micro-Finance and Women's Empowerment in Africa. *Journal of International Development*, 11(7), 957–984. doi:10.1002/(SICI)1099–1328(199911/12)11:7<957:AID-JID623>3.0.CO;2-#.

Miller, S. C. (2017). Reconsidering Dignity Relationally. *Ethics and Social welfare*, 11 (2), 108–121. doi:10.1080/17496535.2017.1318411.

Molyneux, M. (1985). Mobilization without Emancipation? Women's Interests, the State, and Revolution in Nicaragua. *Feminist Studies*, 11(2), 227–254.

Nussbaum, M. C. (2000). Women's Capabilities and Social Justice. *Journal of Human Development*, 1(2), 219–247. doi:10.1080/713678045.

Nussbaum, M. C. (2006). *Frontiers of Justice: Disability, Nationality, Species Membership.* Harvard University Press.

Nussbaum, M. C. (2011a). Capabilities, Entitlements, Rights: Supplementation and Critique. *Journal of Human Development and Capabilities*, 12(1), 23–37. doi:10.1080/19452829.2011.541731.

Nussbaum, M. C. (2011b). *Creating Capabilities: The Human Development Approach.* Harvard University Press.

Paik, S. (2014). Building Bridges: Articulating Dalit and African American Women's Solidarity. *WSQ: Women's Studies Quarterly*, 42(3–4),74–96. doi:10.1353/wsq.2014.0053.

Paik, S. (2020). Dalit Women's Agency and Phule-Ambedkarite Feminism. In S. Arya & A. Singh Rathore (Eds.), *Dalit Feminist Theory: A Reader* (pp. 1–22). Routledge.

Price, S. (2019). The Risks and Incentives of Disciplinary Neoliberal Feminism: The Case of Microfinance. *International Feminist Journal of Politics*, 21(1), 67–88. doi:10.1080/14616742.2018.1454843.

Quayum, M. (2013). *The Essential Rokeya: Selected Works of Rokeya Sakhawat Hossain.* Brill.

Rao, N. (2015). Marriage, Violence, and Choice: Understanding Dalit Women's Agency in Rural Tamil Nadu. *Gender & Society*, 29(3), 410–433. doi:10.1177/0891243214554798.

Rawat, R. S. (2013). Occupation, Dignity, and Space: The Rise of Dalit Studies. *History Compass*, 11(12), 1059–1067. doi:10.1111/hic3.12109.

Reid, E., Waring, M., Enriquez, C. R., & Shivdas, M. (2012). Embracing Disruptions, Responding to Uncertainties, Valuing Agency: Situating a Feminist Approach to Social Protection. *Development*, 55(3), 291–298. doi:10.1057/dev.2012.30.

Roberts, A. (2015). Gender, Financial Deepening and the Production of Embodied Finance: Towards a Critical Feminist Analysis. *Global Society*, 29(1), 107–127. doi:10.1080/13600826.2014.975189.

Rowlands, J. (1997). *Questioning Empowerment: Working with Women in Honduras.* Oxfam GB.

Roy, I. (2013). Development as Dignity: Dissensus, Equality and Contentious Politics in Bihar, India. *Oxford Development Studies*, 41(4), 517–536. doi:10.1080/13600818.2013.835392.

Roy, I. (2019). Disjunctions of Democracy and Liberalism: Agonistic Imaginations of Dignity in Bihar. *South Asia: Journal of South Asian Studies*, 42(2), 344–358. doi:10.1080/00856401.2019.1580829.

Sanyal, P. (2014). *Credit to Capabilities: A Sociological Study of Microcredit Groups in India.* Cambridge University Press.

Sen, A. (1992). *Inequality Reexamined.* Clarendon Press.

Sen, A. (1999). *Development as Freedom.* Alfred A Knopf.

Sen, A. (2004). Capabilities, Lists, and Public Reason: Continuing the Conversation. *Feminist Economics*, 10(3), 77–80. doi:10.1080/1354570042000315163.

Sepúlveda Carmona, M., & Donald, K. (2014). What Does Care Have to Do with Human Rights? Analysing the Impact on Women's Rights and Gender Equality. *Gender & Development*, 22(3), 441–457. doi:10.1080/13552074.2014.963305.

Siegert, R. J., & Ward, T. (2010). Dignity, Rights and Capabilities in Clinical Rehabilitation. *Dignity and Rehabilitation*, 32(25), 2138–2146. doi:10.3109/09638288.2010.483037.

Sonalkar, W. (2020). Ambedkarite Women. In S. Arya & A. Singh Rathore (Eds.), *Dalit Feminist Theory: A Reader* (pp. 88–93). Routledge.

Ward, K. (2017). Cambodia: Managing Work and Care in a Post-Conflict Context. In M. Baird, M. Ford, & E. Hill (Eds.), *Women, Work and Care in the Asia-Pacific* (pp. 102–117). Routledge.

World Bank (2012). *World Development Report: Gender Equality and Development*. https://openknowledge.worldbank.org/handle/10986/4391.

Zavaleta Reyles, D. (2007). The Ability to Go About without Shame: A Proposal for Internationally Comparable Indicators of Shame and Humiliation. *Oxford Development Studies*, 35(4), 405–430. doi:10.1080/13600810701701905.

8 Mobility and the Maintenance of Patriarchy[1]

In the past two decades, with the 'mobilities turn' in the social sciences, there has been increased scholarship on the power dynamics of physical mobility (Cresswell, 2011; Lowe & DeVerteuil, 2020). It is therefore surprising that so little attention has been given to the relationship between physical mobility and women's empowerment programming, which I will explore in this chapter. Increased physical mobility – defined here as the ability to physically move freely across space – is frequently mentioned in the literature on women's empowerment, but without detailed analysis. Instead, studies generally describe physical mobility as one of many indicators of agency and empowerment (Bali Swain & Wallentin, 2012). Most papers conclude that belonging to a women's empowerment programme, such as a self-help group, improves women's mobility, without further examining the significance or limitations of this mobility (Kar (2018a) and Sanyal's (2015) studies are exceptions).

Despite this oversight in the literature, examining the relationship between physical mobility, empowerment and patriarchy is critical for better understanding how to address gender inequality and women's wellbeing. While this chapter focuses on physical mobility, this is connected to wider mobility – including social mobility and imaginative mobility (Urry, 2002). Being restricted in one's movement clearly prevents one from imagining different possibilities for oneself or being open to different opportunities as they arise. Ultimately, limited mobility in all spheres restricts empowerment.

In this chapter I examine the claim that increased mobility leads to improved empowerment outcomes, particularly through empowerment programming (Brody et al., 2017; Weber & Ahmad, 2014). As I have outlined in Chapter 2, empowerment is defined as the process of gaining power, increasing one's autonomy and being able to make meaningful choices (Kabeer, 2012). Empowerment is essentially power in its most productive form – as 'power to' do something (Pansardi, 2012). While much literature has been written on empowerment, greater attention should also be given to the limitations of empowerment, as illustrated through using the lens of physical mobility. While many studies on women's empowerment briefly mention physical mobility, it is presented as an uncomplicated component of

DOI: 10.4324/9781003356400-8

empowerment which requires little attention (Bhaumik & Bera, 2015). By contrast, I argue that by examining empowerment through mobility, we gain a new understanding of how patriarchal power relations are formed and whether these can be substantively ruptured through empowerment programming. In this chapter I provide crucial insights for feminist scholarship as mobility provides a key lens for understanding how gender inequality continues and where and how this may be redressed.

In this chapter I particularly draw on the idea of 'disciplined mobility' (Moran et al., 2012; Packer, 2003) to elaborate on the mechanisms of masculine, domineering power and its control over women's mobility. I find that empowerment programmes must contend with the active discouragement of mobility through the male control of space (Parikh, 2017). In this research I illustrate the way that disciplined mobility manifests through specific restrictions (e.g. not being 'allowed' to leave the house), but more cleverly through surveillance and especially through women self-regulating their own actions, an act of invisible power – a type of power which is difficult to see, but shapes social norms (Lukes, 2005). In this chapter I conclude that patriarchal control is resilient and continues through the act of disciplining women's mobility, ultimately constraining women's empowerment. I therefore argue that women's empowerment programmes are unable to completely dismantle patriarchal norms. While these programmes can increase women's physical mobility, enabling women to move in a wider variety of places, patriarchal norms continue to shape that mobility and limit the possibilities of empowerment.

This research makes a distinct contribution not only to feminist scholarship, but also to the wider mobilities literature, as it illustrates the sheer power of 'disciplined' mobility. It indicates the gendered nature of disciplined mobility, and the extent to which it is an insidious phenomenon. Disciplined mobility is able to structure power relations and societal structures, sometimes overtly, but often invisibly, illustrating why physical mobility requires ongoing attention in scholarship.

Women's Empowerment and Physical Mobility

One key feature of empowerment is agency. The idea of agency is important to explore because physical mobility is most commonly presented as evidence of agency, which then results in scholars concluding that empowerment has been realised (Hashemi et al., 1996). In this chapter I instead argue that the relationship between empowerment and mobility is far more complex. Despite differing approaches, most studies link women's empowerment to the ability to make independent unconstrained choices and fundamentally, to the increased agency of women (Duvendack & Palmer-Jones, 2016; Kabeer, 2011; Kumar et al., 2019; Mukherjee & Kundu, 2017).

One primary indicator of agency, and hence empowerment, used by scholars has been 'women's mobility' – i.e. the extent to which women feel free to physically move around (Huda & Kaur, 2011; Orso & Fabrizi, 2016). Physical mobility has been used as a marker of agency for many years now, with Hashemi et al. (1996) including physical mobility as an indicator for empowerment in their study. In the literature on microcredit, however, physical mobility is represented as one of many different components of empowerment (Bhaumik & Bera, 2015; Mahmud & Tasneem, 2014).

Almost all studies which address women's physical mobility indicate that it improved after joining a self-help group with microcredit (Finnis, 2017; Sanyal, 2014; Sengupta, 2013; Weber & Ahmad, 2014). Most studies from India (excepting Singh (2014)), indicate that belonging to a microcredit initiative challenged entrenched social norms of restricted mobility – including *purdah* – which generally included staying secluded inside the house and not interacting with others (particularly males) outside the family (Sanyal, 2009). Microcredit initiatives are described as a clear catalyst for changing women's mobility – prompting women to leave the house and their local environs to undertake key tasks relating to microcredit activities, such as banking (Bhaumik & Bera, 2015).

While mobility is frequently described in the literature on agency and empowerment, it is usually only one of several indicators listed. The most in-depth coverage comes from Kar (2018b) and Sanyal (2009, 2015). Sanyal (2009) contrasts the situation of isolation and purdah with women's increased movement and self-confidence outside the house after belonging to an SHG. Kar (2018b) in her study of women's interaction with microfinance institutions, highlights the drawbacks of greater mobility and the increased risk of women entering the masculine dominated public sphere. In this research I further build on these findings and illustrate the influence of 'disciplined mobility' and spatial fear.

Why is it then important to address the relationship between mobility and empowerment in greater depth than most studies allow for? Firstly, scholarship indicates that women themselves believed that increased mobility is a form of empowerment (Finnis, 2017; Kabeer, 2012). As Hanson (2010) argues, increased mobility represents a significant opportunity to participate in the public domain. Given the possibilities enabled by increased mobility, there are very few who argue for women's enduring containment (Hanson, 2010). There are, however, ambivalent attitudes in the literature which contest the perceived good of increased mobility. For example, Gilbert (1998) argues that all forms of spatiality have power and that a binary perspective of mobility as good and immobility as bad does not allow for the complexities of each situation. Of course, women's agency and freedom of movement is not uniform and differs depending on characteristics such as class, caste and location (Singh, 2014).

The cultural value of mobility and confinement is highly relevant. In West Bengal, certainly there is an associated privilege with not needing to go out to 'work' outside the home, connected to middle and upper class and caste ideals (Roy, 2019). As I have noted, this research includes participants mainly from scheduled castes, who have had their own particularities of experience in regards to physical mobility. On the one hand, scholars note that scheduled caste women in some instances have had greater physical mobility than other women, as they have not had to conform to such strict notions of proprietary that were expected of 'upper' caste women (Arya & Rathore, 2020). In the areas I visited as part of this research, however, scheduled caste women were similarly cloistered prior to engaging in the SHG programme. When they did leave the house in the past, it was only for economic necessity. Women in this research also indicated a desire to appear 'respectable' (Gopal, 2012; Siwach, 2020). Social norms and the desire to appear virtuous thus restrict women as much as strict prescriptions on their behaviour (Cresswell & Uteng, 2008).

Violence Against Women and Mobility

In the scholarship on women's empowerment, there is a distinct lack of studies exploring restrictions on mobility and how this impacts women's empowerment. Very few studies on women's empowerment examine the violence of restricting mobility and the violence women experience outside the home when women move beyond the confines of the house. Most scholarship on women's empowerment programming has largely focused on domestic violence, alternately indicating that belonging to an empowerment programme, such as a self-help group which distributes microcredit, increases the risk of domestic violence (Ganle et al., 2015), decreases it (Yaron et al., 2020) or makes no difference (Bajracharya & Amin, 2013; Murshid et al., 2016). The connection between violence and mobility is seldom made. Furthermore, there is very little detailed analysis on violence outside of domestic violence, such as sexual violence or harassment. As noted, Kar (2018a) is one exception, arguing that when women enter 'masculine' spaces like the public market, women are confronted with new risks, such as the risk of sexual violence.

Outside of the research on women's empowerment programming, a wide body of literature identifies the restriction of mobility as violence (Brickell, 2008; Cuomo, 2013; Fluri & Piedalue, 2017; Pain, 2014; Tyner & Inwood, 2014). This violence clearly limits women's opportunities for empowerment. Certainly, physically violent relationships restrict spatial movement (Warrington, 2001) but it is important to note that the restriction of mobility is in and of itself violence, as a form of coercive control (Bowstead, 2020; Stark, 2007). Violence clearly goes beyond the physical realm (Balkmar, 2018). Little (2016, p.477) outlines how this physical restriction on movement is a kind of 'entrapment'. She describes the affective component of fear guiding the behaviour of survivors, as they further withdraw from the world. Pain (2014, p.533) further elaborates on this affective dimension of domestic violence as 'emotional warfare'. These affective experiences not only shape the extent to which women feel comfortable moving beyond the house, but also limit women's experience of autonomy and freedom.

Examining wider violence against women and girls, Parikh describes the 'gendered spatialisation of fear' (Parikh, 2017, p.698) which limits women's movement in public locations. This draws on longstanding feminist research which highlights the way that fear regulates women's behaviour, including their ease in going to different spaces (Martin, 2021). The weaponsing of this fear (Pain, 2015) is an effective form of patriarchal control, limiting the extent to which empowerment can be realised.

Mobility and Power

Scholarship on mobility has focused largely on agency and liberty at the expense of coercion and immobility (Moran et al., 2012). The idea of 'disciplined mobility' (Packer, 2003; Sheller, 2015) goes some way to understanding the 'flip' side of mobility by focusing on restricted mobility, with 'disciplinary power' intent on '"fixing" things and people in space, immobilising them' (Philo, 2014, p.496). Scholarship on 'disciplined mobility' largely draws from Foucault, particularly his work in *Discipline and Punish* (1979). Foucault outlined how the modern prison represents all-pervasive power which becomes internalised by prisoners so that physical violence is not even needed to subjugate them. Individuals thus self-regulate their behaviour in accordance with the wishes of the powerful. Scholars have built on Foucault's work to argue that 'disciplined mobility' is best controlled through self-regulation, not force (Moran et al., 2012).

Sandra Bartky (1990) provides essential insights for understanding the impact of 'disciplinary power' on women, arguing that Foucault completely overlooks differences of gender. Bartky (1990) outlines how just as the prisoner feels watched, women always feel the power of the male gaze on them, controlling them and regulating their behaviour. Similarly, as the prisoner self-regulates and believes in his own subjugation, women monitor themselves and their own behaviour so that it meets with the approval of patriarchy. Men do not have to physically subjugate women, women will act in accordance with their wishes regardless. This research illustrates multiple examples of this phenomenon, indicating that a gendered perspective provides the most relevant and pervasive examples of disciplinary mobility.

In understanding the role of disciplinary mobility in shaping women's norms and limiting their empowerment, the idea of 'invisible power' from Stephen Lukes (2005) is helpful. Lukes (2005) outlines three forms of power: decision making power, non-decision making power and invisible power. While the first two forms of power mentioned are explicitly and overtly expressed, invisible power is subtle and shapes an individual's 'very wants'. Invisible power is therefore 'the most effective and insidious' (Lukes, 2005, p.27). Lukes highlights the potency of this power by asking: 'Is it not the supreme exercise of power to get another or others to have the desires you want them to have - that is, to secure their compliance by controlling their thoughts and desires?' (Lukes, 2005, p.27). Invisible power guides social norms and enables people to be subjugated without even realising it. It is both domineering and oppressive. Invisible power maintains structural oppression (Gaventa & Martorano, 2016), shaping individual beliefs to assent to dominant social norms (Petit, 2016). Hierarchies and inequality thus appear 'normal' as invisible power shapes our thoughts (Howard & Vajda, 2016). Invisible power in part helps to explain the reproduction of patriarchy. For example, Rowlands (1997) relates how Lukes' invisible power enables an abused woman to believe in the merits of her own subjugation. In this chapter I draw on this idea of invisible power to illustrate the insidious nature of patriarchal control and how it can discipline mobility without overt force.

Details from Kolkata, South 24 Parganas and Birbhum

Mobility Restrictions

Prior to joining the SHGs, women's physical mobility was 'disciplined' and highly restricted by their husbands and families. One of the dominant themes which emerged from discussions with women and men in communities was that of changes in women's mobility. In both Kolkata and the rural areas, I sat with self-help group members either in their small community halls or in a quiet area outside and had long conversations with them about their lives, aspirations and how they ran their SHGs. Across all locations, women were very chatty and excited, often talking over each other. They were proud of their achievements in their self-help group, from joint agricultural ventures they had engaged in, to saving money. As I detailed in Chapter 5, one of the key questions I asked during visits, was what were the most significant changes (good or bad), in their lives since joining the SHG. Many women indicated that they felt they had 'increased confidence' and an 'ability to move outside the house'.

Women across all locations discussed the restrictions on their mobility before joining the SHG. In all communities, women said that they had largely been confined to their homes and their agricultural fields prior to joining the SHG. Women and men pointed to women's attitude and self-belief as a reason for their mobility being restricted, indicating that fear and a lack of confidence prevented women from leaving the house. For example, men in a focus group discussion in Birbhum agreed with one man, *Hrishab*, who said:

> There was a remarkable change in women – before they couldn't go to the panchayat (local council) or police station – they weren't very courageous. (The NGO) has helped them to gather that courage because of training/awareness.

While men were quick to argue that it was women's lack of confidence which was confining them to the home, it became evident in discussions that women's movement was largely prevented by men and their in-laws. Women frequently used the phrases that they had been 'restricted' to move and were 'not allowed' to travel to certain places before they became involved in the SHG. For example, one woman, *Ankolika*, in South 24 Parganas expressed a sentiment which was iterated multiple times across locations:

> Prior to going to the SHG I was never allowed to go to the bank, I was not allowed to step out of the house – now I have self-confidence due to (the NGO).

Another woman, *Josna*, in South 24 Parganas, had a similar story to tell:

> Initially if any visitors came to my place, I was not allowed to serve food to them, the men would serve the food, I was not allowed to go outside. With the…initiative I have been able to go out.

Women discussed how when the NGO, SPT, first entered communities, the men were very doubtful as to the NGO's intentions and they did not think that it was acceptable for their wives to be leaving the house so frequently and meeting with male staff. This caused a significant number of fights at home, as men expressed that they couldn't trust their wives. For example, *Madhurima*, a woman from South 24 Parganas noted: 'Our husbands used to doubt us - our honesty and fidelity – but now my husband is ok for me to go to meetings'.

Men in focus group discussions concurred with women that men had previously been very upset about their wives leaving the house. For instance, *Partho*, a man in Birbhum said:

> Women are doing well now – they are getting loans, men are supportive. Our outlook was different a few years back – that women should stay at home and not go out. We wanted to know from our wives what (the NGO) was telling them.

Asides from often being restricted to leave the house, women were under close surveillance by their husbands or in-laws. As *Sudeepta*, a woman in South 24 Parganas mentioned in a focus group discussion:

> The trend before was that we were not allowed to go out, our husband and parents-in-law were always monitoring.

In this same community, women confirmed that they used to monitor their daughter-in-law's movements very closely. They had been worried that their daughter-in-law would be visiting places or speaking to others in such a way that it could bring shame to the family. They explained that they felt very suspicious of their daughters-in-law in the past and felt that it was their duty to ensure that their movements were not 'disreputable'. These women said that their attitudes had changed since joining the SHG and they no longer felt the need to closely monitor their daughters-in-law.

Despite changes, some women indicated that they were still being monitored and that their movement continued to be restricted. For example, one woman, *Durba*, noted in a focus group in South 24 Parganas that 'it is now ok to go outside if we communicate with women, but if it is with men then there is a problem, he might say I am having an affair'.

Changes in Mobility

Across all communities, women felt that their physical mobility had improved since joining the SHG – whether that be for practical purposes or for social visits. This change was deemed highly significant for women interviewed. Generally, in the rural locations of South 24 Parganas and Birbhum, women's movement revolved around a few key places, particularly around their agricultural fields and visiting each other's homes in the community. In one focus group discussion in Birbhum, women described their regular movements:

> Sometimes we go to the Gram Panchayat (local council) twice a month, to the bank once a month, once a week to the bazaar, quarterly to the block development office, Suri (the local town): 4–5 times per year to buy sarees or books…sometimes we go to the market, go for enquiry purposes to the police office, we also cook midday meals at the school.

Some women also engaged in paid work, for instance in small-scale micro enterprises or at stone crusher units. Women remarked how the acceptability of this had changed, for example in one village in Birbhum, women agreed with one woman, *Kaberi* who said: 'Initially it was just the men who went to work but now we go to work too'.

Belonging to the SHG programme increased women's sphere of movement in a number of ways. Being part of the SHG meant that women had joined a wider forum of SHGs and could meet with women outside their village. For example, women discussed that they used to feel shy leaving their village but that their involvement with SHG's had helped change this. One woman, *Koel*, in Birbhum explained:

> Members of the SHG meet other people at a higher forum for SHGs – so we had a chance to meet women from other villages. I used to feel out of place when visiting a different village but now I feel ok.

Women in the villages felt that the SHG programme had made it more socially acceptable for women to move beyond their village. Women described that the programme had contributed to this change through: staff encouragement of them and their husbands to enable women to move beyond their homes; SHG leaders undertaking travel outside their homes and setting the example for other women; women moving in groups for safety; and the necessity of needing to go to the bank or local council office meant that it became more acceptable for women to move outside their house. Women described how this SHG related movement resulted in women moving for other activities, such as visiting their friends' houses. Women commented on how their physical mobility was notably greater than that of their mothers or sisters in different villages. Women were significantly proud of their mobility, describing it as an achievement and listing the places where they could travel to.

In Kolkata, in the migrant community areas, women's mobility had also increased. While women may have moved around the streets of their local area before belonging to the SHG, they were largely confined to housework and to socially mixing with their relatives. After joining the SHG, women felt it was more socially acceptable to visit other women in their village and to work outside the house.

Self-Regulation and Fear of Sexual Assault

While women interviewed were pleased with changes in their physical mobility, their mobility continued to be restricted through fear of sexual assault, continued surveillance of their movements and through the endurance of patriarchal social norms. Each of these aspects continued to limit the possibilities of empowerment. The preservation of 'women's honour' was mentioned as one of the reasons for continual monitoring of women and a number of women felt that they were still being monitored by their families. Enmeshed with this idea was the sense that women were 'in danger' outside their villages or small community area. Certainly, a number of examples given illustrated violence against women.

In Birbhum in particular, women expressed that areas outside their village were dangerous. Across the discussions with women in SHGs in Birbhum, women explained that they especially feared sexual assault and harassment, mentioning the dangers at work sites (such as at the stone quarry), railway stations, forests, at the railway station, on buses and walking near the road. Women were worried about the outskirts of their community also. One woman, *Moutushi*, described the issues in Birbhum:

> The forest is a risk, we are scared, we may get sexually assaulted. It is common, one incident happened today. I was fishing and a man tried to grab me. There is a road in the forest but no one wants to go there. A car might pick them up there. There was an incident – a girl was going to school and a truck tried to pick her up but the local men saved the girl.

As with many areas, night was considered a particularly dangerous time. In Birbhum across focus group discussions, a common sentiment was expressed that: 'Women don't go out at night'. Men in focus group discussions noted that they 'prohibited' their wives from going out at night. Women also said that they felt it was unsafe to go out then. For example, one focus group of women discussed recent instances of rape at the railway station. As one woman, *Oindrila*, from a Birbhum community said:

> We are scared of going to the bazaar at night because of traffic – also cars may stop and snatch us, from 7pm it is risky.

There appeared to be less crime in the villages in South 24 Parganas, however many women were still concerned about going far beyond their houses. In South 24 Parganas women were especially concerned about the trafficking and kidnapping of women and expressed that they felt afraid 'far away' and of 'strangers'. For example, in one community, women said they dreaded travelling to Kolkata (a three-hour journey) because they frequently experienced sexual harassment on the train. In this community, however, women said they felt much more confident and that they felt free to walk around. One woman, *Prerna*, said that she felt confident in her community and in regards to sexual harassment: 'If I experienced that here I would beat him'.

In a different community in South 24 Parganas, women discussed the dangers on the outskirts of their community. They said they feared rape at the ferry stop and were afraid of murder in the forest where bandits had killed someone. In this area, alcohol was exchanged illegally, making it increasingly risky. Similarly, in a neighboring village SHG, women described how a woman's body was found in the canal when they ploughed the field which made them feel afraid to leave their nearest confines. Only one older woman was comfortable travelling to Kolkata alone, saying 'I have seen other women do it and I have gained confidence so I am happy to travel there alone'.

In Kolkata, women had greater mobility than in the rural and peri-urban areas of Birbhum and South 24 Parganas. In Kolkata many women worked as domestic servants and walked on the streets at night. The dangerous areas which women were worried about centered on areas near their houses, such as at a bridge on the outskirts of one community settlement. In a focus group discussion, all agreed with one woman, *Sagarika*, who lamented:

> Sexual harassment and rape occurs every day – children in particular are at risk coming home from school.

The focus group discussion in this community described the dangerous situation near their homes and the impunity with which violent perpetrators acted. They discussed the situation of a six-year-old girl who was raped by a 13-year-old boy under the bridge in their community. The girl suffered major injuries and was hospitalised. The boy was taken into custody by police but released after a bribe was paid.

While the women interviewed found this situation tragic, they blamed women for what they perceived to be as an increase in sexual crimes against women. Women shared the sentiment expressed by one woman, *Shrabani*:

> Nowadays the girls wear dresses and the boys go mad – now they are wearing flimsy dresses. Because of this, we can't go out.

Across Kolkata, female self-help group members and staff believed that the situation of sexual harassment and assault was getting worse. Staff talked about changes in women's mobility, with increased numbers of women leaving the house for work. Staff members described how some men resented this, believing that these women were promiscuous through their seemingly unrestricted mobility.

Empowerment and the Violence of Disciplined Mobility

In the first instance, the examples from this research illustrate that women saw changes in their mobility as being highly significant, which they said resulted from being part of the self-help group programme. Visiting banks, the panchayat and other locations for SHG business created a new norm that it was acceptable for women to go beyond their house. This power to move was very significant for women interviewed and they were proud of it. Therefore, despite a societal attachment to the ideal of the 'secluded female' (Kabeer, 2012), women were keen for change and felt that increased scope of movement gave them more confidence and strength. Increased mobility was especially valued by women for its ability to enable greater connections with other women and reduce isolation (Davidson & Sanyal, 2017). This is an important consideration for women's empowerment programming and affirms other studies which indicate that belonging to such a programme can increase women's mobility (Bhaumik & Bera, 2015; Sanyal, 2014; Weber & Ahmad, 2014).

Despite these positive instances, however, the examples from this research indicate that the relationship between empowerment and mobility is more complicated than much of the literature suggests. Mobility is not merely a resource, which is arbitrarily divided between people. Rather, mobility is an act of power and of purposeful distribution, reflecting hierarchies between people (Cook & Butz, 2015). These power relations and hierarchies ensure there is never any equity in who is mobile and who is not (Cook & Butz, 2019; Sheller & Urry, 2006). The 'disciplining' of mobility is the ultimate expression of imbalanced power (Moran et al., 2012). By drawing on this idea of 'disciplined mobility' (Packer, 2003) as a form of pervasive gendered violence, we better understand what women's empowerment programmes can and cannot achieve. While these examples are particularly relevant in the context of India and neighbouring countries where *purdah* is practiced, these findings are by no means limited to these areas. As illustrated in the feminist literature on violence and mobility, the restriction of mobility is a global issue (Bowstead, 2016; Pain, 2014).

In this chapter I have illustrated that disciplined mobility maintains patriarchal control and limits women's empowerment through three distinct acts of violence: first, explicitly through restricting mobility; second, through surveillance and the constant monitoring of women's movement and third, through insidious invisible power (Lukes, 2005) where women regulate their movements to comply with patriarchal expectations. Notably, the examples from the research illustrate that women's restricted mobility was not due to a lack of confidence, ability or choice. Rather, women's mobility was actively *restricted* by men and in-laws, it was *disciplined* in the same way that Bartky (1990) describes the constant surveillance of women's every movement. In these actions of husbands and in-laws 'controlling' and 'monitoring' women's movements, we see evidence of the violence of disciplined mobility. As evidenced, even after their involvement with a microcredit project, women self-regulated their movement and in Kolkata women blamed other women for increased sexual harassment. In this way, the monitored, controlled woman assents to control her own movements and that of other women (Bartky, 1990). These examples illustrate the strength of invisible power (Lukes, 2005) which shapes norms to the extent that the oppressed will partake in their own oppression. These instances shed light on the endurance of restricted mobility and the barriers to empowerment.

These examples further illustrate the resilience of patriarchal control. While much of the literature on women's empowerment programming examines the relationship between microcredit and domestic violence (Murshid et al., 2016; Yaron et al., 2020), much less has been written about the interrelationship with other forms of gendered violence. We see from these examples that women's increased mobility exposes them to male violence in public spaces, as they are seen to transgress the 'male space' of the public sphere (Kar, 2018b) and step away from the virtuous ideal of the cloistered woman (Cresswell, 2006). This research illustrates that in instances where men and in-laws became more accepting of women's increased mobility, the locus of fear merely shifted to outside the house, to fear men in public with their rage and denigration of women (Roy & Bailey, 2021), with women having to contend with 'sexual harassment and rape…every day'. In many cases it was women's understandable fear of sexual harassment and assault which continued to restrict their movement. This 'gendered spatialisation of fear' (Parikh, 2017, p.698) dominating women's movement in public spaces illustrates the limitations on increased mobility (Kar, 2018b). Essentially, the patriarchal 'disciplining' of women's mobility continued but via different means of control. Women had to constantly negotiate fear, social expectations and judgements in their decision to move through space (Wattis et al., 2011).

Conclusion

With millions of dollars invested in women's empowerment programming (Bateman et al., 2019) we need to better understand its constraints and its relationship with mobility. In this chapter I have illustrated that while empowerment is a form of productive power, it is regularly stymied by the vested interests of the powerful (Little, 2016). In this case, increasing women's mobility challenged male patriarchal 'power over' – the kind of domineering power which rules by violence (Battegazzorre, 2017). Women's empowerment is therefore not a neutral process. Indeed, it disrupts existing power dynamics, but this is not a mere transference of power, or a vague abstract concept. Rather, women's empowerment is contingent on the unsettling of patriarchal dominance. Yet, as demonstrated, patriarchy is resilient and able to transform into alternative forms of domination via the disciplinary control of mobility (Moran et al., 2012; Pain, 2014). This domination need not be overt, but can include the subtle pervasiveness of invisible power which shapes social norms and ensures that women self-regulate their own actions. By interpreting women's empowerment through the lens of physical mobility, we see both the productive possibilities and the way that the male control of space continues to limit change in this area.

Note

1 An earlier version of this chapter appeared as 'Disciplinary Mobility and Women's Empowerment: a Complicated Connection' (2022) by Annabel Dulhunty in *Mobilities.* DOI: 10.1080/17450101.2022.2088298. https://www.tandfonline.com/doi/abs/10.1080/17450101.2022.2088298.

References

Arya, S., & Rathore, A. S. (2020). Introduction: Theorising Dalit Feminism. In S. Arya & A. Singh Rathore (Eds.), *Dalit Feminist Theory: A Reader* (pp. 1–22). Routledge.

Bajracharya, A., & Amin, S. (2013). Microcredit and Domestic Violence in Bangladesh: An Exploration of Selection Bias Influences. *Demography*, 50(5), 1819–1843. doi:10.1007/s13524-013-0226-0.

Bali Swain, R., & Wallentin, F. Y. (2012). Factors Empowering Women in Indian Self-Help Group Programs. *International Review of Applied Economics*, 26(4), 425–444. doi:10.1080/02692171.2011.595398.

Balkmar, D. (2018). Violent Mobilities: Men, Masculinities and Road Conflicts in Sweden. *Mobilities*, 13(5), 1–16. doi:10.1080/17450101.2018.1500096.

Bartky, S. L. (1990). *Femininity and Domination: Studies in the Phenomenology of Oppression*. Routledge

Bateman, M., Blankenburg, S., & Kozul-Wright, R. (2019). Introduction. In M. Bateman, S. Blankenburg, & R. Kozul-Wright (Eds.), *The Rise and Fall of Global Microcredit: Development, Debt and Disillusion* (pp. 3–23). Routledge.

Battegazzorre, F. (2017). Some Reflections on the Power to/Power over Debate. *Journal of Political Power*, 10(3), 274–285. doi:10.1080/2158379X.2017.1382169.

Bhaumik, S. K., & Bera, S. (2015). Impact of Micro-Credit Programme on Women's Empowerment. *Journal of Land and Rural Studies*, 3(2), 219–236. doi:10.1177/2321024915598895.

Bowstead, J. C. (2016). Women on the Move: Theorising the Geographies of Domestic Violence Journeys in England. *Gender, Place & Culture*, 24(1), 108–121. doi:10.1080/0966369x.2016.1251396.

Bowstead, J. C. (2020). Private Violence/Private Transport: The Role of Means of Transport in Women's Mobility to Escape from Domestic Violence in England and Wales. *Mobilities*, 15(4), 559–574. doi:10.1080/17450101.2020.1750289.

Brickell, K. (2008). 'Fire in the House': Gendered Experiences of Drunkenness and Violence in Siem Reap, Cambodia. *Geoforum*, 39(5), 1667–1675. doi:10.1016/j.geoforum.2008.04.002.

Brody, C., de Hoop, T., Vojtkova, M., Warnock, R., Dunbar, M., Murthy, P., & Dworkin, S. L. (2017). Can Self-Help Group Programs Improve Women's Empowerment? A Systematic Review. *Journal of Development Effectiveness*, 9(1), 15–40. doi:10.1080/19439342.2016.1206607.

Cook, N., & Butz, D. (2015). Mobility Justice in the Context of Disaster. *Mobilities*, 11(3), 400–419. doi:10.1080/17450101.2015.1047613.

Cook, N., & Butz, D. (2019). *Mobilities, Mobility Justice and Social Justice*. Routledge.

Cresswell, T. (2006). *On the Move: Mobility in the Modern Western World*. Routledge.

Cresswell, T. (2011). Mobilities I: Catching Up. *Progress in Human Geography*, 35(4), 550–558. doi:10.1177/0309132510383348.

Cresswell, T., & Uteng, T. P. (2008). Gendered Mobilities: Towards an Holistic Understanding. In T. Cresswell & T. P. Uteng (Eds.), *Gendered Mobilities* (pp. 1–12). Ashgate.

Cuomo, D. (2013). Security and Fear: The Geopolitics of Intimate Partner Violence Policing. *Geopolitics*, 18(4), 856–874. doi:10.1080/14650045.2013.811642.

Davidson, T., & Sanyal, P. (2017). Associational Participation and Network Expansion: Microcredit Self-Help Groups and Poor Women's Social Ties in Rural India. *Social Forces*, 95(4), 1695–1724. doi:10.1093/sf/sox021.

Duvendack, M., & Palmer-Jones, R. (2016). Micro-Finance, Women's Empowerment and Fertility Decline in Bangladesh: How Important Was Women's Agency? *The Journal of Development Studies*, 53(5), 664–683. doi:10.1080/00220388.2016.1205731.

Finnis, E. (2017). Collective Action, Envisioning the Future and Women's Self-Help Groups: A Case Study from South India. *Indian Journal of Gender Studies*, 24(1), 1–23. doi:10.1177/0971521516678529.

Fluri, J. L., & Piedalue, A. (2017). Embodying Violence: Critical Geographies of Gender, Race, and Culture. *Gender, Place & Culture*, 24(4), 534–544. doi:10.1080/0966369x.2017.1329185.

Foucault, M. (1979). *Discipline and Punish*. Vintage.

Ganle, J. K., Afriyie, K., & Segbefia, A. Y. (2015). Microcredit: Empowerment and Disempowerment of Rural Women in Ghana. *World Development*, 66, 335–345. doi:10.1016/j.worlddev.2014.08.027.

Gaventa, J., & Martorano, B. (2016). Inequality, Power and Participation – Revisiting the Links. *IDS Bulletin*, 47, 11–30.

Gilbert, M. R. (1998). "Race", Space, and Power: The Survival Strategies of Working Poor Women. *Annals of the Association of American Geographers*, 88(4), 595–621.

Gopal, M. (2012). Caste, Sexuality and Labour: The Troubled Connection. *Current Sociology*, 60(2), 222–238. doi:10.1177/0011392111429223.

Hanson, S. (2010). Gender and Mobility: New Approaches for Informing Sustainability. *Gender, Place & Culture*, 17(1), 5–23. doi:10.1080/09663690903498225.

Hashemi, S., Schuler, S., & Riley, A. (1996). Rural Credit Programs and Women's Empowerment in Bangladesh. *World Development*, 24(4), 635–653.

Howard, J., & Vajda, V. (2016). Inclusion as an Agenda for Transformative and Sustainable Change: Addressing Invisible Power through Reflective Practice. *IDS Bulletin*, 47(5), 43–56.

Huda, K., & Kaur, S. (2011). 'It Was as If We Were Drowning': Shocks, Stresses and Safety Nets in India. *Gender & Development*, 19(2), 213–227. doi:10.1080/13552074.2011.592632.

Kabeer, N. (2011). Between Affiliation and Autonomy: Navigating Pathways of Women's Empowerment and Gender Justice in Rural Bangladesh. *Development and Change*, 42(2), 499–528. doi:10.1111/j.1467-7660.2011.01703.x.

Kabeer, N. (2012). Empowerment, Citizenship and Gender Justice: A Contribution to Locally Grounded Theories of Change in Women's Lives. *Ethics and Social Welfare*, 6(3), 216–232. doi:10.1080/17496535.2012.704055.

Kar, S. (2018a). *Financializing Poverty: Labor and Risk in Indian Microfinance*. Stanford University Press.

Kar, S. (2018b). Securitizing Women: Gender, Precaution, and Risk in Indian Finance. *Signs*, 43(2), 301–325. doi:10.1086/693537.

Kumar, N., Raghunathan, K., Arrieta, A., Jilani, A., Chakrabarti, S., Menon, P., & Quisumbing, A. R. (2019). Social Networks, Mobility, and Political Participation: The Potential for Women's Self-Help Groups to Improve Access and Use of Public Entitlement Schemes in India. *World Development*, 114, 28–41. doi:10.1016/j.worlddev.2018.09.023.

Little, J. (2016). Understanding Domestic Violence in Rural Spaces. *Progress in Human Geography*, 41(4), 472–488. doi:10.1177/0309132516645960.

Lowe, J., & DeVerteuil, G. (2020). Power, Powerlessness and the Politics of Mobility: Reconsidering Mental Health Geographies. *Social Science Medicine*, 252, 112918. doi:10.1016/j.socscimed.2020.112918.

Lukes, S. (2005). *Power: A Radical View* (2nd ed.). Palgrave Macmillan.

Mahmud, S., & Tasneem, S. (2014). Measuring 'Empowerment' Using Quantitative Household Survey Data. *Women's Studies International Forum*, 45, 90–97. doi:10.1016/j.wsif.2013.11.009.

Martin, J. H. (2021). Exploring the Affective Atmospheres of the Threat of Sexual Violence in Minibus Taxis: The Experiences of Women Commuters in South Africa. *Mobilities*, 17(3), 1–16. doi:10.1080/17450101.2021.1942171.

Moran, D., Piacentini, L., & Pallot, J. (2012). Disciplined Mobility and Carceral Geography: Prisoner Transport in Russia. *Transactions of the Institute of British Geographers* 37, 446–460. doi:10.1111/j.1475-5661.2011.00483.x.

Mukherjee, A. K., & Kundu, A. (2017). Traditional Institutions and Female Beneficiaries of Mahatma Gandhi National Rural Employment Guarantee in West Bengal. In C. Neogi, A. K. Bhandari, & S. Ghosh (Eds.), *Women's Entrepreneurship and Microfinance* (pp. 41–55). Springer Singapore.

Murshid, N. S., Akincigil, A., & Zippay, A. (2016). Microfinance Participation and Domestic Violence in Bangladesh: Results from a Nationally Representative Survey. *Journal of Interpersonal Violence*, 31(9), 1579–1596. doi:10.1177/0886260515569065.

Orso, C. E., & Fabrizi, E. (2016). The Determinants of Women's Empowerment in Bangladesh: The Role of Partner's Attitudes and Participation in Microcredit Programmes. *The Journal of Development Studies*, 52(6), 895–912. doi:10.1080/00220388.2015.1107046.

Packer, J. (2003). Disciplining Mobility: Governing and Safety. In J. Z. Bratich, J. Packer, & C. McCarthy (Eds.), *Foucault, Cultural Studies, and Governmentality* (pp. 135–163). State University of New York Press.

Pain, R. (2014). Everyday Terrorism. *Progress in Human Geography*, 38(4), 531–550. doi:10.1177/0309132513512231.

Pain, R. (2015). Intimate War. *Political Geography*, 44, 64–73. doi:10.1016/j.polgeo.2014.09.011.

Pansardi, P. (2012). Power to and Power Over: Two Distinct Concepts of Power? *Journal of Political Power*, 5(1), 73–89. doi:10.1080/2158379x.2012.658278.

Parikh, A. (2017). Politics of Presence: Women's Safety and Respectability at Night in Mumbai, India. *Gender, Place & Culture*, 25(5), 695–710. doi:10.1080/0966369x.2017.1400951.

Petit, J. (2016). Why Citizens Don't Engage–Power, Poverty and Civic Habitus. *IDS Bulletin*, 47(5), 89–102.

Philo, C. (2014). 'One Must Eliminate the Effects of … Diffuse Circulation [and] Their Unstable and Dangerous Coagulation': Foucault and Beyond the Stopping of Mobilities. *Mobilities*, 9(4), 493–511. doi:10.1080/17450101.2014.961261.

Rowlands, J. (1997). *Questioning Empowerment: Working with Women in Honduras*. Oxfam GB.

Roy, S. (2019). Precarity, Aspiration and Neoliberal Development: Women Empowerment Workers in West Bengal. *Contributions to Indian Sociology*, 53(3), 392–421. doi:10.1177/0069966719861758.

Roy, S., & Bailey, A. (2021). Safe in the City? Negotiating Safety, Public Space and the Male Gaze in Kolkata, India. *Cities*, 117. doi:10.1016/j.cities.2021.103321.

Sanyal, P. (2009). From Credit to Collective Action: The Role of Microfinance in Promoting Women's Social Capital and Normative Influence. *American Sociological Review*, 74(4), 529–550. doi:10.1177/000312240907400402.

Sanyal, P. (2014). *Credit to Capabilities: A Sociological Study of Microcredit Groups in India*. Cambridge University Press.

Sanyal, P. (2015). Group-Based Microcredit & Emergent Inequality in Social Capital: Why Socio-Religious Composition Matters. *Qualitative Sociology*, 38(2), 103–137. doi:10.1007/s11133-015-9301-8.

Sengupta, N. (2013). Poor Women's Empowerment: The Discursive Space of Microfinance. *Indian Journal of Gender Studies*, 20(2), 279–304. doi:10.1177/0971521513482220.

Sheller, M. (2015). Uneven Mobility Futures: A Foucauldian Approach. *Mobilities*, 11(1), 15–31. doi:10.1080/17450101.2015.1097038.

Sheller, M., & Urry, J. (2006). The New Mobilities Paradigm. *Environment and Planning A*, 38(2), 207–226.

Singh, S. (2014). The Effects of Microfinance Programs on Women Members in Traditional Societies. *Gender, Place & Culture*, 22(2), 222–238. doi:10.1080/0966369x.2013.855627.

Siwach, P. (2020). Mapping Gendered Spaces and Women's Mobility: A Case Study of Mitathal Village, Haryana. *The Oriental Anthropologist*, 20(1), 33–48. doi:10.1177/0972558X20913680.

Stark, E. (2007). *Coercive Control: How Men Entrap Women in Personal Life*. Oxford University Press.

Tyner, J., & Inwood, J. (2014). Violence as Fetish. *Progress in Human Geography*, 38 (6), 771–784. doi:10.1177/0309132513516177.

Urry, J. (2002). Mobility and Proximity. *Sociology* 36(2), 255–274. doi:10.1177/0038038502036002002.

Warrington, M. (2001). 'I Must Get Out': The Geographies of Domestic Violence. *Transactions of the Institute of British Geographers*, 26(3), 365–382. http://www.jstor.org/stable/3650652.

Wattis, L., Green, E., & Radford, J. (2011). Women Students' Perceptions of Crime and Safety: Negotiating Fear and Risk in an English Post-Industrial Landscape. *Gender, Place & Culture*, 18(6), 749–767. doi:10.1080/0966369x.2011.617914.

Weber, O., & Ahmad, A. (2014). Empowerment through Microfinance: The Relation between Loan Cycle and Level of Empowerment. *World Development*, 62, 75–87. doi:10.1016/j.worlddev.2014.05.012.

Yaron, G., Gordon, R., Best, J., & Choudhary, S. (2020). Challenging the Links between Microfinance and Domestic Violence: Evidence from Rural India. *Development in Practice*, 30(3), 345–356. doi:10.1080/09614524.2019.1696282.

9 Solidarity and Connection[1]

While the previous chapter described the impact of power as domination and control, in this chapter I elaborate more on the productive forms of power. As detailed in Chapter 2, an alternative to viewing power solely as domination is to instead understand power as a cluster of concepts such as power 'within', 'to', 'over' and 'with' (Mathie et al., 2017; Rowlands, 1997). There is detailed analysis in the literature on 'power within' as an internal process of change (Jakimow, 2018; McGee, 2016), 'power over' and the dynamics of domination (Battegazzorre, 2017) and 'power to' as capacity (Hartsock, 1983; Pansardi, 2012). 'Power with', however, has received considerably less scholarly attention. 'Power with' can be defined as the collective power gained from relationships of trust and reciprocity (Mathie et al., 2017; Rowlands, 1997; VeneKlasen & Miller, 2002). 'Power with' can form the basis of successful collective action (such as group protests and advocacy against domestic violence or inadequate government services), however 'power with' can also exist independently of collective action, as a trusting relationship between two individuals (Rowlands, 1997). Successful collective action can also strengthen the bonds between individuals and increase 'power with' (Rowlands, 1997).

Redressing the oversight of 'power with' is important for three key reasons. First, 'power with' fundamentally challenges patriarchal discourses on power which are fixated on domination and control. In this way, 'power with' provides an essential counterpoint to masculine mainstream understandings of power and further strengthens feminist theories of power which challenge patriarchy through emphasising collaboration and cooperation. Second, exploring the importance of 'power with' to women reveals the degree of cultural gendered isolation and the extent to which communities are not necessarily sites of collective cohesion. 'Power with' is critical to challenging patriarchal domination, which is enacted through containing women and socially isolating them in the Indian context (Bhattacharyya, 2015). By examining 'power with,' strategies for resistance can be determined to redress controlled isolation and the psychological manifestations of being disconnected from others. Third, 'power with' provides an important framework for challenging neoliberal, economic versions of empowerment which

DOI: 10.4324/9781003356400-9

focus exclusively on individual actions and gains. 'Power with' is thus more important to consider than 'social capital,' a similar but fundamentally different idea, which over-emphasises economic components of empowerment and has readily been adopted by neoliberal theorists (Ferragina & Arrigoni, 2017). While 'power with' shares commonalities with ideas of social capital, it does not focus on economic gains and critically emphasises deeper, psychological processes of empowerment which occur as part of being in a collective or in relation to others (McDaid, 2010).

In this chapter I redress these gaps in the literature and argue that 'power with' is not an afterthought, but a critical component of holistic empowerment. By highlighting 'power with' in empowerment, I challenge both patriarchal mainstream discourses of power and the related rational, economic and individualistic conceptions of empowerment.

Feminist Theories of Power

Even if we are satisfied, however, with the idea that empowerment is inseparable from power, the definition of power itself is even more fervently contested than the term empowerment (Dowding, 2012; Haugaard, 2012). Power was traditionally understood as domineering, aggressive and often repressive, embodied in the authority of the state or elite members of society (Lukes, 1974). Feminist power theorists criticise this version of power as highly limited, arguing that it is distinctly masculine (Hartsock, 1983; Irigaray, 1985; Miller, 1992). At the heart of these critiques is the idea that 'masculine' versions of power focus primarily on domineering 'power over' (Miller, 1992), without considering other forms of power. In contrast to the notion of power as domination, feminist and post-structuralist scholars argue that power is instead a positive productive force or a capacity to act, not necessarily involving control and subjugation (Allen, 1999; Hartsock, 1983).

The idea of productive power is thus closely related to the concept of agency. The works of Amartya Sen (1995, 1997) and Sherry Ortner (2001) shed light on the idea of agency as power. At the heart of Sen (1999) and Nussbaum's (2011) Capabilities framework is the idea of agency, which is distinct from well-being. Rather than viewing the subjects of development (particularly women) as passive recipients of either welfare or domineering 'power over', Sen argues that women should instead be viewed as 'active agents of change' (Sen, 1999, p. 189). Sherry Ortner's work on agency is also instructive for understanding feminist power and how it goes beyond domination and subjugation. Ortner (2001) outlines how agency can be seen as influence, control and domination (thus resembling 'power over') but it can also act as resistance or as a process of following intentions and desires. Agency as resistance and as intention relate closely to the idea of productive 'power to'. Importantly, for Ortner (2001), the agency of intentions is not the agency of a 'grand' hero but is based on fairly ordinary, everyday 'projects' or purposeful actions. In these ideas of agency, we see that agency is a form of productive power, providing further argument against the notion that power is only domineering.

Rather than being either domineering or productive, however, the idea of power can encompass both ideas (Dowding, 2012; Haugaard, 2018; Hearn, 2014; Pansardi, 2012). As I briefly outlined in Chapter 2, development scholars have readily adopted a cluster model of power which is based on four different forms of power: 'power over', 'power within', 'power to' and 'power with' (Mathie et al., 2017; Rowlands, 1997; VeneKlasen & Miller, 2002). In this framework, 'power over' signifies power based on control and subjugation and encompasses traditional ideas of power as domination (Battegazzorre, 2017). 'Power to' instead interprets power as 'energy' and the power to act, for example, to protest against injustice (Hartsock, 1983). 'Power within' focuses on the individual, psychological aspects of inner strength whereas 'power with' is gained from strong relationships which are trusting and reciprocal (Mathie et al., 2017; Rowlands, 1997; VeneKlasen & Miller, 2002).

Collective Versus Individual Power

'Power within' as an individualistic and psychological process has been addressed most frequently in the literature, likely because it can easily be appropriated by neoliberal conceptions of empowerment based on individual change and focused on tangible gains such as increased money, skills or economic participation (Cornwall & Edwards, 2014; Sharma, 2008). Feminist scholars counter this economic version of empowerment by arguing that individual power 'within' is a fundamentally psychological process of self-actualisation (Jakimow, 2018; Kabeer, 1994) which is far more complex than economic definitions. Crucially 'power within' is not constrained by the attitudes of others and is independent of widespread social change. An individual can be 'empowered' through their own critical awareness of reality, and this is particularly significant in contexts of oppression, as the powerful do not even need to be part of the process of empowerment (McGee, 2016). Rather, this process of empowerment is uniquely individual and psychological, based on a person's self-development.

Critics of 'power within' argue, however, that it ignores structurally oppressive power relations that disempower individuals (McDaid, 2010; Sharma, 2008). Critics argue that psychological conceptions of empowerment take the place of political definitions. For instance, mental health programmes that offer promises of 'empowerment' to participants create false expectations of being able to overcome discrimination and inequality (McDaid, 2010). An individualistic conception of empowerment also can fail to recognise social constraints and connections which either limit or enhance empowerment (McDaid, 2010; Sardenberg, 2008; Sengupta, 2013).

McDaid (2010) draws on Hannah Arendt's radical interpretation of power to argue that it is isolation which is fundamentally disempowering. The concepts of isolation and disempowerment are highly significant to the importance of 'power with'. Arendt (1970, p.56) is perhaps one of the strongest advocates of collective 'power with', arguing: 'Power is never the property of an individual; it belongs to a group only so long as the group keeps together' (Arendt, 1970, p. 56). This definition equates power with the ideals of democratic citizenship, of the collective coming together. It challenges domination and as such, Arendt argues that to 'speak of non-violent power…is actually redundant' (Arendt, 1970, p.56).

The idea of 'power with' shares some commonalities with the idea of 'social capital' (Putnam, 1993) but is fundamentally different. 'Power with' is about intimate relationships of trust and reciprocity whereas social capital may include these but focuses more on networks for leveraging relationships (Méndez-Lemus et al., 2017) or for building local leadership (Abe, 2009). Social capital discourses also are notably more closely enshrined with capitalist notions of ambition, enterprise and social advancement (Fine, 2008). 'Power with', by contrast, is far more personal, psychological and is not enmeshed with neoliberalism.

'Power With' and Imagined Communities

One reason why 'power with' is so important to consider is because isolation is so fundamentally debilitating (Franklin, 2012; McLennan & Ulijaszek, 2018). Not only is it difficult to individually stand up for one's rights or to be connected to practical resources and information when alone, isolation is psychologically disempowering (Cacioppo & Cacioppo, 2018; Holt-Lunstad et al., 2010). Much has been written about the role of isolation and disempowerment in the Global North where industrialisation has broken down bonds of familiarity within communities (Cacioppo & Cacioppo, 2018; Franklin, 2012; Holt-Lunstad et al., 2010). There are contrasting understandings of the role of isolation in the Global South, however. On the one hand, a number of post-development scholars argue that societies in the Global South have strong bonds of collective identity that are anathema to Western liberal notions of individualism (Hickel, 2014). On the other hand, several studies indicate that isolation is a real and significant issue in the Global South (Kotian et al., 2018) especially for women (Pinnewala, 2009) and particularly in South Asia where gendered norms prevent women from either leaving the house or from forming friendships beyond their family relationships (Kilby, 2011; Sanyal, 2014).

In understanding the impact of isolation on women in South Asia, it is important to consider the contribution of feminist geographers who argue that the politics of space is highly gendered and a key site of male power (Bhattacharyya, 2015). Even without legal segregation, fear controls women through either the threat of violence or through being judged on social norms (Parikh, 2018; Paul, 2011). This spatial segregation is further exacerbated by intersectional oppressions (Rodó-de-Zárate & Baylina, 2018) – as influenced by discrimination based on caste, class and gender. Spatial segregation is common in South Asia and the resulting isolation is particularly pertinent for women who have to follow strict practices of 'purdah' or seclusion, significantly limiting women's interaction with other people (Stroope, 2015). This spatial segregation is a key component of patriarchal domineering 'power over' which contains women through fear and isolation. These contexts of gendered isolation are further used by critical community development scholars (Bauman, 2001; DeFilippis, 2008; Geoghegan & Powell, 2009; Shaw, 2007) to argue that we should not idealise communities and to refute the claims that Global South communities have natural collective ties of trust and cohesion.

Isolation, SHGs and Collective Action

Across all ten sites, women said that they were significantly isolated before belonging to an SHG; the societal expectation was that women would stay at home and see their family members only. Therefore, the process of joining an SHG and forming relationships with others was regarded as extremely important for women interviewed. For example, one woman from a group in Birbhum, *Debi*, described her happiness in connecting with others:

> Before we were individuals but now we are a group. We did not know each other, we were afraid. We didn't have knowledge of others. So we didn't trust them. No one from outside came to my house. We did not say 'Please sit down'.

In each group, women recounted how prior to joining the SHG they felt 'silent', 'shy' and 'scared of outsiders'. When the SHGs were established, women were quiet for a number of months before they felt comfortable speaking. During the research visits, I found a remarkable difference in talking with women in the ten primary communities who had been involved in SHGs for a long time compared with women who were just joining the SHGs. Women who were established SHG members were much louder and enthusiastic, contrasting sharply with how they described themselves prior to joining the SHG. Even in densely populated urban environments like Kolkata, women stated how previously they needed to remain 'modest' and not draw attention to themselves in public. This meant that women's interactions outside the house were limited and they described feeling lonely. For example, in Kolkata, women from one self-help group explained how much the friendships and solidarity they felt with group members meant to them. One member from this group, *Aadrita*, explained:

> Before we used to cover our heads a lot, otherwise we were loose characters, women could not talk loudly, we really could not talk. Now women are chatting and talking about their lives.

These connections, relationships and bonds of friendship are key examples of 'power with' which is especially important as women described how it made them feel a strong sense of inner confidence, thus shaping their 'power within'. The development of 'power with' frequently led to collective action, most commonly against alcoholism, liquor shops and domestic violence, but also in demanding that the government supply services such as electricity, roads and health care. Nine out of the ten SHG groups in the primary communities studied had undertaken some form of collective action and women reported that they had not been involved in any collective action prior to belonging to the SHG. Women frequently described the importance of their collective strength in undertaking these activities and the extent to which they relied upon strong bonds of friendship and solidarity to be able to confront injustices which they felt they could not address before.

Many instances of collective action focused on reducing domestic violence in communities. Women felt that alcohol consumption significantly contributed to domestic violence and tension at home. They described the problem of illegal liquor shops which had been set up in their communities and were frequented by men. In five out of ten locations, the SHG managed to prevent the sale of liquor at an informal liquor shop, either through burning it down or by advocating with the police to disband it. In one community in South 24 Parganas, women discussed how they banded together as an SHG to confront domestic violence and alcoholism. As one woman, *Joshna*, recounted:

> There was a recent incident of domestic violence, one family in our neighborhood was facing trouble because of alcohol abuse. We intervened as an SHG community. We approached the man and said you have to stop or we will take action. We had to approach the police station and in the end it was solved. So that is an achievement. The police closed the liquor shop and talked to the family. This was five years ago. There is no continuation of domestic violence in that household today. They fear the police and they are much better off today. Less money is spent on alcohol.

SHGs also engaged in collective action to demand their rights from the government. In one community in Kolkata, the SHG successfully lobbied the government for improved housing and in another, they convinced the government to provide electricity to their area. In Birbhum, women in the SHG were also successful in their activism with the local government to institute the midday meal scheme in their village. Women felt that by working together, they could affect change. For example, *Sita*, a woman from Birbhum argued:

> Without the SHG the Gram Panchayat (local government) would do nothing. Until we form a group and demand our rights, nothing will happen.

This successful activism made women feel confident and emboldened. As one woman in Kolkata, *Sharyi*, said:

> If we can approach the local government and get electricity, if women can do this, we can do anything!

Collective action by SHGs was further successful in protecting community assets. Women were very proud of their community halls where they could meet. In one community in South 24 Parganas, after a political party was trying to seize control of the community hall, women from the SHG gathered fifty community members, hired a truck and protested outside the local court some two hours away in order to retain their hall. Women were successful in this initiative and one woman from this SHG reflected on their triumph: 'One lady is equal to one-hundred men!' Similarly, women in one community in Birbhum were successful in banding together with men in their community to protest against a wealthy landowner who tried to claim communal land as his own. Across different locations, women described how the success of their collective action strengthened their sense of power as a group and their sense of individual confidence.

The success of collective action in many cases, however, was contingent on the receptiveness of either the police or the Gram Panchayat (local government) to the group of women. This was important not only for women's collective action for public services, but also for addressing risks in their communities. For example, in locations where women stated that collective action helped to reduce alcoholism, women indicated that the police were supportive. One example arose from a community in South 24 Parganas where women described the various stages of collective action against an abusive husband and the way that they could use the threat of going to the police or government with their issues:

> A girl…married a man from another village who was abusing her. We staged an intervention with four members who met with her husband and her parents-in-law for two rounds of discussion. The girl's in-laws argued that the violence was justified because she didn't have a dowry. The group argued that it was the man's problem because he was abusing her. Again these rounds of discussion didn't result in change but finally we gave a threat of going to the police or the Gram Panchayat office and this created a change.

While women felt motivated to make changes and to demonstrate their collective strength as a group, outside influences such as the competency of police sometimes stymied the efforts of women. In communities where alcoholism continued, focus group participants indicated that police were corrupt or inept. For example, in one community in Birbhum, one woman *Vanhi* explained:

> It's not possible to change alcohol consumption, we went to the police station but nothing changed. Even now children will learn to drink – we cannot stop it. Shop owners paid huge bribes to the police. The police say not to go there and the liquor shops threaten to burn down their homes.

In another group in Kolkata women expressed similar sentiments, with one woman, *Tavishi*, lamenting the situation of male alcoholism:

> If we protest it will create more problems. We prefer not to go to the police. At times we go for help but no one listens.

In these instances where women did not feel that the police or Gram Panchayat would assist, women described feeling defeated and at a loss as what to do to improve their situations.

The Vulnerability of Collective Bonds

Friendship, trust and solidarity could not automatically be assumed to result from forming an SHG, however, as indicated by examples of SHGs which fell apart due to jealousy and rivalry. Rather, the formation of positive group dynamics was tenuous and vulnerable to external influence. Significant numbers of SHGs had become defunct or were only operating at a bare minimum. In each of these cases, women and staff described how group dynamics had broken down and mistrust had taken the place of friendship. In particular, both SHG members and SPT staff commented on the frequent interference by political parties in the functioning of SHGs as political parties tried to recruit members from SHGs and to seize assets like community halls. In West Bengal, especially, political parties have been dominant in the most remote areas with most villagers belonging to a political party (Chandra et al., 2015). One example of politically incurred division arose in a SHG which was largely defunct at the time of research. The leader of this SHG, *Laboni*, was from a different political party than the other members. *Laboni* explained how political parties had increased their presence in the village following the end of the NGO-led programme, creating political divisions between women. This resulted in SHG members trying to oust her as the leader and created an environment of jealousy and mistrust which led to the collapse of the SHG:

> There are arguments in our SHG. They say they have household work, they don't have time – I cannot make them understand. Also there is jealousy in our village – why is she saying do this work, maybe she will gain something out of it? We made some constructions for work but they are lying abandoned, nobody is working. Everyone has equal rights and the opportunity of getting interest but some pay their funds and some don't. Members then say 'if she is not paying, why should I?'

This quotation illustrates the role of trust and reciprocity which underpins the entire operation of SHGs and microcredit activities. Without collective trust, it is understandable that SHG members would feel uncomfortable in paying their fees or in working for the benefit of the community, without worrying that they were being exploited. The role of 'power with' is foundational for the success of an intervention such as SHGs which fundamentally depends on collective unity.

In addition, interviews with women and men further illustrated that communities were far from static creations. For example, migration was a significant component of both women and men's lives with people migrating for work and to escape natural hazards. For the women interviewed in both rural and urban locations, there was constant movement either of themselves or their husbands, combined with regular changes in technologies such as cellphones, internet and farming practices. Communities were constantly changing and were far from ideal places. For example, caste and religious discrimination were clearly worse amongst neighbours in a village setting, contrasting with much greater intermingling of castes outside the community. In Birbhum for instance, women discussed how difficult it would be for their children to marry other castes in their village, compared with in the cities. The friendship and solidarity which women found in SHGs based on trust, went some way to ameliorating poor relationships in communities, but as noted, these bonds were vulnerable to disruption.

One key finding from this research was that SHGs were far easier to establish than to maintain which jeopardised any potential long-term gains of belonging to an SHG. While a number of elements were important to sustaining an SHG – including adequate support provided by the NGO, the leadership and literacy skills of the SHG leaders and access to government schemes – group cohesion demonstrating 'power with' was the most important factor for maintaining SHG operations. Interviews with staff and community members confirmed the importance of interpersonal dynamics and trust in enabling the continued functioning of SHGs. In the ten primary communities I visited with still functioning SHGs, group dynamics were positive and there was a strong sense of reciprocity and friendship between members of the groups.

Beyond Individual Empowerment

This research illustrates that effective SHGs were contingent on the development of 'power with' through strong relationships between members. Importantly, 'power with' did not only function to enable economic empowerment but acted as an essential end in itself (Sen & Majumder, 2015), as illustrated by the importance women placed on forming friendships and feeling less isolated following their involvement in the SHGs. These findings support studies which indicate that the social aspects of belonging to an SHG are most important (Davidson & Sanyal, 2017; Sanyal, 2014), that women can rapidly form strong connections with other women in SHGs (Feigenberg et al., 2010) and that they frequently remain in SHGs for the relationships they have built with other members (Kabeer, 2011; Sen & Majumder, 2015). These examples further demonstrate the flawed logic of neoliberal versions of empowerment which are based solely on individual economic advancement and do not consider the importance of collective power.

Reflecting on the interconnected role of each form of power, I agree with McDaid's (2010) criticism that focusing only on individual empowerment devalues the role of relationships and promotes isolation, especially in regards to neoliberal versions of empowerment which frequently stress the role of 'power within' as an individual process of change without considering the role of collective 'power with' (Commonwealth of Australia, 2016; World Bank Group, 2012). However, I do not deny that 'power within' is a critical component of empowerment nor claim that individuals are less valuable than the collective. While important, I do not support Arendt's (1970) notion that only collective empowerment is genuine. Rather, this case study suggests that the individualistic, internal and psychological components of 'power within' which foster women's self-confidence, are significantly supported by 'power with' and are difficult to sustain without relationships and connection. Hence, 'power within' must be complemented by 'power with'.

While 'power with' is particularly important for SHG and microcredit initiatives, it is necessary for all development initiatives that aim to 'empower' participants. Strong relationships were essential not only for microcredit activities but also for discussing and strategising about deeply personal and sensitive topics such as family violence, marital relations and health issues. Drawing on connections with others enabled women in this case study to feel more confident to assert themselves in their communities, at home and with the government and police. The bonds of friendship and trust formed through 'power with' were hence important for establishing other forms of power in the cluster model of power such as 'power to' (Mathie et al., 2017; Rowlands, 1997; VeneKlasen & Miller, 2002).

The development of 'power with' was especially important for promoting collective action. This research found that SHGs were well situated to promote collective action (Chakravarty & Chaudhuri, 2012; Finnis, 2017), and while the activities were limited to environments on a smaller scale (Huda & Kaur, 2011), the results were still significant, with much valued changes for communities. When successful, collective action demonstrates the productive, generative power of 'power to' which challenges 'power over' (Rowlands, 1997). Successful collective action enhanced women's sense of agency (Ortner, 2001; Sen, 1999) and positively ruptured their previously held limited beliefs of themselves (Kabeer, 2011), as demonstrated by the quote: 'One lady is equal to one-hundred men!' These examples add to feminist critiques of power *only* as domination and subjugation (Allen, 1999; Hartsock, 1983; Irigaray, 1985). Instead, the strength of women resisting the domineering 'power over' of marital violence or civic injustice indicates that power can also be affirming and life-giving (Hartsock, 1983). This research adds to this feminist literature by demonstrating that the ability to resist 'power over' is best enhanced through 'power with', especially in contexts of gendered isolation.

While successful collective action was life changing, this research also shows the negative impact of unsuccessful collective action and of women feeling it wasn't even worth trying, challenging women's sense of capability and power. As Sanyal (2015) notes, collective action against domestic violence and alcoholism are especially important. While this research certainly indicated similar results, it also found that the success of these actions was highly dependent on the competency and relations with the police and Gram Panchayat (local council), illustrating the crucial role of government services in women's empowerment.

'Power With', Gendered Isolation and Ideal Communities

Women repeatedly emphasised the importance of forming friendships and connections. These findings support the idea that isolation is highly gendered in many Global South societies, particularly South Asia (Kilby, 2011; Pinnewala, 2009; Sanyal, 2014; Sanyal, 2015; Stroope, 2015) and that spatial segregation is used as a tactic of patriarchal power and control (Bhattacharyya, 2015; Parikh, 2018). Therefore, while there may be more literature on isolation in the Global North, we cannot assume that individuals are automatically well connected and bonded by collective ideals in the Global South. Collectivist interpretations of communities fail to address the role of mistrust and tension within these spaces (Lenette, 2015; Pittaway et al., 2016). Friendship, trust and understanding could not automatically be assumed to result solely from group formation, as indicated by the example of the defunct SHG. While I agree with scholarship (Davidson & Sanyal, 2017; Finnis, 2017; Knowles & Luke, 2018; Sanyal, 2009; Sanyal, 2014) arguing that significant trust can form out of belonging to an SHG, these findings also indicate that trusting relationships were highly precarious. Trust was easily undermined by external influences such as political interference or jealousy, illustrating that 'power with' is tenuous, mutable and never static. This corresponds with other examples of SHGs in India, such as in Brody et al. (2017), Sabhlok (2011) and Lahiri-Dutt and Samanta (2006) which highlight the way that caste inequalities, religious differences and political allegiances led to the demise of SHGs. This damaging force of mistrust among women indicates that female solidarity cannot be taken for granted (Lenette, 2015).

The idea of 'power with' as contingent on the strength of relationships also illustrates that empowerment is not a 'fixed' good but can change rapidly (Cornwall, 2016; Kabeer, 2001). This concept of empowerment thus challenges the communitarian notion of the 'community' as a reified imaginary ideal (Bauman, 2001; DeFilippis, 2008; Geoghegan & Powell, 2009). Instead, communities are in a constant state of flux and are constantly being shaped by different internal and external interests, power dynamics and influences (DeFilippis, 2008).

Conclusion

By emphasising the role of 'power with', I argue that researchers and practitioners must be aware of power dynamics within communities and the inside and outside influences which can break down trust and cohesion. Practically, this can involve NGOs engaging communities in open discussions about political interference and conflict resolution. Practitioners can facilitate groups to develop charters around rights and responsibilities and spend time building group rapport before dispensing credit. NGOs can also undertake power mapping and analysis with communities and enable better linkages between SHGs and groups which can aid in successful collective action, such as with female task forces in the police (if they exist) and with women's rights groups. In all instances, empowerment should not be viewed as an achievable result within a programme but should instead be seen as an ongoing, tenuous process of change.

This chapter therefore demonstrates how the idea of empowerment is dependent on 'power with', drawing on feminist interpretations of power as a cluster of concepts. 'Power with' illustrates the agency of women and the importance of the often overlooked role of relationships, friendships and trust in development projects. SHGs and microcredit programmes are only effective if the group has developed enough trust and solidarity with each other. These ideas counter neoliberal individualistic versions of empowerment which ironically have frequently promoted microcredit initiatives. This chapter further demonstrates that while tenuous, the development of 'power with' contests the spatial segregation and patriarchal control of women and hence provides an important site of resistance for feminists.

Note

1 A previous version of this chapter appeared as 'Gendered isolation, idealised communities and the role of collective power in West Bengal self-help groups' (2021) by Annabel Dulhunty in *Gender, Place & Culture, 28(5)*, 725–746, DOI: 10.1080/0966369X.2020.1754167.

References

Abe, A. (2009). Social Capital Formation and Local Capture in Decentralization: The Case of Zambézia, Mozambique. *Progress in Development Studies*, 9(1), 63–79. doi:10.1177/146499340800900106.

Allen, A. (1999). *The Power of Feminist Theory: Domination, Resistance, Solidarity.* Westview.

Arendt, H. (1970). *On Violence*. Harcourt, Brace & World.

Battegazzorre, F. (2017). Some Reflections on the Power to/Power over Debate. *Journal of Political Power*, 10(3), 274–285. doi:10.1080/2158379x.2017.1382169.

Bauman, Z. (2001). *The Individualized Society*. Polity Press.

Bhattacharyya, R. (2015). Understanding the Spatialities of Sexual Assault against Indian Women in India. *Gender, Place & Culture*, 22(9), 1340–1356. doi:10.1080/0966369x.2014.969684.

Brody, C., de Hoop, T., Vojtkova, M., Warnock, R., Dunbar, M., Murthy, P., & Dworkin, S. L. (2017). Can Self-Help Group Programs Improve Women's Empowerment? A Systematic Review. *Journal of Development Effectiveness*, 9(1), 15–40. doi:10.1080/19439342.2016.1206607.

Cacioppo, J. T., & Cacioppo, S. (2018). The Growing Problem of Loneliness. *The Lancet*, 391(10119), 426. doi:10.1016/S0140-6736(18)30142-9.

Chakravarty, A., & Chaudhuri, S. (2012). *Strategic Framing Work(S): How Microcredit Loans Facilitate Anti-Witch-Hunt Movements Mobilization*, 17(2), 175–194.

Chandra, U., Heierstad, G., & Bo Nielsen, K. (2015). Introduction. In U. Chandra, G. Heierstad, & K. Bo Nielsen (Eds.), *The Politics of Caste in West Bengal* (pp.1–18). Routledge India.

Commonwealth of Australia (2016). Gender Equality and Women's Empowerment Strategy, February 2016. Department of Foreign Affairs and Trade. http://dfat.gov.au/about-us/publications/documents/gender-equality-and-womens-empowerment-strategy.pdf.

Cornwall, A. (2016). Women's Empowerment: What Works? *Journal of International Development*, 28(3), 342–359. doi:10.1002/jid.3210.

Cornwall, A., & Edwards, J. (2014). *Feminisms, Empowerment and Development: Changing Women's Lives*. Zed Books.

Davidson, T., & Sanyal, P. (2017). Associational Participation and Network Expansion: Microcredit Self-Help Groups and Poor Women's Social Ties in Rural India. *Social Forces*, 95(4), 1695–1724. doi:10.1093/sf/sox021.

DeFilippis, J. (2008). Paradoxes of Community-Building: Community Control in the Global Economy. *International Social Science Journal*, 59(192), 223–234. doi:10.1111/j.1468-2451.2009.00694.x.

Dowding, K. (2012). Why Should We Care About the Definition of Power? *Journal of Political Power*, 5(1), 119–135. doi:10.1080/2158379x.2012.661917.

Feigenberg, B., Field, E. M., & Pande, R. (2010). Building Social Capital through Microfinance. National Bureau of Economic Research Working Paper Series, Working Paper 16018.

Ferragina, E., & Arrigoni, A. (2017). The Rise and Fall of Social Capital: Requiem for a Theory? *Political Studies Review*, 15(3), 355–367. doi:10.1177/1478929915623968.

Fine, B. (2008). Social Capital in Wonderland: The World Bank Behind the Looking Glass. *Progress in Development Studies*, 8(3), 261–269. doi:10.1177/146499340800800304.

Finnis, E. (2017). Collective Action, Envisioning the Future and Women's Self-Help Groups: A Case Study from South India. *Indian Journal of Gender Studies*, 24(1), 1–23. doi:10.1177/0971521516678529.

Franklin, A. (2012). A Lonely Society? Loneliness and Liquid Modernity in Australia. *Australian Journal of Social Issues*, 47(1), 11–28. doi:10.1002/j.1839-4655.2012.tb00232.x.

Geoghegan, M., & Powell, F. (2009). Community Development and the Contested Politics of the Late Modern 'Agora': Of, Alongside or against Neoliberalism? *Community Development Journal*, 44(4), 430–447. doi:10.1093/cdj/bsn020.

Hartsock, N. (1983). *Money, Sex and Power: Towards a Feminist Historical Materialism*. Northeastern University Press.

Haugaard, M. (2012). Rethinking the Four Dimensions of Power: Domination and Empowerment. *Journal of Political Power*, 5(1), 33–54. doi:10.1080/2158379x.2012.660810.

Haugaard, M. (2018). Justification and the Four Dimensions of Power. *Journal of Political Power*, 11(1), 93–114. doi:10.1080/2158379x.2018.1433759.

Hearn, J. (2014). On the Social Evolution of Power to/Over. *Journal of Political Power*, 7(2), 175–191. doi:10.1080/2158379x.2014.927963.

Hickel, J. (2014). The 'Girl Effect': Liberalism, Empowerment and the Contradictions of Development. *Third World Quarterly*, 35(8), 1355–1373. doi:10.1080/01436597.2014.946250.

Holt-Lunstad, J., Smith, T. B., & Layton, J. B. (2010). Social Relationships and Mortality Risk: A Meta-Analytic Review. *PLOS Medicine*, 7(7), 1–20. doi:10.1371/.

Huda, K., & Kaur, S. (2011). 'It Was as If We Were Drowning': Shocks, Stresses and Safety Nets in India. *Gender and Development*, 19(2), 213–227. doi:10.1080/13552074.2011.592632.

Irigaray, L. (1985). *This Sex Which Is Not One*. Cornell University Press.

Jakimow, T. (2018). Beyond 'State Ibuism': Empowerment Effects in State-Led Development in Indonesia. *Development and Change*, 49(5), 1143–1165. doi:10.1111/dech.12374.

Kabeer, N. (1994). *Reversed Realities: Gender Hierarchies in Development Thought*. Verso.

Kabeer, N. (2001). Conflicts over Credit: Re-Evaluating the Empowerment Potential of Loans to Women in Rural Bangladesh. *World Development*, 29(1), 63–84. doi:10.1016/S0305-750X(00)00081-4.

Kabeer, N. (2011). Between Affiliation and Autonomy: Navigating Pathways Ofwomen's Empowerment and Gender Justice in Rural Bangladesh. *Development and Change*, 42(2), 499–528. doi:10.1111/j.1467-7660.2011.01703.x.

Kilby, P. (2011). *NGOs in India: The Challenges of Women's Empowerment and Accountability*. Routledge.

Knowles, G., & Luke, B. (2018). Creating Conflict or Harmony? The Impact of Microfinance Programs and Self-Help Groups on Social Order in Poor Communities. *Third Sector Review*, 24(2).

Kotian, D. B., Mathews, M., Parsekar, S. S., Nair, S., Binu, V. S., & Subba, S. H. (2018). Factors Associated with Social Isolation among the Older People in India. *Journal of Geriatric Psychiatry and Neurology*, 31(5), 271–278. doi:10.1177/0891988718796338.

Lahiri-Dutt, K., & Samanta, G. (2006). Constructing Social Capital: Self-Help Groups and Rural Women's Development in India. *Geographical Research*, 44(3), 285–295. doi:10.1111/j.1745-5871.2006.00390.x.

Lenette, C. (2015). Mistrust and Refugee Women Who Are Lone Parents in Resettlement Contexts. *Qualitative Social Work*, 14(1), 119–134. doi:10.1177/1473325013517924.

Lukes, S. (1974). *Power: A Radical View*. Palgrave Macmillan.

Mathie, A., Cameron, J., & Gibson, K. (2017). Asset-Based and Citizen-Led Development: Using a Diffracted Power Lens to Analyze the Possibilities and

Challenges. *Progress in Development Studies*, 17(1), 54–66. doi:10.1177/1464993416674302.

McDaid, S. (2010). Redefining Empowerment in Mental Health: An Analysis Using Hannah Arendt's Power Concept. *Journal of Power*, 3(2), 209–225. doi:10.1080/17540291.2010.493701.

McGee, R. (2016). Power and Empowerment Meet Resistance: A Critical, Action-Oriented Review of the Literature. *IDS Bulletin*, 47(5), 103–118. doi:10.19088/1968-2016.170.

McLennan, A. K., & Ulijaszek, S. J. (2018). Beware the Medicalisation of Loneliness. *The Lancet*, 391(10129), 1480. doi:10.1016/S0140-6736(18)30577-4.

Méndez-Lemus, Y., Vieyra, A., & Poncela, L. (2017). Peri-Urban Local Governance? Intra-Government Relationships and Social Capital in a Peripheral Municipality of Michoacán, Mexico. *Progress in Development Studies*, 17(1), 1–23. doi:10.1177/1464993416674297.

Miller, J. B. (1992). Women and Power. In T. E. Wartenberg (Ed.), *Rethinking Power* (pp. 240–248). SUNY Press.

Nussbaum, M. C. (2011). *Creating Capabilities: The Human Development Approach*. Harvard University Press.

Ortner, S. B. (2001). Specifying Agency: The Comaroffs and Their Critics. *Interventions*, 3, 76–84.

Pansardi, P. (2012). Power to and Power Over: Two Distinct Concepts of Power? *Journal of Political Power*, 5(1), 73–89. doi:10.1080/2158379x.2012.658278.

Parikh, A. (2018). Politics of Presence: Women's Safety and Respectability at Night in Mumbai, India. *Gender, Place & Culture*, 25(5), 695–710. doi:10.1080/0966369x.2017.1400951.

Paul, T. (2011). Space, Gender, and Fear of Crime: Some Explorations from Kolkata. *Gender, Technology and Development*, 15(3), 411–435. doi:10.1177/097185241101500305.

Pinnewala, P. (2009). Good Women, Martyrs, and Survivors: A Theoretical Framework for South Asian Women's Responses to Partner Violence. *Violence Against Women*, 15(1), 81–105. doi:10.1177/1077801208328005.

Pittaway, E. E., Bartolomei, L., & Doney, G. (2016). The Glue That Binds: An Exploration of the Way Resettled Refugee Communities Define and Experience Social Capital. *Community Development Journal*, 51(3), 401–418. doi:10.1093/cdj/bsv023.

Putnam, R. (1993). *Making Democracy Work: Civic Traditions in Modern Italy*. Princeton University Press.

Rodó-de-Zárate, M., & Baylina, M. (2018). Intersectionality in Feminist Geographies. *Gender, Place & Culture*, 25(4), 547–553. doi:10.1080/0966369x.2018.1453489.

Rowlands, J. (1997). *Questioning Empowerment: Working with Women in Honduras*. Oxfam GB.

Sabhlok, S. G. (2011). Development and Women: The Role of Trust in Self-Help Groups. *Indian Journal of Gender Studies*, 18, 241–261.

Sanyal, P. (2009). From Credit to Collective Action: The Role of Microfinance in Promoting Women's Social Capital and Normative Influence. *American Sociological Review*, 74(August), 529–550. doi:10.1177/000312240907400402.

Sanyal, P. (2014). *Credit to Capabilities: A Sociological Study of Microcredit Groups in India*. Cambridge University Press.

Sanyal, P. (2015). Group-Based Microcredit & Emergent Inequality in Social Capital: Why Socio-Religious Composition Matters. *Qualitative Sociology*, 38, 103–137. doi:10.1007/s11133-015-9301-8.

Sardenberg, C. M. B. (2008). Liberal Vs. Liberating Empowerment: A Latin American Feminist Perspective on Conceptualising Women's Empowerment. *IDS Bulletin*, 39(6), 18–27. doi:10.1111/j.1759-5436.2008.tb00507.x.

Sen, A. (1995). Gender Inequality and Theories of Justice. In M. Nussmaum & J. Glover (Eds.), *Women, Culture and Development* (pp. 153–198). Clarendon Press.

Sen, A. (1997). Human Capital and Human Capability. *World Development*, 25(12), 1959–1961.

Sen, A. (1999). *Development as Freedom*. Alfred A. Knopf.

Sen, D., & Majumder, S. (2015). Narratives of Risk and Poor Rural Women's (Dis)-Engagements with Microcredit-Based Development in Eastern India. *Critique of Anthropology*, 35(2), 121–141. doi:10.1177/0308275x15569850.

Sengupta, N. (2013). Poor Women's Empowerment: The Discursive Space of Microfinance. *Indian Journal of Gender Studies*, 20(2), 279–304. doi:10.1177/0971521513482220.

Sharma, A. (2008). *Logics of Empowerment: Development, Gender, and Governance in Neoliberal India*. University of Minnesota Press.

Shaw, M. (2007). Community Development and the Politics of Community. *Community Development Journal*, 43(1), 24–36. doi:10.1093/cdj/bsl035.

Stroope, S. (2015). Seclusion, Decision-Making Power, and Gender Disparities in Adult Health: Examining Hypertension in India. *Social Science Research*, 53, 288–299. doi:10.1016/j.ssresearch.2015.05.013.

VeneKlasen, L., & Miller, V. (2002). Power and Empowerment. *PLA Notes*, 43, 39–41.

World Bank (2012). *World Development Report: Gender Equality and Development*. https://openknowledge.worldbank.org/entities/publication/51c285f6-0200-590c-97d3-95b937be3271.

10 Conclusions and Recommendations

In this book I have outlined the complex relationship between microcredit, SHG programming and women's empowerment. While the examples from this research come from a small number of programmes in West Bengal, they provide insight into the possibilities and barriers to women's empowerment and the contributing role of SHG microcredit programming. In combination with a detailed review of other studies conducted on microcredit, SHGs and women's empowerment, it is possible to draw conclusions as to the benefits and drawbacks of SHG microcredit programmes. In summary, SHG microcredit programmes are no panacea for the redistribution of resources required for the alleviation of poverty. Neither are all SHG microcredit programmes empowering, as there is a broad range of programme styles and implementers. Yet neither can we say that all microcredit or SHG programmes are exploitative and harmful to women. Rather, SHG programmes can play an important role in establishing connections between isolated women, in harnessing collective action and advocacy for the achievement of women's rights, and in establishing solidarity and group strength to respond to community issues. The ability of an SHG microcredit programme to achieve these ends depends very much, however, on the programme model used and the extent to which a programme adopts a transformational model of community development and of achieving gender equality. In this final chapter I outline the overarching conclusions from this research, both for SHG and microcredit programming and for the pursuit of women's empowerment. Inherent in these conclusions are recommendations for better practice.

Women's Empowerment and Gender and Development

Can women's empowerment and Gender and Development (GAD) be revitalised and extracted from neoliberal co-option? While this is difficult to determine, I would argue that while the *language* of empowerment, even GAD, may remain contested, the initial ideas of empowerment based on conscientisation, collective action and reflection on power relationships remain relevant today. As argued by feminist scholars, empowerment means all things to all

DOI: 10.4324/9781003356400-10

people (Cornwall, 2016). For corporations, NGOs and governments gripped by neoliberal ideas of the rollback of the state, empowerment can signify a focus on the individual freed from governmental control (Batliwala, 2007). This clearly is far removed from the intentions of those initially advocating for women's empowerment – yet as empowerment has been so readily adopted by mainstream development institutions, its initial meaning has been challenged. It is easier to 'sell' the idea of empowerment as a technical solution (Mosedale, 2014) or as a means to achieving the end of economic growth (Chant & Sweetman, 2012) than it is to market the idea of radical transformational change which would subvert power relations.

Interestingly and sadly, it can seem as though 'smart economics' is merely a redo of Women in Development (WID), with the same criticisms of WID applicable to 'smart economics'. Despite the similarities between WID and 'smart economics' however, there are also some key differences. While WID was arguably an uphill battle to convince development actors to focus on women, there is a much wider belief today amongst these organisations that investing in women is a key driver of economic growth (World Bank, 2012). Importantly, as global capitalism has expanded, there is a widespread understanding that money is to be made through giving poor women access to credit (Keating et al., 2010). These seemingly 'untapped' markets provide a host of opportunities for a cacophony of actors, all with the desire to create profit from impoverished populations (Calkin, 2015). This global landscape is hence highly different from the environment of the 1970s and 80s and the reach of global capitalism at that time.

The rise of GAD appeared to provide hope for a more holistic and feminist oriented approach to development. GAD emerged as a radical contestation of WID's narrow focus on investing in women. It criticised WID's inability to challenge the underlying power assumptions of gender relations (Rathgeber, 1990). Yet it seems that many of the core principles of GAD have been largely ignored in recent years. Certainly, the phrase 'gender equality' may be more frequently used than 'women's equality' today, but the majority of women's empowerment programming largely still resembles WID – as seen through many microcredit and business training programmes for women. This is disappointing, especially given: the clarity of feminist critique of these programmes from the 1980s onward; the hopes invested in a rights based approach to women's empowerment from the Beijing Platform for Action in 1995 and the obvious focus on holistic, liberatory empowerment in many GAD frameworks (Sardenberg, 2008). This regression illustrates, however, the ease with which liberatory ideals are co-opted (Cornwall, 2007) and the fact that feminist fights are never linear: one step forward, one or perhaps two steps back. Furthermore, despite the large body of scholarly work on GAD, we must also never assume that this research has been well communicated throughout development institutions. The disconnect between theory and practice is especially evident in NGOs or donor agencies which are not primarily focused on gender equality – many of the more radical demands of

GAD become lost as they are 'mainstreamed' into the systems of wider agencies (Moser & Moser, 2005).

Intersectional Feminism and Decolonising Feminism

The critiques of how gender was addressed in development in the 1990s (Kabeer, 1994; Rowlands, 1997) are just as relevant today, if not more so, as women's rights have been affronted by conservative backlash globally. Yet there is opportunity also to redress some of the weaknesses of different GAD frameworks, such as its lack of attention to intersectionality and to issues of race and coloniality (Marchand, 2009). In the past decade, there has been a growing recognition of the importance of intersectional feminism and feminism based on difference. Whether that be greater emphasis to differences in sexuality (Monro & Richardson, 2010) or attention to race (Wilson, 2011), it is evident that merely focusing on gender difference is inadequate for meaningful change and empowerment. The Black Lives Matter movement and subsequent Dalit Lives Matter movement also highlight the need to redress caste and race based discrimination. If GAD is to be revitalised in any way it clearly must represent this diversity.

What then, of criticisms that GAD and feminist frameworks in 'development' are Western impositions (Tripathy, 2010)? Certainly gender programmes have the potential to be top-down or 'Western', particularly if they rely on Western gender 'experts' implementing programmes. Yet these criticisms do not give ample recognition to the long and diverse history of feminist organising from the Global South. It is true that these movements have been undervalued in global feminism (Menon, 2015), yet there is a richness of scholarship, not just empirical examples, from the Global South which can guide 21st Century GAD. The rise of Dalit feminism, for example, as a theoretical framework (Paik, 2021) provides an opportunity to remake GAD discourse and practice. While Dalit feminism is much broader than 'development' programming and encompasses a holistic theory, many of its key ideas – from a focus on the most marginalised, to an exposition on shame and an emphasis on human dignity and self-respect (Arya & Rathore, 2020), provide a useful way of reframing GAD.

In addition, expertise in gender-transformative change is hardly limited to scholarship and practice from the Global North, yet Global South voices need to be given far greater prioritisation and recognition. It is important to learn from the multitude of disruptive and inspirational NGOs and grassroots women's organisations working for feminist change in the Global South and their experience in implementing gender-transformative programmes. Using a GAD approach then does not mean that we need to 'transport' feminist ideas from the North to the South, rather we should promote, uphold and fund feminist organisations from the Global South. We can further learn from the new era of feminism in India and its rich history, drawing from both historical and contemporary feminism. For example, the writing of early feminists such as Savitribai Phule for Dalit rights and Begum Rokeya Sakhawat Hossain in Bengal also provide inspiration. Rokeya's writings on the power of education resonates with informal GAD based educational programmes today which aim to go beyond literacy, also attempting to enable 'power within'. Rokeya's work provides a useful reference for this type of work, advocating that education must reject misogyny and be fundamentally premised on promoting the 'inner faculties of the individual' (Quayum, 2013, p.29).

The history of feminism in India is also enlightening for its promotion of class based rights, particularly in the struggle against colonialism and neo-colonialism, as encapsulated by the Indian feminist contribution to the DAWN document and to the rise of postcolonial feminism (Banerjee, 2017). For GAD to remain relevant it must continue to engage in the ideas of global class based oppression and question the very foundations of development. Numerous projects are carried out in the name of 'development', yet how many of these actually aid the most marginalised? While GAD was initially influenced by the Marxist Women and Development (WAD) movement, any synergies have since become less obvious. While WAD had its issues, its focus on addressing *global* inequality and exploitation should further influence current GAD discourse.

Furthermore, learning from feminisms in India can further revitalise GAD through adopting the strategic use of social media for organising feminist action as seen in the Indian context. Online platforms have increasingly been used as an organising mechanism for multiple women's rights campaigns in India and for creating solidarity amongst otherwise disparate groups (Madabhushi et al., 2015), resulting in a significant expansion of the feminist movement. While this form of organising cannot be the *only* mechanism of activism, given that it necessarily excludes those without internet connectivity, it can be viewed as one component of current feminist strategising, which should not be overlooked for its importance.

It is important also to note that as is the case globally, all feminist organisations can themselves reflect other hierarchies (e.g. based on caste and class in India). There is no one homogenous feminism, either within the Global South or in India. As such, focusing on feminist organisations which are led by and support the work of the most marginalised women is of key importance. The contemporary focus amongst many in India on caste, diversity and sexuality can further inform contemporary GAD theory. Rather than seeing any 'splintering' of feminist causes as a weakness, there is instead richness in this diversity (Roy, 2022), to ensure that feminism and feminist based programming is inclusive for all.

Dignity

A focus on human dignity should also be prioritised within GAD or any form of community development programming. Kant's (2012/1785) insistence that each and every person is an *end* in themselves, not a *means* to an end, is still relevant today. Feminist critiques of Kant (Hay, 2013; Nussbaum, 2011), are particularly important to draw from, in their arguments that dignity should not only be premised on ideas of the public citizen or rationality. Dalit feminist conceptions of dignity are also important, emphasising the role of selfhood and self-respect (Rao, 2015). Dalit feminism also highlights the extent to which others' actions constantly affront our own sense of dignity. While another's viewpoint does not erode one's intrinsic worth, it can make an individual believe that they are worthless. Gender and development programmes therefore need to encourage both a sense of inner dignity and self-respect and also respect from others. The framework for feminist dignity which I outlined in Chapter 7 draws on these ideas and it is worth repeating the core questions here. It is meant to be used by community development practitioners, both in the design and implementation of programmes, to enable programmes to ensure that the dignity of *all* is inherent in the programme.

The core principle of the framework is that individuals are ends in themselves and the key questions are:

1. Does the programme encourage inner dignity?
2. Does the programme enable dignity from others?
3. Does the programme promote holistic dignity, beyond masculinist notions of 'public' dignity?
4. Does the programme enhance equality of dignity through redressing power imbalances?

This framework asks the practitioner to examine whether the programme promotes dignity and self-respect in the individual in addition to enhancing respect from others. Moreover, by taking an explicitly feminist approach, this framework demands that dignity not be tied to the public sphere. This underscores the fact that an individual's sense of self-worth is frequently linked with their earnings or public contributions, ignoring the necessary role of care and household work. This was documented in the examples given in Chapter 7 when women were proud of themselves and felt increased self-confidence, but this appeared to be tied to their earnings and their ability to see themselves as 'contributing' to the household. This framework further indicates the need to address imbalances in how people are treated with dignity in communities. Programmes should try to promote a sense of dignity amongst *all* and for *all*– focusing on redressing inequalities, whether that be based on gender, caste or class.

Power

A nuanced understanding of power and willingness to challenge power inequalities is also key to transformative practice in women's empowerment and community development programming. Rowlands' (1997) differentiation between 'power within', 'power over', 'power with' and 'power to' is a useful framework for guiding our understanding of power. As I have argued in Chapter 9, too frequently power has been thought of only as a top-down aggressive form of power, as 'power over' others. Yet other forms of power are also important, particularly when we draw from feminist ideas of power as *productive* (Allen, 1999; Hartsock, 1983) and as a critical component of empowerment (Kabeer, 1994). 'Power within', for example, is a highly important process of acknowledging the differentiation of self, of understanding one's agency and in being able to see the construction of social norms. This 'power within' involves the development of critical consciousness (Kabeer, 1999). While this has rightfully been given significant attention, the role of 'power with' is equally important. This idea is premised on the fact that we are not isolated individuated units but live and exist with others. Isolation and withdrawal from others disempowers the individual (McDaid, 2010). Networks with others and social relations is hence critically important to developing this sense of 'power with' others and enabling solidarity and the capacity for collective action. With the formation of 'power within' and 'power with', the power to act, or 'power to' is enhanced and people may demonstrate their strength in challenging damaging social norms or in contesting discriminatory practices. These are all critical elements of empowerment.

While these forms of power are positive, disciplinary, negative 'power over' others still shapes social relations and it is critical that women's empowerment and community development programmes do not ignore this. 'Power over' can be overt and explicit e.g. men telling women not to leave the house or they will be punished for engaging in the SHG, as documented in Chapter 8. This form of power controls women's mobility and can be challenged by women's empowerment programmes which enable women to have greater mobility outside the home. Yet 'power over' is not so easily disabled. Instead, 'power over' also functions in a more subtle, insidious way – shaping people's norms and expectations and resulting in them disciplining their own actions to conform with others. This type of power can be conceived of as 'invisible power' as per Stephen Lukes' (2005) theory or as Bourdieu's *doxa* (Bourdieu, 1977). Feminist criticisms and adaptations of Foucault (Bartky, 1990) are also helpful in their arguments that women are constantly controlled by disciplinary power, shaping women's every movement and consideration. While women's empowerment and community development programmes cannot completely overturn 'power over', they can help communities to understand the extent to which rigid gender norms can control and limit women's fulfilment and empowerment.

From Mainstreaming to Transformative Approaches

Throughout these chapters I have regularly contrasted gender mainstreaming with more transformational approaches. Despite criticisms, gender mainstreaming has continued to dominate development programming, after gaining widespread support since the 1995 Beijing Platform for Action. Ultimately, however, the outcomes of gender mainstreaming remain limited as it becomes another add-on tick box exercise to development programming. A focus on gender is important but it can be easily misunderstood to mean equally addressing the needs of women *and* men *and* girls *and* boys. This becomes somewhat self-defeating as it essentially prioritises the needs of no one. The question then is how to ensure that a project focuses on women's empowerment?

The differentiation between gender-neutral, gender-sensitive and gender-transformative programming (Dworkin et al., 2013) is a useful framework for understanding how a programme can go beyond gender mainstreaming. Any transformational approaches require significant investment and resources in staff and must go beyond a 'light touch' of adding gender as an additional 'cross-cutting' component. Gender-transformative approaches must fundamentally address social norms, which are not superficial, but are deeply embedded and constitutive of social structures. The examples from this research illustrate that to try to change social norms, a didactic approach by NGO staff whereby large lectures on megaphones are given to communities, is unlikely to work. Rather Freirean 'learning circles' (Freire, 1970) where well trained frontline staff sit with smaller groups of community members and facilitate discussions, is more likely to be useful. Similarly, no gender 'training' should be a one off occurrence, given that this almost never succeeds in prompting normative change (Currier & Carlson, 2009).

Furthermore, social norm change cannot just focus on women, as if women alone are responsible for creating social norms. Too many projects provoke changes in attitudes amongst women, providing greater awareness amongst women of women's rights, but the thinking of men remains unchanged (Caridad Bueno & Henderson, 2017). While some feminist critics (Brush & Miller, 2019) have argued against focusing efforts on working with men for gender-transformative change, findings from this research indicate that if men are *not* engaged in a programmatic intervention, then violent backlash may occur. In addition, even if women are educated about their rights, changes in communal social norms are unlikely to occur unless men also have an understanding of gender equality. Engaging men and boys in small group discussions as to the existence of gender inequality is hence important. Conscientisation processes are paramount for both women *and* men. Yet as Dworkin and Baker (2019) argue, the method involved in implementation is crucial: how successful a programme is depends in many ways on how it is adapted for local purposes, while retaining the core ideas of transformative gender change. In many examples from this research it was clear that even when women described that they were aware of their rights, they felt despair when they said that their husbands did not respect them, or even more so when they saw that their sons lacked respect for them. In Birbhum, there was a dangerous combination of frustration, boredom and lack of hope amongst men which arguably exacerbated situations of domestic violence. Admittedly it is also harder to engage men in gender equality programmes in many instances. Women potentially have something to gain from believing in gender equality, whereas men may have something to lose. Whether empowerment is zero sum (where one person's empowerment causes another to lose power) (Read, 2012) depends on the type of household and community relations, whether they are conflictual or collaborative. Ultimately, however, any women's empowerment programme is going to be highly limited unless it can help change the mindsets of men.

Programmes must therefore find a way of engaging men and can tie in gender awareness sessions with skills building, or other activities which may be of interest to men. Furthermore, as Dworkin, Fleming & Colvin (2015) argue, an intersectional approach to working with men is also paramount. Many men in these locations are also treated poorly by 'higher' castes in the village, by their employers or by the wealthy middle class on the streets. Processes of conscientisation which focus on multiple forms of oppression may aid men to empathise with the situation of women and may also enable collective consciousness of the limiting social norms and oppressions governing their lives.

Organisational Support

To promote transformational change, the role of front line workers or 'field staff' is especially important. As Chapter 6 documented, many NGO programmes operate within a hierarchy whereby the frontline workers are at the most junior level. Across many organisations, it will be the frontline staff who are least remunerated, who work in the most hazardous conditions and who have the least amount of organisational support. Yet it is in their face to face work with communities and in their method and style of working that enables either the success or failure of a community development programme. Providing good salaries and conditions is hence fundamental to a good programme.

In addition, in many contexts, women face additional barriers in working in communities. In many cases, frontline staff are expected to travel alone, sometimes at night, frequently on bicycles or motorbikes. Women may either perceive this as risky, or as was the case with SPT, they viewed it as an organisational risk to have women employed in this capacity. Yet without adequate numbers of female frontline staff, undoubtedly a masculinist perspective will be employed in communities. Ultimately NGOs and donor organisations need to factor in additional costs for supporting female SHG staff. When women's safety may be compromised by frontline work, the following considerations are important: providing funds to women so that they may travel with another woman, enabling women to access a car and allowing that it may take longer to implement a project due to shorter days (and prioritising returning before dark). Rather than look for cost cutting solutions, women must be given adequate support to work with communities.

There is a role for donors here too who frequently review programme salaries asking for 'value for money' and cost cutting measures. Donors can instead prioritise funding frontline workers with good salaries and conditions. They can further ask what is being done to support female frontline staff and what provisions are in place for female frontline workers, with the expectation that extra support will cost more. In addition, donors can expect that organisations have strong procedures for preventing and responding to sexual exploitation, abuse and harassment in the workplace. No procedure is foolproof and there needs to be channels for whistleblowers and the most vulnerable to provide feedback and complaints.

It must also be acknowledged that working on any gender programme has the possibility of causing harm, particularly in acknowledgement that being seen to promote any 'deviance' in maintained gender norms can provoke backlash (Hattery, 2022). As I have documented throughout this book, men's initial opposition to their wives attending the NGO programmes was severe and some responded with violence. A programme intervention cannot be rushed and time needs to be spent with men in the initial stages also, not just with the 'target' group of women. Any rush to try to establish large volumes of SHGs or the rapid dispensing of microcredit loans can do significant harm. The rigidity of NGO timeframes is problematic when taking into account the complexity of behaviour change (Van der Hoogte & Kingma, 2004). NGO timeframes hence have to acknowledge the crucial preliminary participatory steps at the commencement of a programme. Donors also have a role in not 'rushing' any SHG programme or any project aimed at achieving 'women's empowerment'. Instead, meaningful participatory processes take time (Chambers, 1995).

Microcredit

Moving now to the topic of microcredit, in this work I have shown the divergences of opinion as to the value of microcredit. In essence, microcredit is access to loans for poor individuals or groups which can result in multiple outcomes. That said, given that microcredit has been in circulation for some time now and given the fact that poverty and gender inequality persist (including in populations 'tapped' by microcredit), it seems that microcredit is no magic solution. At its best, microcredit provides individuals who are poor with a greater number of options. Instead of going to the local money lender, they may go to the microcredit provider which may have better rates and may (or indeed may not) be less likely to harass them. In this way, access to microcredit can improve human agency and choice, as per Amartya Sen's 'Development is Freedom' (Sen,1999). For individuals who are entrepreneurial and not in dire situations, access to credit means they may be able to put their business ideas into action without being constrained by a lack of access to funds.

Just as there is no one model of microcredit, however, there is no one lender and regulations differ greatly by country. In India for example, recent

Reserve Bank of India regulations were loosened, enabling Non-Bank Financial Companies (NBFCs) to set their own interest rates. This diversity of lenders and minimised regulations means that there is a much greater likelihood of there being 'loan sharks', as Yunus (2011) has rallied against. It is interesting to note that the recent spate of RCTs concluded that microcredit had no adverse effects on individuals (Banerjee et al., 2015). Yet these findings are impossible to generalise – the practices of loan recovery differ significantly by lender. For some lenders, harassing clients to repay, turning up at their homes or places of work (even visiting the clients in hospital) is all part of their strategy of repayment (Finch & Kocieniewski, 2022). So the question remains, as microcredit is deemed to be a more and more attractive prospect for global investors and local companies looking for profit, are these predatory practices likely to decrease or increase? Without adequate and strict government regulation, microcredit certainly has the capacity to do significant harm and it seems likely that we will see more predatory lenders.

In addition, while it is helpful for SHG members to build connections with other women, it is not a substitute for state protections, secure employment or welfare. In the neoliberal rush to prioritise markets, it is easy to see how microcredit SHG programming can be seen as a counterpoint to government intervention. Through the lens of 'smart economics', microcredit is pitched as a low cost solution – empower women through giving them access to credit and then grow the economy! Yet the process of empowerment is oversimplified in this version and does not take into account the structural constraints surrounding women. The initial development of 20th Century microcredit programmes such as SEWA in India and under Muhammed Yunus in Bangladesh had little to do with neoliberalism. Rather they were a means for seeing that the poor had access to a resource (loans) which they did not have previously. While Yunus (2005) overestimated the potential impact of these loans for solving poverty, they weren't enmeshed with neoliberalism as microcredit is more frequently today. The growth of the idea of 'smart economics' (World Bank, 2012) and investment in 'Women's Economic Empowerment' has further supported today's flourishing of microcredit. While government support for microcredit SHG programmes has some value, it is problematic if it is used as an excuse to ignore significant more beneficial poverty alleviation measures for impoverished women and their communities. If it is merely a process of enabling women access to the 'market' under a neoliberal ideal of reduced state involvement, this is not ultimately going to benefit the poor. In addition, viewing women as a *means* to the end of economic growth, denies women of their inherent dignity. The flurry of excitement that focusing on women's empowerment could lead to economic growth in the vicinity of $12 trillion USD (Woetzel et al., 2015) illustrates the extent to which women are used as conduits for the overarching aims of global capitalism.

How to then consider microcredit programmes overall? Ultimately, they are another tool, another option for poor households which may be helpful in some circumstances but in other instances have the ability to cause harm in cases where lenders feel emboldened to harass clients or to charge excessive rates. Given the increasing interest from private investors in accumulating profit from the microcredit industry, it is imperative that governments create tight regulations to curb the predatory actions of some lenders. In addition, microcredit should not be viewed as a solution to poverty and inequality. It may help some people in some cases, but there are no grounds for government divesture from redistributive schemes, job creation and social protection for citizens. Enthusiastic claims that microcredit is a 'solution' for poverty or gender inequality are unfounded.

Studies on the link between credit-only microcredit and women's empowerment also vary in their outcomes. Studies conflict in respect to whether a microcredit programme increases women's empowerment or not, with some indicating no changes (Banerjee et al., 2015) and others indicating some varied positive effects (Brody et al., 2017). There are two salient lessons from this. First, microcredit may not increase women's empowerment because it has such little effect on women's income that it doesn't really change women's status. In addition, funds can easily be controlled by men, and in some cases, women are the mere conduits of funds. Second, even if women's income did change, this may improve some aspects of women's empowerment (ability to move outside the house; potentially viewed differently at home) but it doesn't go to the root causes of gender discrimination.

Credit Plus Models

There is clearly a far greater argument to be made for credit-plus models of microcredit and SHG programming. Women in this study stated that they most valued changes in their confidence, mobility and sense of having gained new knowledge. These aspects of belonging to an SHG appeared to be more important than any financial gains made, perhaps in part because financial gains were small anyway. As Chapter 9 indicates, the role of SHGs in enabling a sense of solidarity amongst women, in facilitating collective action and in decreasing isolation was highly significant. Enabling group advocacy for state resources such as electricity, secure housing and access to government schemes was particularly important. In addition, focusing only on the distribution of credit in a singular microcredit programme, as highlighted in Chapter 5, was not necessarily advantageous to women. While access to credit may be one of many tools which the poor may use to alleviate the symptoms of poverty, this is unlikely to change women's status. Instead, as Chapter 7 shows, the SPT programme could have gone further in promoting transformational gender change, replicating their South 24 Parganas programme in other areas. SHGs are able to provide the most benefit to women through enabling collective solidarity and through transformational gender programming. Moreover, trying to set up multiple SHGs quickly can also be a cause for harm as male backlash can be significant and groups may not be adequately supported to be sustainable. Instead groups need intensive support from frontline staff, not only in how to keep records or establish bank accounts, but also in how to advocate for their rights in communities.

So then, are credit-plus models the answer to women's empowerment? Certainly there are promising examples, both from within this research and from similar studies (Kabeer, 2011; Sanyal, 2014). Setting up an SHG with a tangible benefit such as microcredit can provide a platform for engaging women and enabling collaborative strength. Yet it is no guarantee. Groups fall apart, disrupted by political interference, poor administration or lack of interest amongst members.

In addition, as stated, microcredit and SHG programmes are no substitute for state solutions for poverty reduction. Adequate taxation and redistributive measures can support a social protection floor (Standing, 2017). Yet the political pressure of elites to maintain the status quo makes any redistributive efforts difficult. While SHG microcredit-plus programmes may provide scope for some small income generating opportunities, ultimately this only brings women into further informal employment which is haphazard, transitory and without security.

Advocating for Rights

It is important also to note that credit-plus models themselves differ and no NGO programme is equal. Rather than just advocate for a credit-plus programme, there are key features which are important in good practice, including that implementers adopt a transformational approach to gender and that they promote critical consciousness. Moreover, NGOs ideally should draw on rights based principles where communities are made aware of their rights and can advocate with government and others for fulfilment of those rights. NGO programmes should also be based on principles of anti-oppressive practice (Dominelli & Campling, 2002), reflecting on relationships of power between the communities and the NGO (Jackson, 2012).

Rights are holistic and incorporate the rights to housing, food and security – all aspects which SPT assisted communities in advocating for. Ultimately, drawing on a rights based approach counters neoliberal ideas of state withdrawal. It holds the state accountable (Gready, 2008) and instead of seeing SHG microcredit programmes as a substitute for state intervention (Sengupta, 2013), it uses this very mechanism to demand services from the state. Certainly different NGOs have differing levels of skills in their understanding of rights based approaches and their willingness to push back and hold the state accountable. Indeed the role of NGOs must also be to strengthen the skills of communities to advocate for themselves and to engage in community organising and animation, a mindset which may differ from many managerial models of NGO programming today (DeFilippis, 2008). NGOs can also play a role in connecting communities with other like-minded groups to build a coalition for social change (Green, 2016). This is more likely to be sustainable and to be supportive for communities past the life of a programme intervention.

Conclusion

In this book I have attempted to draw together a diverse array of theories based on different forms of community development, feminism and understandings of contemporary microcredit. I have used these frameworks to argue that women's empowerment is not a straight forward idea and is not easily achieved through financial-only models of microcredit. Rather, women's empowerment is far more difficult to realise, as it involves critically destabilising existing power relations. As such, microcredit programming can only play some part towards an overall agenda for women's equality and empowerment. In its worst form it can also be exploitative, harming women who are harassed and pursued by predatory lenders. Implementers of SHG programming also need to consider the prospect of male backlash and the ongoing maintenance of invisible power 'over', shaping social norms which punish those who deviate from those norms. In its best form when credit-plus transformative models are adopted through SHG programming, they have the ability to produce meaningful social networks, solidarity amongst women, increased confidence and capacity for collective action. Even with these positive examples, however, credit-plus microcredit programming is not a panacea for women's empowerment, rather it can complement other strategies for the improvement of gender equality and women's lives.

References

Allen, A. (1999). *The Power of Feminist Theory: Domination, Resistance, Solidarity.* Westview.

Arya, S., & Rathore, A. S. (2020). Introduction: Theorising Dalit Feminism. In S. Arya & A. Singh Rathore (Eds.), *Dalit Feminist Theory: A Reader* (pp. 1–22). Routledge.

Banerjee, A., Karlan, D., & Zinman, J. (2015). Six Randomized Evaluations of Microcredit: Introduction and Further Steps. *American Economic Journal: Applied Economics*, 7(1), 1–21. doi:10.1257/app.20140287.

Banerjee, N. (2017). Feminism at the Crossroads: Where Do We Go from Here? *Indian Journal of Gender Studies*, 24(1), 98–110. doi:10.1177/0971521516678540.

Bartky, S. L. (1990). *Femininity and Domination: Studies in the Phenomenology of Oppression.* Routledge.

Batliwala, S. (2007). Taking the Power out of Empowerment – an Experiential Account. *Development in Practice*, 17(4–5), 557–565. doi:10.1080/09614520701469559.

Bourdieu, P. (1977). *Outline of a Theory of Practice.* Cambridge University Press.

Brody, C., de Hoop, T., Vojtkova, M., Warnock, R., Dunbar, M., Murthy, P., & Dworkin, S. L. (2017). Can Self-Help Group Programs Improve Women's

Empowerment? A Systematic Review. *Journal of Development Effectiveness*, 9(1), 15–40. doi:10.1080/19439342.2016.1206607.

Brush, L. D., & Miller, E. (2019). Trouble in Paradigm: "Gender Transformative" Programming in Violence Prevention. *Violence Against Women*, 25(14), 1635–1656. doi:10.1177/1077801219872551.

Calkin, S. (2015). "Tapping" Women for Post-Crisis Capitalism. *International Feminist Journal of Politics*, 17(4), 611–629. doi:10.1080/14616742.2015.1071994.

Caridad Bueno, C., & Henderson, E. A. (2017). Bargaining or Backlash? Evidence on Intimate Partner Violence from the Dominican Republic. *Feminist Economics*, 23 (4), 90–116. doi:10.1080/13545701.2017.1292360.

Chambers, R. (1995). The Primacy of the Personal. In M. Edwards & D. Hulme (Eds.), *Non-Governmental Organisations - Performance and Accountability: Beyond the Magic Bullet* (pp. 207–217). Routledge.

Chant, S., & Sweetman, C. (2012). Fixing Women or Fixing the World? 'Smart Economics', Efficiency Approaches, and Gender Equality in Development. *Gender & Development*, 20(3), 517–529. doi:10.1080/13552074.2012.731812.

Cornwall, A. (2007). Buzzwords and Fuzzwords: Deconstructing Development Discourse. *Development in Practice*, 17(4/5), 471–484. doi:25548244.

Cornwall, A. (2016). Women's Empowerment: What Works? *Journal of International Development*, 28(3), 342–359. doi:10.1002/jid.3210.

Currier, D. M., & Carlson, J. H. (2009). Creating Attitudinal Change through Teaching: How a Course on "Women and Violence" Changes Students' Attitudes About Violence against Women. *Journal of Interpersonal Violence*, 24(10), 1735–1754. doi:10.1177/0886260509335239.

DeFilippis, J. (2008). Paradoxes of Community-Building: Community Control in the Global Economy. *International Social Science Journal*, 59(192), 223–234. doi:10.1111/j.1468-2451.2009.00694.x.

Dominelli, L., & Campling, J. (2002). *Anti-Oppressive Social Work Theory and Practice.* Palgrave MacMillan.

Dworkin, S. L., & Barker, G. (2019). Gender-Transformative Approaches to Engaging Men in Reducing Gender-Based Violence: a Response to Brush & Miller's 'Trouble in Paradigm'. *Violence against Women*, 25(14), 1657–1671. doi:10.1177/1077801219872555.

Dworkin, S. L.. Fleming, P. J., & Colvin, C. J. (2015). The Promises and Limitations of Gender-Transformative Health Programming with Men: Critical Reflections from the Field. *Culture, Health & Sexuality*, 17(sup2), 128–143. doi:10.1080/13691058.2015.1035751.

Dworkin, S. L., Treves-Kagan, S., & Lippman, S. A. (2013). Gender-Transformative Interventions to Reduce Hiv Risks and Violence with Heterosexually-Active Men: A Review of the Global Evidence. *AIDS and Behavior*, 17(9), 2845–2863. doi:10.1007/s10461-013-0565-2.

Finch, G., & Kocieniewski, D. (2022, 3 May). Big Money Backs Tiny Loans That Lead to Debt, Despair and Even Suicide. *Bloomberg*. https://www.bloomberg.com/graphics/2022-microfinance-banks-profit-off-developing-world/?leadSource=uverify%20wall.

Freire, P. (1970). *Pedagogy of the Oppressed.* Herder & Herder.

Gready, P. (2008). Rights-Based Approaches to Development: What Is the Value-Added? *Development in Practice*, 18(6), 735–747. doi:10.1080/09614520802386454.

Green, D. (2016). *How Change Happens.* Oxford University Press.

Hartsock, N. (1983). *Money, Sex and Power: Towards a Feminist Historical Materialism*. Northeastern University Press.

Hattery, A. J. (2022). Feminist Lecture: (Re) Imagining Gender-Based Violence as a Strategy for Enforcing Institutional Segregation and Reproducing Structural Inequalities. *Gender & Society*, 36(6), 789–812. doi:10.1177/08912432221128665.

Hay, C. (2013). *Kantianism, Liberalism, and Feminism*. Palgrave Macmillan.

Jackson, C. (2012). Speech, Gender and Power: Beyond Testimony. *Development and Change*, 43(5), 999–1023.

Kabeer, N. (1994). *Reversed Realities: Gender Hierarchies in Development Thought*. Verso.

Kabeer, N. (1999). Resources, Agency, Achievements: Reflections on the Measurement of Women's Empowerment. *Development and Change*, 30(3), 435–464.

Kabeer, N. (2011). Between Affiliation and Autonomy: Navigating Pathways of Women's Empowerment and Gender Justice in Rural Bangladesh. *Development and Change*, 42(2), 499–528. doi:10.1111/j.1467-7660.2011.01703.x.

Kant, I. (2012/1785). Groundwork of the Metaphysics of Morals. In M. Gregor & J. Timmermann (Eds.), *Immanuel Kant: Groundwork of the Metaphysics of Morals*. Cambridge University Press.

Keating, C., Rasmussen, C., & Rishi, P. (2010). The Rationality of Empowerment: Microcredit, Accumulation by Dispossession, and the Gendered Economy. *Signs: Journal of Women in Culture and Society*, 36(1), 153–176. doi:10.1086/652911.

Lukes, S. (2005). *Power: A Radical View* (2nd ed.). Palgrave Macmillan.

Madabhushi, T., Wahlang, M. G. T., & Joshua, G. (2015). Locating 'Hyderabad for Feminism' in the Present Struggle against Violence. *Economic and Political Weekly*, 50(34), 38–46.

Marchand, M. H. (2009). The Future of Gender and Development after 9/11: Insights from Postcolonial Feminism and Transnationalism. *Third World Quarterly*, 30(5), 921–935. doi:10.1080/01436590902959149.

McDaid, S. (2010). Redefining Empowerment in Mental Health: An Analysis Using Hannah Arendt's Power Concept. *Journal of Power*, 3(2), 209–225. doi:10.1080/17540291.2010.493701.

Menon, N. (2015). Is Feminism About 'Women'? A Critical View on Intersectionality from India. *Economic and Political Weekly*, 50(17), 37–44.

Monro, S., & Richardson, D. (2010). Intersectionality and Sexuality: The Case of Sexuality and Transgender Equalities Work in Uk Local Government. In *Theorizing Intersectionality and Sexuality* (pp. 99–118). Springer.

Mosedale, S. (2014). Women's Empowerment as a Development Goal: Taking a Feminist Standpoint. *Journal of International Development*, 26(8), 1115–1125. doi:10.1002/jid.3050.

Moser, C., & Moser, A. (2005). Gender Mainstreaming since Beijing: A Review of Success and Limitations in International Institutions. *Gender & Development*, 13 (2), 11–22. doi:10.1080/13552070512331332283.

Nussbaum, M. C. (2011). Capabilities, Entitlements, Rights: Supplementation and Critique. *Journal of Human Development and Capabilities*, 12(1), 23–37. doi:10.1080/19452829.2011.541731.

Paik, S. (2021). Dalit Feminist Thought. *Economic and Political Weekly*, 56(25), 127–136.

Quayum, M. (2013). *The Essential Rokeya: Selected Works of Rokeya Sakhawat Hossain*. Brill.

Rao, N. (2015). Marriage, Violence, and Choice: Understanding Dalit Women's Agency in Rural Tamil Nadu. *Gender & Society*, 29(3), 410–433. doi:10.1177/0891243214554798.

Rathgeber, E. M. (1990). WID, WAD, GAD: Trends in Research and Practice. *The Journal of Developing Areas*, 24(4), 489–502.

Read, J. H. (2012). Is Power Zero-Sum or Variable-Sum? Old Arguments and New Beginnings. *Journal of Political Power*, 5(1), 5–31. doi:10.1080/2158379x.2012.659865.

Rowlands, J. (1997). *Questioning Empowerment: Working with Women in Honduras*. Oxfam GB.

Roy, S. (2022). *Changing the Subject: Feminist and Queer Politics in Neoliberal India*. Duke University Press.

Sanyal, P. (2014). *Credit to Capabilities: A Sociological Study of Microcredit Groups in India*. Cambridge University Press.

Sardenberg, C. (2008). Liberal Vs. Liberating Empowerment: A Latin American Feminist Perspective on Conceptualising Women's Empowerment. *IDS Bulletin* 39 (6), 18–27. doi:10.1111/j.1759-5436.2008.tb00507.x.

Sen, A. (1999). *Development as Freedom*. Alfred A Knopf.

Sengupta, N. (2013). Poor Women's Empowerment: The Discursive Space of Microfinance. *Indian Journal of Gender Studies*, 20(2), 279–304. doi:10.1177/0971521513482220.

Standing, G. (2017). *Basic Income: And How We Can Make It Happen*. Penguin UK.

Tripathy, J. (2010). How Gendered Is Gender and Development? Culture, Masculinity, and Gender Difference. *Development in Practice*, 20(1), 113–121. doi:10.1080/09614520903436901.

Van der Hoogte, L., & Kingma, K. (2004). Promoting Cultural Diversity and the Rights of Women: The Dilemmas of 'Intersectionality'for Development Organisations. *Gender & Development*, 12(1), 47–55. doi:10.1080/13552070410001726516.

Wilson, K. (2011). 'Race', Gender and Neoliberalism: Changing Visual Representations in Development. *Third World Quarterly*, 32(2), 315–331. doi:10.1080/01436597.2011.560471.

Woetzel, J., Madgavkar, A., Ellingrud, K., Labaye, E., Devillard, S., Kutcher, E., Manyika, J., Dobbs, R., & Krishnan, M. (2015). The Power of Parity: How Advancing Women's Equality Can Add $12 Trillion to Global Growth. https://www.mckinsey.com/featured-insights/employment-and-growth/how-advancing-womens-equality-can-add-12-trillion-to-global-growth.

World Bank (2012). *World Development Report: Gender Equality and Development*. https://openknowledge.worldbank.org/entities/publication/51c285f6-0200-590c-97d3-95b937be3271.

Yunus, M. (2005). Microcredit Changes Lives. *Appropriate Technology*, 32(1), 6.

Yunus, M. (2011, 14 January). Sacrificing Microcredit for Megaprofits. *The New York Times*. https://www.nytimes.com/2011/01/15/opinion/15yunus.html.

Index

For Product Safety Concerns and Information please contact our EU
representative GPSR@taylorandfrancis.com
Taylor & Francis Verlag GmbH, Kaufingerstraße 24, 80331 München, Germany

www.ingramcontent.com/pod-product-compliance
Ingram Content Group UK Ltd.
Pitfield, Milton Keynes, MK11 3LW, UK
UKHW020001200926
475702UK00015B/2417

* 9 7 8 1 0 3 2 4 1 1 3 0 9 *